ALSO BY STEPHEN FLYNN

AMERICA THE VULNERABLE

THE EDGE OF
DISASTER

THE EDGE OF
DISASTER

REBUILDING A
RESILIENT NATION

STEPHEN FLYNN

RANDOM HOUSE • NEW YORK

IN COOPERATION WITH THE COUNCIL ON FOREIGN RELATIONS

Founded in 1921, the Council on Foreign Relations is an independent, national membership organization and a nonpartisan center for scholars dedicated to producing and disseminating ideas so that individual and corporate members, as well as policymakers, journalists, students, and interested citizens in the United States and other countries, can better understand the world and the foreign policy choices facing the United States and other governments. The Council does this by convening meetings; conducting a wide-ranging Studies program; publishing *Foreign Affairs,* the preeminent journal covering international affairs and U.S. foreign policy; maintaining a diverse membership; sponsoring Independent Task Forces; and providing up-to-date information about the world and U.S. foreign policy on the Council's website, www.cfr.org.

THE COUNCIL TAKES NO INSTITUTIONAL POSITION ON POLICY ISSUES AND HAS NO AFFILIATION WITH THE U.S. GOVERNMENT. ALL STATEMENTS OF FACT AND EXPRESSIONS OF OPINION CONTAINED IN ITS PUBLICATIONS ARE THE SOLE RESPONSIBILITY OF THE AUTHOR OR AUTHORS.

Copyright © 2007 by Stephen Flynn

Published in the United States by Random House, an imprint of The Random House Publishing Group, a division of Random House, Inc., New York.

RANDOM HOUSE and colophon are registered trademarks of Random House, Inc.

ISBN 978-1-4000-6551-6

Library of Congress Cataloging-in-Publication Data

Flynn, Stephen E.
    The edge of disaster : rebuilding a resilient nation / by Stephen Flynn.
      p. cm.
    Includes bibliographical references and index.
    ISBN 978-1-4000-6551-6
    1. Emergency management—United States. 2. Terrorism—Prevention—Government policy—United States. 3. Civil defense—United States. 4. National security—United States. I. Title.
HV551.3.F62 2007
363.34'5250973—dc22   2006050405

Printed in the United States of America on acid-free paper

www.atrandom.com

987654321

First Edition

Book design by Lynn Newmark

To JoAnn and Christina,
the two great loves of my life

CONTENTS

INTRODUCTION

Consider this. It's a warm Friday evening in late June, and nearly forty thousand baseball fans are gathered at Philadelphia's Citizens Bank Park to watch the home team play the New York Mets. Summer break for the city's public-school students has begun with the dismissal of classes earlier in the day. The stands are crowded with carefree children and their parents rooting for their Phillies. Most of the stadium's 21,000 parking spaces are filled, many by cars owned by Mets fans who have traveled from New York and northern New Jersey. Just a few hundred yards away, Interstate 95 is crowded with weekend travelers heading for Atlantic City, the Jersey Shore, and New England. Two miles due west, workers on the night shift are starting to arrive at the thousand-acre Sunoco oil refinery on the banks of the Schuylkill River. A light breeze is blowing toward the east—ideal conditions for a terrorist operation that has been nearly two years in the making.

Three young men gather in a vacant lot in Camden, New Jersey, across the Delaware River from Philadelphia. The leader of the group is a British national who spent much of 2004 in Iraq. Angered by the U.S. invasion, he had journeyed across Europe to Turkey and slipped into the country to join other foreign insurgents waging war on American forces. A second-generation Pakistani with a university degree in mechanical engineering, he comes from a middle-class family in Liverpool. He has received training in bomb making from an Iranian tutor in southern Iraq and participated in two attacks on Iraqi oil refineries.

In the spring of 2005, a few months after returning from the insurgent front lines in Iraq, the British-born jihadist traveled to the United States on a flight from London's Heathrow Airport. Having never run afoul of the law in the United Kingdom, his name is not on the traveler watch list of the Transportation Security Administration (TSA). Further, as a British subject he was able to travel to New York without a visa. Upon arrival at Kennedy airport, he calmly answered the standard entry questions posed by the customs and border protection official, who snapped a digital photograph, scanned his fingerprints, stamped his passport, and welcomed him to the United States.

With a letter of introduction from a radical British sheikh, he found his way to a Jersey City mosque. There, the local imam put him in contact with two Americans: an undergraduate who belonged to a Muslim Student Association at a local college and his cousin, who was in his midtwenties. The cousins, whose parents are first-generation Egyptians, had been recruited to the mosque by its imam, who had helped to organize a college-student-association event for a visiting Egyptian Salifi speaker. The speaker had made a strong impression on the two men, and the imam had invited them to a small dinner gathering afterward. With the encouragement of the speaker, the imam had agreed to provide the men with private lessons in the teachings of the radical Egyptian philosopher Sayyid Qutb. They had been attending the mosque for well over a year when the British operative arrived.

The three hatched a plan to use a commercial tanker truck to target the Sunoco refinery in southern Philadelphia. The choice of weapon was not a novel one: a tanker truck was used in the bombing of the Khobar towers in Saudi Arabia on June 25, 1996. For that attack, terrorists had purchased a large truck used for sewage treatment and loaded it with three to five thousand pounds of explosives. They parked the truck next to an eight-story building that housed U.S. Air

Force personnel and detonated the explosive. Nineteen U.S. service-men and one Saudi were killed, and 372 servicemen and civilians were wounded. Commercial trucks have also been used in the 2002 attack on a synagogue in Djerba, Tunisia, and in suicide bombings in Iraq, including the attack on the United Nations headquarters housed in the Canal Hotel on August 19, 2003.

Thousands of tanker trucks operate in the tristate area of New York, New Jersey, and Connecticut. The older American cousin held a commercial driver's license, earned at a certified truck-driving school in Elizabeth, New Jersey, and had been a truck driver for over five years. In the summer of 2006, he provided biographical information and fingerprints to the Transportation Security Administration to get a hazardous materials endorsement added to his license. Since he had no criminal record and had never been involuntarily committed to a mental institution, he had no problem obtaining the TSA endorsement.

When a gasoline tanker trailer was stolen from Pennsauken, New Jersey, in April 2004, the Federal Bureau of Investigation issued a nationwide alert; law enforcement officials were worried that the tanker might be used as a part of a terrorist attack. The Jersey City group had no desire to attract this kind of attention. After they had moved to southern New Jersey, the older cousin obtained a job driving for an independent gasoline distributor. The younger cousin got a job as an apprentice painter with one of the thousand contractors who work on the Sunoco facility each day. His mission was to scout out the best target and the truck route to get to it.

In the late afternoon before the Phillies-Mets game, the older cousin drives his truck to the Valero Energy terminal and receives a full load of premium gasoline. He will not make his first scheduled stop, a Camden-area service station. Instead, he drives to a rendezvous point a few blocks away to join up with his two co-conspirators. The younger cousin is there with a pickup truck. Resting behind the cab, hidden under a tarpaulin, is a small fertilizer bomb. The British operative opens his car trunk and carefully removes two suicide vests he has constructed. Each vest is packed with explosives and armed with detonators. On the evening before, the two cousins had dressed in white, sat in front of a camcorder, and recorded their martyrdom videos.

Shortly after 7:00 P.M., as the fans at the ballpark rise to sing the national anthem, the tanker truck and pickup cross the Delaware River. Ten minutes later, the vehicles exit Interstate 76 and head west along the street that runs parallel to the Sunoco facility. The tanker truck slows down to allow the smaller vehicle to pull ahead. As the pickup turns in to the entrance, the driver accelerates and drives directly at the guard shack, detonating the explosives. The explosion knocks out the roll-away gate, allowing the larger truck unobstructed access into the facility.

A moment later, the older cousin brings his vehicle to an abrupt stop near a large storage tank that is well marked with hazard placards. Crying out "Allah is great!" he detonates his vest. The explosion sends up a ball of flame two hundred feet high, killing everyone within one hundred yards of the truck immediately. The secondary explosions kill or injure many of the other employees and contractors on the facility, crippling the refinery's ability to put in place its emergency response plan.

Two miles away, the fans at Citizens Bank stadium suddenly go quiet as the concussive force and noise of the explosion reach them. The umpire calls a halt to the game as security officials scramble to get more information about what has happened. The secondary explosions have also ruptured pipelines to several smaller pressurized tanks that contain thousands of gallons of anhydrous hydrogen fluoride. The warm evening and the heat of the raging fires nearby cause the hydrofluoric acid to quickly evaporate and form a highly concentrated, colorless vapor cloud, which stays close to the ground. With the light westerly wind, the toxic plume moves slowly across the interstate and toward the blue-collar neighborhood north of Roosevelt Park. Many of the windows in these homes have been shattered by the pressure waves created by the explosions, adding to the risk that the residents will be overcome by the toxic gas that is heading their way.

The plume moves over the residences and toward the ballpark at six miles per hour. After a few minutes, an announcement that there has been an accident at the nearby refinery comes over the public-address system. The crowd is directed to calmly evacuate the stadium and move as rapidly as possible toward the Delaware River and in a northerly direction.

As families scramble to get to their cars, a pungent odor reaches them. They experience a burning sensation in their noses and mouths, and children complain that their throats and eyes are bothering them.

Gridlock sets in almost immediately. Interstate 95 was already congested with weekend travelers, and Interstate 76 has been shut down as dozens of emergency vehicles head for the refinery. Twenty thousand vehicles cannot all get onto the highway at the same time, and there are few police officers available to direct the stadium traffic. Thousands of people are trapped in their cars as the hydrofluoric cloud slowly drifts over them. Those who don't close their windows and shut off their engines draw the chemical vapors into their vehicles through the air ventilation system.

The acid begins to burn the eyes and eyelids of the trapped occupants. Victims soon experience a dry, hacking cough. Breathing becomes increasingly labored and painful as they gasp in more of the chemical. Their lungs become inflamed and congested, depriving them of oxygen and leading to seizures. Ultimately, many people fall into a coma.

Without immediate medical attention, everyone caught in the toxic plume will die within ten hours.

This is only a scenario, of course, but one that sadly remains plausible more than five years after the attacks on New York and Washington on

September 11, 2001. Many readers may be shocked to learn that an oil refinery has the potential to pose such a threat. Be assured that terrorists are not in the dark. Al-Qaeda has been acquiring experience in these kinds of attacks in Iraq and Saudi Arabia, and sharing the details of constructing improvised explosive devices in Internet chat rooms. All the information on the dangers of hydrofluoric acid and the vulnerability of the Sunoco facility can be found in publicly available reports that can be readily accessed with the click of a mouse.

Increasingly, Americans are living on the edge of disaster. Like reckless teenagers, we have been embracing risks while shrugging off the likely consequences. We allow chemical facilities and oil refineries to operate next to crowded neighborhoods without requiring that the industry use safer materials and technologies. We build new homes on floodplains while neglecting to maintain the levees that hold the water back. We demand more electricity for our air conditioners and computers while allowing the electrical grid to deteriorate. We know that terrorists can be citizens of the United States, or nearly any other country, and can operate in our midst, yet for the most part we have allowed local police forces to be sidelined in the war on terrorism. Finally, our emergency responders who are straining to keep up with the everyday demand for their services have little to no surge capacity to handle large-scale events.

This is madness. There are things we can and must be doing, right now, to make America a more resilient society. Each year, hurricanes will form in the Atlantic Ocean and threaten the East and Gulf coasts. It is only a matter of time before subterranean plates shift and the earth opens up along continental fault lines near Los Angeles and San Francisco. Heavy rains will cause seasonal flooding in the Mississippi Valley. The chemical sector, including major oil refineries, will experience industrial accidents that will endanger thousands of lives. Terrorist acts will never be eradicated, because they are relatively easy to accomplish and remain the most effective way for the weak to challenge the strong.

We can prepare for these eventualities. We can reduce the use of highly toxic, volatile, or flammable chemicals within large cities. We can invest in maintaining flood protection systems. We can build more power transmission lines to keep the lights on when the temperature rises. We can make sure that our emergency management and public health systems have adequate resources, so that when things go wrong qualified people can come to our rescue. We can do a better job protecting the things that make the most attractive and destructive targets. It is the height of folly for the world's wealthiest nation not to make these kinds of prudent investments.

Despite all the rhetoric since September 11, 2001, and some new federal spending on homeland security, America remains dangerously unprepared to prevent and respond to acts of catastrophic terrorism on U.S. soil. Even the disastrous handling of Hurricane Katrina's aftermath by all levels of our government failed to serve as a wake-up call. Managing the risk associated with predictable large-scale natural and man-made disasters remains far from the top of our national priorities.

In 2005, I organized a series of meetings for a group of private-sector executives at the Council on Foreign Relations, where I serve as a senior fellow. My objective was to enlist a nonpartisan group of corporate leaders in informing, and ideally becoming advocates for, a series of recommendations that could help redress our most glaring homeland vulnerabilities. What we concluded was that the capabilities of the private sector to help make the country safer had been largely untapped. This neglect could be traced to a mistaken assumption by many in Washington that market mechanisms would provide adequate levels of security to address the modern terrorist threat. As a result, the federal government had been adopting an essentially hands-off approach to protecting critical infrastructure.

While the group was primarily focused on identifying incentives for advancing public and private cooperation to deal with the post–9/11 terrorist threat, the discussions often ended up considering other major hazards that could have large economic and societal consequences. The most prominent among these was the risk of a pandemic flu outbreak. My Council colleague Laurie Garrett spoke about this issue at a February 2005 meeting. Laurie is a Pulitzer Prize–winning writer and the author of the seminal work on the topic of infectious diseases, *The Coming Plague.* Given our counterterrorism focus, we began the session by examining the hypothetical danger of terrorists spreading disease as a malicious act. However, we soon found ourselves talking about the danger of a global pandemic spawned by bird flu.

Laurie described how quickly avian flu had spread among the Eurasian bird populations and that it had a 90 to 100 percent mortality rate among chickens, ducks, and turkeys. Domesticated birds often went from infection to death within forty-eight hours. In the few human cases associated with the avian flu outbreaks in Asia and parts of Europe, more than half of the people infected have died. The good news is that the H5N1 virus in its current form does not usually infect people. The bad news is that viruses are always mutating, and H5N1 could adapt to spread very easily from one person to another. If that happens, hundreds of millions of people will become infected, and many of them will die. The virus is terribly lethal, because humans have little to no immune protection to fight it.

During this sobering discussion, it occurred to several of us that, like our elected leaders in Washington, we had become so preoccupied since 9/11 with potential man-made dangers that we had been overlooking what might well be the higher-probability and higher-consequence risk arising from naturally occurring events. I came away convinced that there is something fundamentally wrong with expending virtually all of our intellectual energies, political capital, and resources on combating terrorists when a daunting array of other perils is more likely to injure or kill us. A fundamental obligation of government is to provide for the safety and well-being of its people. From a potential victim's standpoint, it does not matter how your life is being threatened; what matters is that reasonable measures have been taken both to protect you from that threat and to assist you when you are in trouble. The folly of a myopic focus on terrorism became abundantly clear when Hurricane Katrina struck New Orleans and the Gulf Coast of Mississippi and Alabama in late August 2005.

The day that Hurricane Katrina became a Category 5 storm, I was literally half a world away. On August 28, 2005, I had just arrived in Hong Kong to help the port devise a method for reducing the risk that a cargo container might be used as a poor man's missile. As I checked in to my hotel room overlooking the world's busiest harbor, I flipped on the television to see what had happened during my eighteen-hour flight from New York. Filling the screen was a meteorological map of the Gulf of Mexico, showing a storm 150 miles wide, 225 miles from making landfall, and with maximum sustained winds of 175 mph. The National Hurricane Center warned that the storm would generate a storm surge that would produce flooding along the coast, reaching eighteen to twenty-two feet above normal tide levels. I then watched with dismay as the cable networks broadcast live images of families lining up at the Superdome to pass through security so that they could gain entry to the city's "shelter of last resort." I assumed that the city soon would be under water once a storm of that force hit. The fact that these people were not being evacuated I found bewildering.

I have visited New Orleans only a few times, either as a tourist or to attend conferences. My pre-Katrina knowledge of the vulnerabilities of the city's levee system came from the research I did for my 2004 book, *America the Vulnerable*. I had been inventorying America's potentially softest targets that could produce catastrophic consequences. A series of articles published by the New Orleans *Times-Picayune* led me to look at the city's levees as possible terrorist targets. What if a couple of fertilizer trucks such as those used in the Oklahoma City bombing in 1995 were detonated next to the levees along the Industrial Canal, which connects the Mississippi River to Lake Pontchartrain? If there had been a major storm and the river waters were running high, the bombing of the levees would cause those waters to rush into the Ninth Ward of the city with none of the warning that precedes a hurricane. No one would have a chance to evacuate. Tens of thousands of residents would be trapped as the floodwaters quickly rose. Many who are elderly or disabled would drown in their homes.

In the end, I decided not to write about this theoretical attack. While the consequences would be severe, I presumed that levees strong enough to withstand a Category 3 hurricane would not make a particularly soft target. As a retired Coast Guard officer, I instead focused on a threat that I was more familiar with: a weapon of mass destruction being shipped in a cargo container.

Ironically, just as New Orleans was about to be nearly destroyed by the failure of its badly neglected levee system, I was twelve time zones away working to prevent a still-hypothetical "bomb-in-the-box" scenario. While watching with growing frustration the mismanagement of Hurricane Katrina's aftermath, I was struck by the fact that as dangerous and disruptive as the container threat could be, only a nuclear warhead could begin to match the damage wrought by this storm. When I landed back in New York on September 1, I made up my mind to broaden my homeland security focus to include natural disasters. This decision formed the genesis for this book.

Conducting the research that informs the pages ahead has involved treading both familiar ground and exotic territory. For two decades I have been involved in national security, both as an academic and as a practitioner. Examining the issues surrounding the threat of catastrophic terrorism is something I have been deeply immersed in for much of that time. However, I began as no more than a reasonably informed layman on such issues as climate change, contagious diseases, the energy industry, and flood management systems. Undoubtedly, readers with expertise in these areas may find evidence that I did not always gain mastery of their subjects. But hopefully any missteps I might have inadvertently made by walking down unfamiliar paths are offset by the value of discovering that these roads lead to the same destination: America needs to make building national resiliency from within as important a public policy imperative as confronting dangers from without.

Yossi Sheffi, a professor of engineering systems at the Massachusetts Institute of Technology, recently invoked the concept of resiliency in a book written to guide companies on how to cope with major random disruptions. Resilience, he points out, is a concept used in the materials sciences and represents "the ability of a material to recover its original shape following a deformation." Professor Sheffi posits that resilient enterprises are those that can quickly "return to their normal performance level following a high-impact/low probability disruption."

Applying this notion of resiliency to our society at the national level involves two things: mobilizing the means to reduce our vulnerabilities and increasing our capacity to swiftly bounce back from major manmade or natural disasters. Embracing national resiliency (as opposed to homeland security) as the organizing principle to confront our perilous age has three important benefits. First, it can engender widespread public support, so that our leaders can tap the greatest source of America's strength: our civil society and the private sector. Second, it has the potential to help generate economic growth and provide dual societal benefits that will strengthen the competitive position and quality of life for current and future generations of Americans. Finally, it supports the national security imperative of confronting the ongoing terrorist threat. A society that can match its strength to deliver a punch with the means to take one makes an unattractive target.

Nearly 90 percent of Americans are currently living in locations that place them at a moderate-to-high risk of earthquakes, volcanoes, wildfires, hurricanes, flooding, or high-wind damage. This translates into virtually all of us having a direct stake in our national capacity to mitigate the risks associated with these perils. Consequently, an all-hazards approach provides a compelling rationale for mobilizing and sustaining a broad cross section of our society in constructing safer communities and reducing the overall fragility of the nation. By contrast, only a small percentage of us are likely to find ourselves in the crosshairs of terrorists. Further, counterterrorism initiatives tend to be restricted to a limited cadre of officials and professionals who have been vetted and hold clearances.

Another advantage of investing in resiliency is that it can produce economic and social gains that amply offset the upfront costs. The model here is the interstate highway system that was launched a half-century ago. President Dwight D. Eisenhower justified undertaking this vast federal public works project as essential to our national security. Drawing on his experience as a career Army officer, Ike argued that a robust transportation system was essential in supporting the rapid mobilization of the nation should the Cold War with the USSR become a hot one. Thankfully, the highway system never had to perform that task; but it proved to be a windfall for economic development, especially for the rural states around the country.

Over the past two decades, we have stopped thinking about the elements of our physical infrastructure as national security assets. In fact, increasingly it seems that we have stopped thinking about infrastructure altogether. America once had a transportation system that was the envy of the world. Now we are better known for our over-crowded highways, second-rate ports, third-rate passenger trains, and a primitive air traffic control system. Many of the great public works projects of the twentieth century—dams and canal locks, bridges and tunnels, aquifers and aqueducts, and even the Eisenhower interstate highway system—are now old and are not aging gracefully.

We should be racing to shore up these foundations, even if we were not living in an age that portends protracted conflict and environmental turbulence. First, there are real costs associated with our neglect. As anyone who has failed to keep up with their car tune-ups knows, when things are not well maintained, the cost of repairs goes up exponentially. When critical systems become unreliable, businesses have to invest in backup capabilities to sustain their operations. Over time, this can weaken the competitive position of companies in the international marketplace.

Alternatively, a national effort to repair and upgrade these systems would bolster the attractiveness of investing, working, and living in the United States. Company supply chains would be more efficient and reliable. Corporations could channel some of their investments in continuity-of-operations contingencies back into their core businesses. Insurance costs would be reduced. Commuters would spend less time in traffic jams. Infrastructure renewal projects would also provide higher-paying employment opportunities for skilled workers.

Finally, there is a national security benefit to be derived from reversing the corrosive condition of U.S. critical infrastructure. Acts of terrorism will have substantial political and military value for our adversaries as long as these operations promise to generate large costs or produce political changes that advance their interests. It follows that the more fragile U.S. vital systems are, the more likely it is that terrorists will assume they can cause the kind of fallout that makes these attacks worth pursuing.

Our current adversaries have limited resources and a relatively small pool of potential operatives to carry out terrorist acts on U.S. soil. Once they attack, they face almost certain retribution. Therefore, they must weigh the risks of taking their battle to our shores. If an attack on our critical infrastructure or on innocent civilians is unlikely to be successful or consequential, going after softer targets outside the United States becomes more attractive. This is not to say that all acts of terrorism can be deterred. However, the strategic value, particularly for an adversarial nation state, of sponsoring or conducting terrorist attacks on the United States can be substantially reduced if we make investments that advance domestic resiliency.

In the private sector, resilient companies end up having a competitive advantage over those that remain unprepared to cope with major disruptions. This advantage arises from the most important quality for achieving resiliency: flexibility. Building flexibility, in turn, requires participation from all parts of a firm, because it often involves making fundamental changes in the way a company conducts its business.

Regrettably, Washington has shown no inclination to adopt a similar posture for dealing with the disruptive threat posed by terrorism. Instead, we are becoming an ever more brittle society, while the vast majority of Americans remain outside the process of making the United States more secure. This is perhaps the greatest shortcoming in the Bush administration's response to the 9/11 attacks. The White House has never made a serious attempt to engage the American people in a national enterprise whose aim is to reduce our myriad vulnerabilities at home. What was initially advertised as a two-front effort quickly became a lopsided strategy in which protecting our homeland has been neglected while the vast majority of our resources and political capital have been expended in "taking the battle to the enemy." President George W. Bush and Vice President Richard Cheney have consistently argued that by engaging our enemies overseas, we have been spared having to fight them here. But one consequence of investing so heavily in our military efforts abroad has been to leave the rest of us without much to do. Most of us have chosen to live our lives pretty much like we had before 9/11.

It can be argued that the Bush administration's counterterrorism strategy has bought us some time, by focusing the energies of al-Qaeda on our occupation forces in Iraq. Even if this is the reason for the lack of attacks on the United States since 9/11, we have not been making productive use of that time. Our infrastructure continues to grow frailer while our politics have become more divisive. Neither of these trends bodes well for dealing with the ongoing risk of disaster. We are becoming a less flexible nation just as the likelihood of mass disruptions continues to gather steam.

How would a focus on resiliency help to deal with the frightening scenario I laid out at the beginning of this introduction? As a starting point, we must acknowledge that none of our current overseas efforts can help us to foil an operation that involves a radicalized British national working with two U.S. citizens who are willing to sacrifice their lives so as to turn a domestic industrial facility into a weapon of mass destruction. On the contrary, however things may turn out in the long term, the current assessment of the U.S. intelligence community is that the war in Iraq is abetting the radical jihadist recruitment efforts beyond the Middle East while advancing the means to develop such skill sets as constructing suicide vests and improvised explosive devices.

What then can be done to protect the citizens of Pennsylvania and New Jersey, and other Americans who live near oil refineries? The key to the solution can be found by focusing less on the terrorists and more on the prospective target. The most destructive element of the scenario is not the bombing of the refinery but the release of hydrofluoric acid into a densely populated area. This should lead to the question: Can refineries near major urban areas change the way they are doing business and use an alternative to hydrofluoric acid that poses less of a danger to the surrounding community? It turns out that they can.

Lawrence Wein, a professor of management science at the Stanford Business School, has determined that for a conversion cost of $20 million to $30 million per refinery, sulfuric acid could replace hydrofluoric acid in the alkylation process used to manufacture high-octane gasoline. Sulfuric acid can pose dangers as well, but unlike hydrogen fluoride it does not form a dense cloud when it is released. If Sunoco were using this alternative, it would have a nasty chemical spill on its hands as a result of the hypothetical attack I have posited. However, the ball game could have gone on without the people in the stands facing the risk of inhaling lethal doses of a toxic gas.

Ninety-eight refineries already are using sulfuric acid or another safer alternative, which is to modify hydrofluoric acid with an agent that causes most of the acid in the cloud to fall to the ground. The multimillion-dollar price tag for making the conversion may sound pretty steep to the average American. However, that sum represents what Americans have been spending every two to three *hours* on the war in Iraq, a war that has been costing U.S. taxpayers $250 million per day since the invasion in March 2003. In order to reduce the current risk posed to so many citizens living around the refinery, the federal government could provide a tax break to Sunoco for investing in this change. But even if Washington simply mandated the change, Sunoco could afford it. A major refinery produces about one billion gallons of gasoline per year. That means that if the cost of the refinery conversion were amortized over three years, it would raise the production cost by one cent per gallon. The people living in the Philadelphia area are likely to view that as a penny well worth spending at the pump.

Embracing a safer chemical has the added benefit of simultaneously reducing the risk associated with industrial accidents, which cannot always be prevented. Nearly two decades ago, the citizens of Texas City had a narrow brush with a hydrofluoric acid disaster. On October 30, 1987, a crane at Marathon Oil's Texas City refinery dropped its load, severing two pipelines leading to the top of a storage tank of anhydrous hydrogen fluoride. The pressurized tank released 6,548 gallons of its hazardous contents over a forty-four-hour period, forming a vaporized cloud that prompted the evacuation of a fifty-block residential area adjacent to the plant. Trees were defoliated all along the route that the chemical traveled, and 1,037 people ended up in hospitals for treatment of respiratory problems and skin rashes. Altogether, the U.S. National Response Center's Emergency Response Notification System reported four hundred incidents at refineries and other facilities involving hydrofluoric acid or hydrogen fluoride from 1990 to 2005. In light of the fact that there are substitutes and safer technologies, reducing the use and storage of hydrofluoric acid would be worth pursuing even in the absence of the ongoing terrorist threat.

This introductory chapter provides a preview of how this book approaches the subject of America's growing flirtation with disaster. The Philadelphia refinery scenario dramatically highlights the fact that we remain a very vulnerable society; however, it turns out that there are reasonable measures we can take to dramatically reduce risks. In a similar fashion, the first five chapters contain ominous warnings of current and pending perils, while the next five ask the reader to take a deep breath and consider a menu of actions we could undertake right now that would allow us to manage these dangers.

Chapter 1 presents the argument that what makes a disaster a true catastrophe has more to do with our own acts of omission or commission than with the forces that lie beyond our control. Chapter 2 outlines how that fragility could be exploited in a frightening way by a terrorist attack on the ports of Boston and of Long Beach, California. Chapter 3 makes the case that our recklessness is more of a contemporary development than a historical one. In the past, Americans learned from disasters and acted on those lessons, but in contemporary times we seem unwilling or unable to muster the political will to change our increasingly reckless ways. Chapters 4 and 5 establish that the problem of neglecting critical infrastructure and exacerbating our perils is not an isolated problem but a truly national one. These chapters portend dark consequences if we do not confront our own folly.

While we are poised on the edge of disaster, the second half of the book makes clear that we have the means to step back from the brink. Chapter 6 suggests that the starting point for building a resilient society is to reconsider some of the conventional thinking that has determined how the war on terrorism is being waged. It presents a critical analysis of the post–9/11 reliance on our military forces to fight back, outlining how more could be constructively done to confront the terrorist threat within our own borders. It also presents the case that there is deterrent value to reducing our vulnerabilities at home. Chapter 7 sketches out a plan for Washington to move from a focus on homeland security to one that makes building national resiliency our top public policy priority. Chapters 8 and 9 provide a plan of action for tapping the nation's greatest asset—we the people. They include guidance for how business leaders and everyday Americans can be substantially involved with mitigating disaster. The concluding chapter lays out the major findings and recommendations to be drawn from these pages.

As this manuscript was being completed, a major fire at a chemical facility was in the headlines. In the middle of the night on October 5, 2006, seventeen thousand people fled their homes ahead of a plume of toxic fumes rising over an industrial chemical storage facility in Apex, North Carolina. The plume was created by a raging fire fed by pesticides, oxides, bulk sulfur, contaminated lead, and chlorine gas, which were being stored in a warehouse just east of the town's center. The stinging cloud of smoke sent thirteen police officers and a firefighter to hospitals with respiratory problems and chemical burns. Shifting winds emptied downtown streets as thousands of residents sought refuge from the choking airborne mix of contaminants. In the end, the quick evacuation left the citizens of Apex shaken but largely unharmed. However, the incident provides yet another warning of how abruptly our lives can be interrupted by the dangers that surround us, and highlights the importance of being prepared to respond to emergencies when they happen.

Coming to grips with perils that can lead to catastrophic consequences is not about living in a perpetual state of fear. We become fearful only when a sense of imminent danger is coupled with a feeling of powerlessness. But there is no reason to doubt our ability to confront and manage these risks. Every American generation has had to confront serious dangers, and they have always passed the test. While we must be prepared to acknowledge that there are dark clouds on the horizon, it is vital that we not lose sight of our most important and endearing national trait: our sense of optimism about the future and our conviction that we can change it for the better.

THE EDGE OF
DISASTER

ONE

A BRITTLE NATION

THE UNITED STATES HAS BECOME a brittle superpower. We are the world's economic and cultural 900-pound gorilla and spend more on our military muscle than the rest of the world combined. Yet we increasingly behave like the occupants of a grand old mansion who have given up on investing in its upkeep. We depend on complex infrastructure built by the hard labor, capital, and ingenuity of our forbears, but we seem oblivious to the fact that it is aging—and not very gracefully. Bridges are outfitted with the civil engineering equivalent of a diaper. Public works departments construct "temporary" patches for dams that leave those living downstream one major storm away from waking up to a wall of water rolling through their living rooms. Our electricity comes to us via a decades-old system of power generators, transformers, and transmission lines that has utility executives holding their breath on every hot day in July or August.

It is not just modernity's hardware that is being neglected. Two decades of taxpayer rebellion have stripped away the means for emergency workers to help us when we need them. Today, most city and state public health departments are not adequately funded to manage their routine work. A flu pandemic would completely overwhelm them. A growing number of firehouses have been shuttered in recent years, and firefighters must make do with radios that often are unable to support communications with neighboring departments. In many cities across the country, there are fewer police officers on the streets today than there were in 2001, and those still on the beat have only limited access to the kind of protective equipment that would allow them to operate in a contaminated environment. Emergency room services have been a major casualty of medical care belt-tightening, forcing ambulances to routinely engage in countywide scavenger hunts for a place to bring their patients. Federal agencies such as the Coast Guard operate with a rickety fleet of aged ships and aircraft that routinely break down during patrols. In short, on any given day, our first responders are barely treading water. That means that there is little to no capability to deal with large-scale disasters such as major hurricanes, terrorist attacks, and disease outbreak.

Like the spoiled offspring of well-off parents, we seem blissfully ignorant of what is required to sustain the quality of our daily lives. Washington has shown little interest in challenging this national state of complacency. Rather than address the myriad soft targets within the U.S. border, the White House has defined the war on terrorism as something to be managed by actions beyond our shores. The rallying cry of the Bush administration and its allies on Capitol Hill has been "We must fight terrorists over there so we don't have to fight them here." What this ignores is that terrorists can still come here—and, worse yet, are being made here. When it comes to natural disasters, both ends of Pennsylvania Avenue rationalize their passivity by citing deference to governors and mayors and the private sector. With the exception of the nation's capital and military bases, our national infrastructure lies within the jurisdictions of individual states and cities and is largely owned and operated by private entities. And emergency response has traditionally been a local responsibility.

The most compelling lesson we should have learned on 9/11 is that our borders are unable to provide an effective barrier against the modern terrorist threat. The al-Qaeda operatives who carried out the attacks on New York and Washington had been residing in the United States. They did not strike us with weapons of mass destruction provided by a rogue state but turned four domestic airliners into their equivalents. The Madrid train attacks in March 2004, the suicide bombings of the London Underground in July 2005, the June 2006 arrests of seventeen radicalized Canadians in Toronto, and the August 2006 arrests of two dozen British citizens intent on bombing U.S.-bound flights from London all highlight the growing reality that advanced democratic societies are not immune to incubating the homegrown terrorist threat.

The central lesson to be learned from Hurricanes Katrina and Rita is that major natural disasters are likely to overwhelm states' and localities' capacities to respond. Those two storms caused damage to more than 90,000 square miles of land and destroyed 360,000 households. Washington's exhortations to governors and mayors to do more will not alter documented reality. In a report on disaster preparedness released in June 2006, the U.S. Department of Homeland Security found that only one quarter of state emergency operations plans and 10 percent of municipal plans are sufficient to cope with a natural disaster or terrorist attack. The majority of plans "cannot be characterized as fully adequate, feasible or acceptable to manage catastrophic events."

Denial and a fatalistic sense of resignation seem to be conspiring to immobilize us. Superficially, on an individual level there is an underlying logic to our inertia. Most of us will not be in the wrong place at the wrong time when terrorists attack, the earth rumbles, the tsunami hits, or the hurricane makes landfall. Of course, there will be victims, but odds are that individually we will not be counted among them. On the flip side, if fate does place us directly in the crosshairs of a disaster, anything we may have done in advance to protect ourselves is likely to be overwhelmed by the destructive forces aligned against us. So why worry about forces that lie beyond our control?

But this kind of rationalization is silly and irresponsible. Anyone who has ever prepared for a camping trip or gone to sea on a small vessel knows that having plans for coping with emergencies does not rob these activities of their enjoyment. However, not having plans could eat away at your peace of mind and put lives needlessly at risk should misfortune strike. We rightfully condemn as a fool anyone who marches off into the wilderness or leaves shore without the basic survival skills and tools for coping when things go wrong.

The fact is that we are living in increasingly complicated and perilous times and we have to stop pretending that disasters are extremely rare and unforeseeable. Even if we personally are usually lucky enough to be outside the primary strike zone, we are unlikely to escape the fallout. The things we depend on are becoming more and more interconnected and interdependent. A disruption of pipelines and refineries on the Gulf Coast means that gasoline quickly becomes in short supply everywhere. The closure of a major seaport such as Los Angeles means a nationwide shortage of the things that retailers and manufacturers—and ultimately consumers—need to keep operating. And in an age when long daily commutes and frequent air travel are facts of life, there is little hope that the rapid spread of a contagious disease can be contained by a simple quarantine.

The danger from man-made attacks is growing despite the more-than-five-year reprieve the United States has enjoyed since 9/11. We have been hedging most of our security bets on open-ended military campaigns to combat terrorism overseas, a gamble that appears to have worsening odds. When we were focused on containing the Soviet Union during the Cold War, relying on the projection of our military power beyond our shores made sense. However, today, we are seeing that the far-flung radical jihadist threat cannot be encircled by deploying our armed forces to the Middle East and Central Asia. Indeed, those efforts have had the unintended consequence of attracting more recruits, including "self-starter" groups of first- and second-generation Muslim immigrants in advanced democratic societies such as the Netherlands, the United Kingdom, and Canada. The use of sabotage by insurgents in Iraq has also helped to proliferate the number of individuals who possess the skills and technology to target critical facilities such as refineries, pipelines, water management systems, power generators, and electrical transformers. Whatever the long-term prospects for a more peaceful Middle East—and they do not look good for the foreseeable future—the global terrorist risk is going to get worse before it gets better. It is simply a matter of time before the United States is attacked again.

Compounding the risk is that we are living our lives in ways that increasingly tempt both fate and our enemies. At the micro level, most of us are blithely depleting the reservoir of self-sufficiency that once got us through emergencies. Our just-in-time lifestyles rely on ATM machines to provide us with cash when we need it and twenty-four-hour stores to provide us with food and gas on demand. When the power goes out and these modern conveniences fail, we quickly become incapacitated. Within hours after storms hit, thousands of people end up standing in line for clean water, a hot meal, and basic shelter. Then we are dismayed to find that the public safety and public health sectors that we have been starving of resources during the good times are unable to help us when the times get bad.

We have raised our exposure to harm in other ways as well. For one thing, we have been unwilling to invest in the infrastructure that supports our lives. In 2005, the American Society of Civil Engineers assigned grades to fifteen categories of infrastructure based on a review of hundreds of studies and reports and a survey of more than two thousand engineers. Grades were assigned on the basis of condition and capacity, and funding versus need. It was not the kind of report card you would have wanted to bring home to your parents: four Cs, ten Ds, and one incomplete. The narrative reads like a survey that might have been conducted on the eve of the collapse of the Roman Empire. Roads, dams, water purification facilities, the power grid, canal locks, roads, and wastewater management systems have gone from very bad to worse in the past four years. More than 3,500 dams around the country are unsafe and many pose a direct risk to human life should they fail. The nation's inland waterway system is literally falling apart, which is especially bad news for Midwesterners, who depend upon it to move agricultural exports, bring coal to power plants, and transport chemicals and other bulk commodities. Nearly one half of its 257 locks are functionally obsolete, and that number is projected to rise to 80 percent by 2020. The report also documents that while the U.S. power system is in urgent need of modernization, maintenance expenditures have been dropping by 1 percent per year since 1992.

Demographic trends are also contributing to our growing fragility. Over the past two decades, Americans have been moving to coastal cities and communities in growing numbers. Half of the U.S. population currently lives within fifty miles of the coast just as scientists are predicting that we are at the start of a cycle of severe weather that promises more frequent—and probably more dangerous—storms. Hurricanes Katrina and Rita highlighted a fact that we should already have known: the poorest and neediest among us are especially vulnerable in these areas. Those who cannot afford to own cars may be stranded in homes that lie in flood zones or are easily damaged by high winds.

The stakes transcend the unnecessary loss of innocent lives and the risk of major disruptions to our economy and our society. Our elected leaders' failure to provide meaningful leadership in addressing America's gravest vulnerabilities endangers the durability of the social contract between the governed and the government. The poststorm collapse of the New Orleans levee system showed that government at all levels was unwilling to undertake prudent measures to protect us in the face of a foreseeable and inevitable threat. Increased public cynicism has been the inevitable by-product. A poll conducted on the eve of the first anniversary of the Katrina disaster found that 57 percent of Americans feel the country is ill prepared for a disaster. After the next major terrorist attack on U.S. soil, the post-9/11 homeland security efforts will again be placed under a blistering spotlight. Americans will then painfully discover that our elected and private-sector leader have been barely going through the motions. Beyond passenger line security, few meaningful measures have been put into p^ construct a credible counterterrorism deterrent at home or that the emergency plans laid out on paper can actually be c in reality.

Thinking about and preparing for when things can go very need not be about becoming a nation of Chicken Littles. It is f and self-destructive to oscillate between immobilizing fear, on th hand, and blithely going about our lives playing a societal versio Russian roulette, on the other. Natural disasters will happen, and not all terrorist attacks can be prevented. However, what is preventable is the cascading effects that flow from these disasters and attacks. The loss of life and economic fallout that disasters reap will always be magnified by our lack of preparedness to manage the risk actively and to respond effectively when things go wrong.

As a stepping-off point, we must be open to rethinking how the business of national security and emergency preparedness is done.

On the home front, we continue to leave it up to city and and state governments to manage natural disasters, with Washington admonishing mayors and governors that in case of a disaster they will be on their own for at least seventy-two hours. In an earlier era, relying almost exclusively on local means to deal with calamities was the only real option, given the substantial barriers that geographic distance presented to effective communication and transportation. But today assistance from afar can be just a few hours away. Within twenty-four hours after Katrina made landfall, the perennially underfunded and undermanned Coast Guard managed to get one third of its aviation assets—some from as far away as Alaska—operating within the Gulf Coast area. By the time the 82nd Airborne arrived in New Orleans six days later, Coast Guard men and women had already rescued more than 33,000 people trapped in the floodwaters. The service never waited for direction from above. On its own initiative it brought in resources from around the country, locating and assisting Americans who were in need. Other elements of the federal government, including the Pentagon, could potentially have responded as the Coast Guard did. That they did not and do not has been a matter of choice, largely having to do with resources and who will pay for them. If the American people would choose to invest in a more active federal capability to help us in times of need, we could have one.

While the Bush administration has assigned the federal government a decidedly backseat role in dealing with natural disasters, it has undertaken an essentially "go-it-alone" approach to the war on terrorism. The White House has not mobilized the nation to wage this war, only our national security establishment, on which the administration is willing to spend freely. In 2006, the defense budget was more than half a trillion dollars, which accounted for more than 50 percent of the federal government's budget for discretionary spending. Not only are we spending this extraordinary amount so that our military can wage the war on terror, but the Pentagon has also asked for and received $16.5 billion to protect itself from terrorist attacks.

This is insane. The Department of Defense is spending twenty-three times more protecting its own military bases, naval ships, and barracks—two thirds of which are located inside the United States—

than the federal government is spending to help local governments protect our major cities. The U.S. Navy is bankrolling a Coast Guard force to protect its vessels moving into and out of Puget Sound that is several times larger than the entire Seattle port police force, which is responsible for protecting that city's long waterfront. Any objective analysis would conclude that terrorists would be more interested in targeting civilian infrastructure on U.S. soil than taking on the U.S. military. Yet Washington sees no imbalance in providing billions of dollars to the Pentagon to protect its hardware while providing a paltry $710 million for cities around the country to use to safeguard critical and largely unprotected infrastructures. Since the White House has chosen to combat terrorism as essentially a military and intelligence activity, it treats homeland security as a decidedly second-rate priority. The job of everyday citizens is to just go about their lives, shopping and traveling, while the Pentagon, Central Intelligence Agency, and National Security Agency wage the war.

In short, we have a war on terrorism that is being waged almost entirely by our armed forces and intelligence community, and we have a disaster management system where the bulk of the burden falls on local and state shoulders. What we actually need is an approach to both these imperatives that will engage all levels of government to a far greater extent.

But our most important and largely untapped national assets are everyday citizens and the private sector that powers our economy. On December 9, 1941, two days after the Japanese attacked Pearl Harbor, President Franklin Roosevelt said to the American people:

We are now in this war. We are all in it—all the way. Every single man, woman, and child is a partner in the most tremendous undertaking of our American history. We must share together the bad news and the good news, the defeats and the victories—the changing fortunes of war.

Company executives traded in their pinstripe suits for uniforms and led the effort to adapt America's industrial base to support the war effort. Women left their homes to work in factories, while neighbors and grandparents provided child care. Americans grew "Victory Gardens" and volunteered to be air wardens.

Americans have not lost their willingness to give of themselves. Many of the rescues made in the aftermath of Hurricane Katrina were done by good Samaritans. Volunteers have helped to rebuild churches and homes. People opened up their purses and wallets and donated to charities in record numbers. What has been missing is the kind of leadership that Lincoln and Roosevelt exemplified when the nation faced its darkest hours.

The presidential scholar James MacGregor Burns has said that transformational leaders are always "relentlessly optimistic." Even when circumstances seem grim and the hurdles for achieving progress appear insurmountable, a leader retains his faith that change for the better is not only possible but inevitable. This does not mean that leaders must be starry-eyed idealists. Just the opposite is the case; few followers are willing to hitch their fate to someone who is not grounded in their current reality. So leadership must always start from a clear-eyed view of how things really are. Only then can we begin to address how we can get from where we are to where we need to be. That is the aim of this book: to create a more resilient nation.

TWO

READY TO BLOW

A T 10:03 A.M. on September 11, 2001, United Airlines Flight 93 crashed into a reclaimed coal strip mine in Somerset County, Pennsylvania. None of the seven crew members and thirty-seven passengers aboard the Boeing 757 survived the fiery impact. Among the fatalities were four hijackers who, when faced with the imminent assault by passengers intent on recapturing control of the plane, opted to end their suicide mission in a remote field 140 miles short of their intended target in Washington, D.C.

What happened aboard United 93, the last of the four aircraft hijacked on 9/11, epitomized the contradictions of that tragic day. In the face of horrific acts of violence perpetrated on people who had the misfortune of being in the wrong place at the wrong time, we saw glimpses of ordinary Americans at their very best.

The story is documented by the 9/11 Commission, reenacted in a 2006 feature film, and etched in most of our collective memories of that day. United 93 was scheduled to leave Newark International Airport at 8:00 A.M., bound for San Francisco. Due to air traffic congestion on the runway, it did not actually lift off until 8:42 A.M. When the plane was finally in the air, the passengers were able to learn, through urgent air phone calls to families, friends, and colleagues after the hijackers took control of their plane, that the World Trade Center towers and the Pentagon had been hit by three other planes. Aware that they were about to share the same fate of having their airliner serve as a missile, several of the passengers decided to fight back. As the passengers struggled to break into the cockpit, the lead hijacker, Ziad Jarrah, turned the control wheel hard right, rolling the plane onto its back. With one of the hijackers shouting "Allah is the greatest!" United 93 crashed nose first into an empty field.

The events aboard United 93 deserve retelling in no small part because they illustrate what is possible when everyday citizens are armed with information about threats that affect both their individual fates and the safety of the community at large. We will never know if the passengers aboard the first three flights that struck the Twin Towers and the Pentagon would have acted in the same heroic way if, like those aboard Flight 93, they had been aware of the likely intentions of their hijackers. However, we do know that there were a number of people inside the U.S. government who had collected intelligence that pointed to a growing risk of terrorists' hijacking passenger airliners and using them as weapons. Because that information was viewed as sensitive, it was never shared with the American public.

At 8:24 A.M. on September 11, twenty-two minutes before American Airlines Flight 11 struck the North Tower of the World Trade Center, Mohamed Atta, the ringleader and pilot of the first hijacked aircraft, was recorded calmly saying "We have some planes. Just stay quiet, and you'll be okay. We are returning to the airport." Apart from an initial violent scuffle in the first-class cabin, it appears that the passengers complied with the hijackers' demand.

Complying was an appropriate response for people who would have assumed that hijackings always involve hostage taking while the hijackers negotiate with the authorities over their demands. As had been dramatized in a steady stream of Hollywood thrillers, the pre-9/11 protocol was to do what you were told and leave it to professional negotiators or SWAT teams to deal with your captors after the plane landed.

But what if the directors of the FBI and CIA, along with the secretary of transportation, had convened a press conference in August 2001? Suppose that at the briefing, they had announced that they were monitoring intelligence reports suggesting that al-Qaeda appeared to be involved in active plans to attack the United States. Additionally, while acknowledging that the information was sketchy, what if they had warned that among the possible attack scenarios, there was a risk that terrorists might seize a plane, as had been attempted on an Air France flight in December 1994, with the intent to explode it over a major city or crash it into a landmark?

What if some of the men and women who ended up on American Airlines Flight 11, United Airlines Flight 175, and American Airlines Flight 77 had followed the news coverage surrounding this hypothetical briefing? Would they have been more alert to the possibility that they were not involved in a conventional hijacking? Would they have decided to marshal a counterattack?

Sadly, what makes this press briefing seem entirely implausible is not that senior officials would legitimately have wanted more definitive intelligence than they had available to them at the time. It is, rather, that even if they had had a clearer picture of the threat, it would not have occurred to them that they should share it in such a public way. The resistance to doing so would have been considerable. The airline industry would have expressed its concern that the briefing might unduly panic the public, leaving their planes depopulated of all but hard-core business travelers. Intelligence operatives would have raised concerns that a premature announcement might compromise their sources or ongoing investigations. Some transportation security officials might have asserted that the warnings would actually encourage the very thing that they were working to prevent, as potential terrorists might perceive a public warning as an official admission that existing security measures were inadequate to prevent such a hijacking.

But what happened aboard Flight 93 should have exposed how wrongheaded these kinds of rationalizations are. The safety of the people on the ground and aboard four hijacked planes turned out to be in the hands of private citizens. But the U.S. government lacked both the ability and inclination to provide them with critical information that could have led them to fight back.

Before 9/11, would people have stopped flying had they been told what the intelligence community had uncovered about the new hijacking risk? People are flying today in record numbers even though 9/11 happened and the threat to passenger airliners remains. Would ongoing investigations have been compromised? Perhaps. But more likely there would have been a more alert public, particularly within the aviation industry, that could have provided helpful information in support of those investigations. Would the warnings have been a green light to terrorists because they suggested that officials had little faith in the existing security measures? This is the most fallacious argument of them all. The security measures in place were indeed woefully inadequate. More important, no effort was being made to improve them. Part of the problem was that the agencies primarily responsible for those measures were out of the intelligence loop. The secretary of transportation, Norman Mineta, and the head of the Federal Aviation Administration, Jane Garvey, testified to the 9/11 Commission that they were not aware of the intelligence that had been collected about the plane-as-a-weapon scenario. An inclination to openness and inclusion in assessing the threat would have prevented this kind of bureaucratic ineptitude. Likewise, it would have helped to generate the public support required for doing the things we have done since 9/11, such as hardening cockpit doors and improving passenger screening.

The problem is that we have a deeply embedded culture within the national defense and federal law enforcement communities that embraces secrecy and prevents public disclosure of information. Since the end of World War II—the last war when the entire society was mobilized—our national security establishment has paternalistically anointed itself as our sole protector against all enemies, foreign and domestic. The Bush administration's penchant for secrecy and executive independence has only accentuated this trend. Everyday citizens are not seen as potential allies in advancing our security. At best, it is assumed that we would be unwilling or unable to grasp the nuances and severity of the stakes involved and overreact, underreact, or simply get in the way. At worst, our government acts as though its citizens are potential security risks. Citizenship buys us no presumption of loyalty against a tenacious enemy it is sworn to protect us from.

At its core, politics is about making choices among competing interests. For a democracy to function properly, this process must be an open one. The post-9/11 slide toward greater levels of secrecy, particularly when it involves our domestic vulnerabilities, must be reversed. In the end, security is a public good and the public must be actively involved in providing it. We would do well to heed Thomas Jefferson's famous admonition "A nation's best defense is an educated citizenry."

There were no federal air marshals aboard United 93. The Defense Department's North American Aerospace Defense Command could not defend Washington from the commandeered airliner—it had no advance notice that it had been hijacked. In the words of the 9/11 Commission, what prevented the terrorist pilot Ziad Jarrah from crashing his airliner into the U.S. Capitol or the White House was that "he was defeated by the *alerted*, unarmed passengers of United 93." (The italics are mine.) It is both remarkable and ironic that the two centers of a government created "to provide for the common defense" were themselves ultimately protected by an alert and heroic citizenry.

The American people should draw inspiration from their fellow countrymen aboard United 93. But they should also be expressing outrage at a government that continues to treat them as though they were small children. No matter how bravely and professionally our dedicated men and women in uniform fight in Iraq, they cannot prevent the spread of radical Islam and the tactics unleashed by Osama bin Laden. Our borders have never served as a meaningful barrier against determined people intent on reaching the United States. They never will.

Terrorism will increasingly be like the flu: the only thing we can safely predict is that each season there will be new strains. Thus it is only prudent to bolster the odds that our immune system can successfully fend off the known strains. This requires our identifying the most likely and attractive targets and striving to protect them from potential attacks. At the same time, we must also assume that not every attack can be prevented. This makes it critical that we be able to respond effectively when disaster strikes and have the means to rapidly restore what is damaged. In short, it will require a far greater engagement of our civil society. It will also require making investing in our own national resilience a top public policy priority.

The foregoing discussion is an essential starting point for the pages that follow. I am convinced that we must err on the side of candor when it comes to contemplating potential catastrophic terrorist attacks. As a practical matter, it is impossible to put the information genie back in the bottle. Criminals and terrorists know our soft spots. They will seek to exploit or target our vulnerabilities as long as we do nothing to address them. But the only way to muster the political will to reduce our exposure to malicious acts is to acknowledge our weaknesses and to openly discuss the options for addressing them.

One such major terrorist risk we face involves our seaports. I have been writing about this potential Achilles' heel for more than a decade. I have presented testimony at Senate and congressional hearings on more than a dozen occasions since 9/11. I have briefed senior members of the Bush administration from the White House on down. But the frightening scenario I outline below remains all too plausible. There are pragmatic measures we could have been undertaking and can still undertake to minimize this risk, some of which I will outline in future chapters. But I am convinced that our government will continue to drag its feet unless the American public is aware of the stakes involved. Like the passengers on United 93, we must overcome our understandable inclination to remain in our seats and hope someone else will rescue us from peril. We can meet the dangers that lie before us. But we need to be far better informed and assertive if we are to do so.

What follows is a scenario roughly based on two real-world post-9/11 terrorist attacks: one on the French oil tanker *Limburg* off the coast of Yemen in October 2002, the other on Iraq's Khor al-Amaya and al-Basra oil terminals in April 2004. The operating premise is this: terrorists operations that are undertaken on foreign shores will ultimately find their way to our shores. The characters are fictional, but they are based on the profiles of real individuals apprehended over the past two years by European authorities. All the details on the ports where the hypothetical attacks take place come from open-source information, nearly all of which can be found by way of searches on the Internet.

Most of America's major cities have been built around water. There is a straightforward reason for this: ports are our economic lifelines. The most efficient and affordable way to move the goods we trade and consume is by water. This is true for America's heartland as well as along the coasts. Each year, 310 million tons of grain, petroleum, steel, ore, soybeans, and corn move up and down the Mississippi River, and 90 percent of our imports from and exports to Asia, Europe, Africa, and South America move by sea. In 2005, more than eleven million containers loaded with imported cargo from every corner of the world arrived in our ports.

Ports also play host to some of our nation's most critical and potentially hazardous facilities. An example of this is a liquefied natural gas (LNG) terminal that sits less than two miles away from the gold-leaf-covered dome of the Massachusetts State House. Once a week a ship carrying more than three billion cubic feet of LNG arrives at the French-owned Distrigas terminal on Boston's Mystic River to off-load its cargo. To get there, the vessel travels over three tunnels and under a major bridge and passes within a mile of the homes and workplaces of approximately 100,000 people, Logan International Airport, Boston's financial district, and historic landmarks like Faneuil Hall, Old North Church, and the USS *Constitution*.

Long before anyone gave much thought to terrorist attacks on U.S. soil, the Distrigas terminal was constructed on the industrial waterfront of Everett, Massachusetts. It began operation in 1971, and in the ensuing years, residential housing has steadily closed in on the facility as the demand for Boston-area real estate has soared. The terminal has been on the receiving end of nearly half of all the LNG imported into the United States, and it provides 20 percent of New England's gas for power generation and home heating. Through a direct pipe connection to the 1,550-megawatt Mystic Station power plant, Distrigas provides the fuel that in turn generates enough electricity for approximately 1.5 million homes in the Greater Boston area. The lights in the metro Boston area would literally go out were it not for LNG, and the demand for electricity continues to climb.

Another example of a vital and vulnerable waterfront facility lies just south of Los Angeles. Californians depend on the daily importation of petroleum to keep millions of vehicles on the road, jets flying at the state's airports, and machinery operating throughout the region. The Port of Long Beach is the West Coast's most important source for crude oil shipments, having received more than 30 million metric tons of petroleum products in 2005. Located in the East Basin, just inside the Middle Harbor, lies the largest oil terminal, which is managed by British Petroleum. Pier T accommodates some of the world's largest oil tankers, off-loading crude oil into storage tanks within the port or pumping it several miles away to facilities in the city of Carson via 42-inch and 24-inch pipelines.

Although California's appetite for fossil-based fuels shows no sign of abating, the system that feeds the region's energy needs is an increasingly concentrated and time-sensitive one. At any given moment there is only a week to ten days of refined gasoline available in people's cars, at the filling stations, in the tank trucks servicing the filling stations, and in storage at the refineries. Maintaining a larger energy inventory is not attractive for several reasons. First, building new refineries is expensive and unpopular—no new refinery has been built on the West Coast in more than thirty years. Second, residents don't like large storage tanks in or around their neighborhoods. Third, California's strict environmental requirements translate into a refinement process that is more technically complex and expensive than elsewhere in the country. The bottom line is that for the oil companies, it is more profitable to sell fuel as quickly as it is produced than to have it sitting around. As long as there is no interruption in the importation of crude oil, this works out fine. But should the shipping channel into Long Beach become blocked, oil tankers will be unable to off-load their shipments of crude oil to the refineries. Even with rationing, gas pumps could go dry within two to three weeks.

In short, the Port of Long Beach and the Port of Boston are attractive targets for would-be terrorists. This is why the next attack by a tenacious adversary could evolve like the following.

On a rainy Sunday in early spring, three passengers—all Dutch nationals—arrive at Boston's Logan airport, traveling on different airlines from different European capitals. They are three of the more than 12,000 international passengers who together with 75,000 domestic passengers pass through the airport each day. On this particular day, the airport is operating at full capacity because a deluge of Boston-area college students is returning from spring break.

Three thousand miles away, two British nationals arrive at Los Angeles International Airport, the world's fifth busiest passenger airport, which receives more than 45,000 foreign travelers each day. In addition to traveling college students, LAX's Tom Bradley International Terminal and its eight domestic terminals are filled with tourists who have been drawn to the southern California sunshine.

None of the passports for the Dutch and British travelers shows that a year earlier they were all in Iraq as foreign insurgents. Like hundreds of other radicalized European Muslims, they had joined the jihadist cause to push the Americans out of the country that al-Qaeda has dubbed "the sacred land between the two rivers." The travel for that earlier experience had been more circuitous, including a boat ride from southern Spain to Morocco, a trip across northern Africa by truck and bus to Syria, and a return trip via rental car and rail from Turkey. Officially, there was no record of their having been in Iraq, since they had slipped into and out of the country across its poorly policed borders.

The three terrorists arriving in Boston had first met in Amsterdam, where they had grown up as children of Moroccan and Syrian parents who had immigrated to Holland in the early 1970s. As young men, they attended the technical university at Eindhoven, receiving degrees in engineering, chemistry, and computer science, respectively. Upon graduation, they found themselves among the 40 percent of immigrant youths in the Netherlands who are unemployed.

Khalid, the leader of the group, interned for a short time at an engineering firm after he graduated, but that had ended with no offer of a paid position. He had alternated between unemployment and a series of dead-end temp jobs, spending his plentiful free time playing soccer with his former schoolmates and hanging out in a local café popular with the Muslim diaspora. Inevitably the conversation among his comrades would turn to the plight of being young and Muslim in a country they felt did not want them. One day, one of the regular café patrons invited them to attend the Friday services of a young imam who operated a nearby mosque above a storefront.

The imam tutored them in Islamic teachings and law according to the radical Hanbali school. They read the Koran and collections of the Hadiths, the sayings of the Prophet Mohammed. They immersed themselves in the writings of Ibn Taymiyya, the thirteenth-century fundamentalist Islamic philosopher, and his twentieth-century Egyptian counterpart, Sayyid Qutb. They came to see the Netherlands and the West as blighted by depravity and moral corruption. Amsterdam's bustling red-light district was tolerant of every sin and vice, yet the native Dutch were often contemptuous of the cultures and religious traditions of immigrant laborers, who did much of the menial work that kept the society running.

Khalid and his two comrades became convinced that the U.S. invasion of Iraq presented a cataclysmic threat to the cradle of the Muslim world. If left to stand, Western decadence would destroy Islam's holiest lands. They asked to join the fight and were given a contact in Spain who could help to enlist them in the cause. The next week, Khalid spoke to his parents. He told them that one of his colleagues at the engineering firm at which he had interned had sent a letter on his behalf to a German engineering company in Bremen. Khalid said that he been offered a six-month contract and had accepted. His parents were overjoyed about his change in fortune.

Two days later, his parents saw him off at the train station. He waved to them from the train as he headed northeast in the direction of Hamburg. At the first stop, he got off, purchased a ticket to Madrid, and in a small café waited the three hours for the next train. As he headed south across the mountains from France to Spain, he marveled at how easy it was for a European to travel across borders that had once been so heavily fortified and over which so much blood had been shed over the centuries. Now a businessman or tourist could move from Portugal to Finland without ever showing a passport or obtaining a visa.

At a nondescript apartment outside Madrid, Khalid met his contact, from whom he received a folded envelope that included a Lebanese passport with his picture on it and a stack of U.S. currency. He was driven to the coastal town of Málaga in a rental car and boarded a fishing vessel, where he found his two friends, who had come separately by similar routes. The captain's primary income came not from fish but from smuggling migrants from North Africa into Spain and beyond. More than one million illegal immigrants, mostly from Morocco, are thought to be in Spain. In 2004, the Spanish government apprehended more than fifteen thousand people trying to enter the country illegally, but local authorities are much less mindful of those who are leaving. The captain gave them coveralls so they could appear to be part of the crew. Two nights later, a small speedboat with its navigational lights extinguished pulled up alongside the vessel while they were trawling off the coast of Morocco and took them off.

Once they were ashore in Morocco, it took three weeks for the trio to travel across North Africa, through Lebanon, and arrive at the Syrian-Iraqi border. When they reached Iraq, Khalid and his colleagues found that their technical backgrounds were in high demand. They traveled to a training camp in eastern Iraq and there learned from Iranian tutors how to construct the latest version of the improvised explosive device, or IED. These weapons were effectively neutralizing the ability of American soldiers to patrol in tanks and personnel carriers. Sophisticated "shaped" charges or explosively formed projectiles (EFPs) are a kind of pipe bomb that uses a high explosive to generate a shock wave through a large copper slug. The slug then becomes a molten jet of metal capable of penetrating even the thick armor of a 70-ton M1 Abrams tank. (Pentagon experts are working around the clock trying to find an effective countermeasure for this low-tech weapon, but so far have come up dry.)

After three months of working on explosive devices, Khalid was assigned to an operation whose aim was to destroy one of Iraq's largest oil refineries in the town of Baiji in northern Iraq. Early one morning, two groups departed from a nearby village. Their goal was to arrive at the facility as the day and night shifts were changing. The plan was for the first unit to drive a car bomb into the guard station located at the entry gate, killing the sentries and creating chaos, which would allow Khalid's unit to slip into the facility. The second group would head for a storage tank near the refinery and attack it with an IED. The subsequent conflagration would destroy the refinery.

On the day of the attack, the operation was tripped up by an unexpected roadblock manned by U.S. troops a short distance from the facility. When two GIs approached the first car, the driver set off the explosive device. Khalid's car, traveling a short distance behind, was able to turn around and speed away before being apprehended.

A week after the failed refinery attack, Khalid, along with his Dutch friends and two fellow insurgents from the United Kingdom, were given a new assignment. They were told they could make a greater contribution to confronting the enemies of Islam by returning to their home countries and applying their newly acquired war-fighting skills there. Three days later, they slipped across the Iraqi border into Turkey. Once they crossed the border into Greece with their Dutch and British passports, they were able to move freely across Europe without attracting any undue attention.

During their travels, Khalid urged his colleagues to think ambitiously. The nation that led "the crusader alliance" and that was most responsible for advancing the cult of the individual and the secularization of modern society had been unbloodied on its own soil since 9/11. Why should the group not follow the example of Khalid Sheikh Mohammed, who had masterminded the audacious strikes on New York and Washington? But this time, instead of an attack from the air, they should strike the infidels from the sea, as their Yemeni counterparts had done against the USS *Cole* in October 2000. If a small boat laden with conventional explosives could blow a forty-by-forty-foot gash in the hull of the *Cole*, imagine what a shaped charge would do to a ship carrying liquefied natural gas or oil! The October 2002 suicide bombing of the 1,090-foot French tanker *Limburg* had set it on fire, spilling 90,000 barrels of oil into the Gulf of Aden. Osama bin Laden had observed that "by striking the oil tanker in Yemen with explosives, the attackers struck at the umbilical cord of the Christians." Instead of the cord, why not target the womb, by bombing a tanker inside a U.S. harbor?

Nabih—one of the British nationals—responded that while Khalid's idea was both audacious and appealing, there were practical issues that would have to be addressed. The group had proven themselves in battle on land, but conducting an attack at sea was more complicated. A shaped charge had not yet been used against a ship, and it would be difficult to practice attack techniques without attracting attention. The Americans had been investing in port security, so they would need to investigate the measures that were in place that might raise the risk of failure. Nabih said they were all ready to die for martyrdom, but such sacrifice was justifiable only if they could be successful in carrying out the mission.

The group agreed that they should proceed cautiously, but an attack on America's Achilles' heel—its dependency on imported energy—was a worthy mission. When they arrived back in Amsterdam, they began planning in earnest. They quickly decided that their goal would be to carry out simultaneous attacks on both the East and West coasts.

A Web search unearthed media reports from the period just after 9/11 that pointed to one very attractive potential target. Each week, a ship more than three football fields long, 150 feet wide, and twelve stories high, loaded with 30 million gallons of liquefied natural gas, sails into Boston Harbor. (Liquefied natural gas is natural gas that has been frozen to −260 degrees Fahrenheit, making it six hundred times as dense as than its normal volume so it can be shipped economically.) The vessel steams through the inner harbor of Boston and under the Tobin Bridge—a major vehicle artery into Boston—and ties up at an LNG facility at the mouth of the Mystic River.

After the attacks on the Twin Towers, Boston Fire Commissioner Paul Christian and several fire chiefs from neighboring communities met with Boston's mayor, Thomas Menino, to brief him on the destruction that could be wrought should a terrorist strike at one of these ships. They told the mayor that they had a limited ability to respond to such a scenario, which would place the lives of thousands of their citizens in danger. After the briefing, Mayor Menino publicly called for a ban on LNG deliveries.

The Coast Guard responded by denying entry to the Norwegian-operated LNG tanker *Matthew* on September 27, 2001, while it reviewed the matter. The agency then put into place new requirements. These include requiring vessels carrying LNG to stay in constant communication with the Coast Guard from the time they sail from their port of departure until they arrive offshore. Inspectors board LNG tankers as they approach Boston harbor and examine them before allowing them to enter the port. There is an expanded legal zone around the ship that other vessels are prohibited from entering, and several Coast Guard small boats are assigned to escort LNG ships on their harbor transits. Bridge traffic is shut down, and flights to Logan are diverted until the ship passes. The Boston Police Department and Massachusetts State Police also step up their shore patrols whenever an LNG-carrying tanker is in the harbor.

For a while these new security measures helped to quiet down the furor, but in November 2003 Menino renewed his call for an end to LNG shipments after U.S. government scientists confirmed that an LNG tanker attack would have dire consequences. Menino accused federal and industry officials of playing "Russian roulette" with the safety of the city.

Even though the ruckus had largely quieted down, there continued to be calls to close down the Everett facility. Securing the ships' transits has become routine—which meant, from a terrorist's perspective, that they were potentially vulnerable to a surprise attack. Khalid also liked the symbolism of striking so close to Logan airport, which had served as one of the stepping-off points of the 9/11 attacks. If they succeeded, it would help reinforce the message that committed jihadists could strike where and when they pleased.

On the West Coast, San Pedro Bay is home to a massive port complex shared by Los Angeles and Long Beach. Surfing the Internet, Nabih discovered that all the main pipelines to the major refineries are located on the Long Beach side of the harbor. This meant that large oil tankers, such as the 300,000-ton *Limburg,* would have to enter from the sea by way of the Long Beach channel. If the main channel could be blocked by a sabotaged tanker and the resultant massive oil spill, other ships would not be able to enter or leave. Containing the oil spill and salvaging the sunken vessel would be a daunting and time-consuming challenge.

A bit more research revealed that when the 629-foot freight ship *New Carissa,* of Panamanian registry and carrying 400,000 gallons of fuel, ran aground off of Coos Bay, Oregon, in February 1999, it took more than three months and the involvement of fifty-eight agencies and more than seven hundred people to deal with the resulting wreck and oil spill. Marine accidents on the West Coast have become increasingly rare, which has translated into there not being enough demand to support a commercial salvage industry there. This means that it would likely take weeks to clear a major wreck sunk in Long Beach Harbor. In the interim, the region's refineries would be idled within a week and the nation's most populous region would literally run out of gas.

Nabih also learned that while the Americans seemed to be talking a great deal about port security, they had really not done much about it. The Port of Los Angeles has 7,500 acres of waterways and facilities and forty-three miles of waterfront. This infrastructure is being protected by a port police force of just over one hundred officers, and a diverse collection of private security services hired by the marine terminals. Long Beach's equivalent area of waterways and facilities is even more exposed: just a dozen Long Beach police officers and a small cadre of port security personnel patrol a waterfront protected primarily by private security guards hired by the terminal operators. There are other federal, state, county, and city agencies that have some level of jurisdiction in this massive port complex, but all maintain only a tiny presence. Too often, confusion over who should be in charge leaves many security gaps unattended. In the five years since 9/11, Los Angeles had received just $25 million dollars in federal grants to improve its port security, less than what Washington spends on airport security every two days.

By surfing the Web, the terrorist planner was able to find a July 2006 *Seattle Times* article describing the experiences of a reporter who easily penetrated the security of ports in Los Angeles–Long Beach and Seattle. All he had to do was hitch a ride from a few immigrant truck drivers coming to drop off and pick up cargo. The one time when the reporter was asked for identification, he flashed an expired driver's license to a uniformed guard standing fifteen feet away, who then waved him through the gate.

Regarding the Americans' ability to deal with the risk of a small-boat attack, beginning in 2002, the Coast Guard had deployed armed maritime safety and security teams to operate out of thirteen U.S. ports, including Los Angeles, Long Beach, and Boston. However, even the commandant of the U.S. Coast Guard seemed apprehensive that the service was not ready to deal with the threat. Admiral Thad Allen had publicly declared that while its own threat and vulnerability analysis had confirmed there was a real risk, "We haven't put nearly as much thinking in science and technology and (general) thought into the small-vessel threat as we need to."

Part of the problem the Coast Guard or any port police force faces is discerning a terrorist needle in a mammoth haystack of legitimate recreational boaters. The United States has no national registry or national system of operator licensing for the eighteen million recreational boats in the United States. The only way to anticipate whether a boater may pose a threat is by observing the vessel and its operator's behavior. The Coast Guard does not usually provide an escort for tankers carrying crude oil, so there often is not even anyone available to make this call. For LNG, the Coast Guard has established a half-mile exclusion zone on either side of a tanker—essentially a regulatory no-man's-land that boaters are supposed to steer clear of. But a small boat traveling at 50 knots can enter that zone and be alongside a ship in just over thirty seconds. Once the LNG tanker is inside the harbor, the channel may be only a few hundred yards wide, a distance that can be traveled in the blink of an eye. This leaves virtually no time for the Coast Guard escort vessels to determine that they are facing an imminent attack as opposed to a reckless or ignorant everyday boater. Firing on the attacking boat is very problematical. Even if there were not all the risks associated with using automatic firearms near a waterfront where people live, work, and play, it is extremely hard to hit a small vessel moving at a high speed from another moving vessel.

As for securing a small boat to carry out an attack, Khalid, Nabih, and their compatriots learned that purchasing a Zodiac boat with a powerful outboard motor in the United States was about as easy as buying a plasma television. It could then be outfitted with an improvised shaped charge constructed with explosive materials and technology readily available within the United States. The best way to gain access to the water without drawing much attention to themselves would be to transport their Zodiacs on a trailer pulled behind a SUV to an open public boat ramp. Once inside the harbor, two Zodiacs traveling at the speed of 40-plus knots could pull out of a nearby marina, penetrate the Coast Guard's security perimeter, and be alongside a lumbering vessel with little risk of being intercepted. It would be a suicide mission, but Allah would surely reward them for carrying out such a bold strike on the infidels.

Confident now that their plan was a viable one, the group met with their imam, who commended them for their unwavering commitment to defeating the crusaders. He provided them with contacts at mosques in the Los Angeles and Boston areas. The five men decided they would leave within a month on different flights to Logan and LAX.

Once in the United States, their preparations began in earnest. Their goal was to carry out the attack within six months, ideally as close to the 9/11 anniversary as possible. Khalid and his compatriots screened several possible candidates referred to them by the local imam. They settled on two first-generation Pakistani immigrants whom the imam had successfully radicalized. Both had been arrested for their involvement in a car theft ring that specialized in stealing luxury automobiles in the New York area and shipping them to Latin America in containers for resale on the black market. While serving time in the New York State prison system, they had become devout Muslims. A prison chaplain suggested that after they were released, they should reach out to a friend of his who was the imam of a mosque in northern Massachusetts. He said his friend would be happy to help them find jobs and a place to live. The chaplain was right; the imam found them an apartment and lined them up with jobs in nearby Nashua, New Hampshire. Meanwhile, he took them under his wing, taking a very personal interest in their religious education.

The reason Khalid needed additional recruits was that he had determined that it would take a minimum of two Zodiacs to carry out the attack on the LNG ship. First, there was always a chance that the Coast Guard would get lucky and intercept or succeed at firing at and hitting one of the boats before it reached the target. Second, according to reports he had read, there was some debate among experts as to whether the rupture of a single six-million-gallon double-walled cargo tank would be sufficient to ignite the entire vessel and its load of 30 million gallons. A safer bet would be to breach two of the ship's five tanks.

Because LNG is stored at such low temperatures in liquid form, it does not explode. However, it does burn at extremely high temperatures. Once started, a gas fire cannot be extinguished; it has to burn itself out. In a report released by Sandia National Laboratory in December 2004, scientists determined that should a large LNG spill on water be ignited, it would burn at 3,000 degrees Fahrenheit for thirty minutes to an hour, throwing off enough heat to incinerate everything within four-tenths of a mile of the vessel. This includes steel, which melts at 2,300 degrees Fahrenheit and has no strength left if it is exposed to a temperature of 1,200 degrees for ten minutes. Beyond that range, the threat to most buildings would be from secondary explosions of hazardous materials within the area of the original fire or the result of failed efforts by firefighters to contain it. Even in protective clothing, firefighters could get no nearer than 1.3 miles away from the fire until it started to burn itself out. Those people outside this range but within the second mile radius of the fire would suffer second-degree burns on unprotected skin within about thirty seconds. However, most would likely be able to get to shelter and avoid this exposure.

On the West Coast, Nabih made the decision to keep his operation simpler, using only his comrade and one Zodiac. His target would not be escorted. His plan was to attack the oil tanker toward the rear of the ship just as it cleared the harbor breakwater. If things worked out as planned, he would be able both to set the vessel on fire and to cause enough damage to the vessel to make it unmaneuverable, so that it would ultimately sink in the channel.

Early one Friday morning before the Labor Day weekend, two boat trailers arrived at the boat ramp in Mary O'Malley Park on the Mystic River Reservation, just a few miles north of the Everett facility. Khalid and his four colleagues brought along fishing poles, bait, and a cooler. The IED had been loaded into the boat and covered with a blue tarp. Their destination was a marina just south and west of the Tobin Bridge, a short distance from the Charlestown Navy Yard, where the USS *Constitution* was moored. To buy themselves some time, they purchased some ice for their supposed fishing trip. Meanwhile, on the opposite coast, an SUV backed a Zodiac down the Cabrillo Beach boat ramp in San Pedro, California. After parking the vehicle, Nabih and his accomplice headed out toward the breakwater at the entrance of Los Angeles Harbor.

It was just before 10:00 A.M. when the LNG tanker *Matthew*—ironically, the very vessel that had been stranded outside Boston Harbor after 9/11—steamed past the runways of Logan airport and turned north for the final two miles of its voyage to the Everett facility. There were Coast Guard vessels in front and along either side of the tanker. When the ship reached Boston's North End, the harbor narrowed to about 750 feet across.

Khalid waited until the *Matthew* was making its final turn to transit under the bridge. The two Zodiacs then darted out from the Shipyard Quarters Marina. By the time the Coast Guard vessel on the port side of the *Matthew* saw them, the Zodiacs were moving at full speed only 250 feet away. The petty officer in charge of the escort vessel reached for his bullhorn to warn the boats to steer clear. That cost him precious time. By the time he realized that the Zodiacs were heading directly for the LNG tanker, it was too late. The Zodiacs drew alongside the tanker, roughly 150 feet apart. As the Coast Guard scrambled to remove the safeties on their weapons, a man stood up in each boat and pressed an object to the hull, then disappeared in a blinding light.

Soon there was a torrent of liquefied gas spilling out of two gaping holes in the tanker's hull. As the gas came into contact with the warm air outside, it started to vaporize, and then the vapors ignited.

On the West Coast, Nabih's Zodiac arrived at the breakwater shortly before 6:00 A.M., West Coast time. As planned, they traveled eastward, staying close to the inside of the breakwater, and then intercepted the 300,000-ton, Panamanian-flag vessel *Mercury Glory* as it was entering the Long Beach channel. As the Zodiac approached the vessel, Nabih gave a friendly wave. Then the Zodiac suddenly turned around and drew alongside the rear of the vessel. Nabih stood up, held the EFP against the hull, and set off the detonator.

In Boston, the burning hull of the *Matthew* was drifting toward the Tobin Bridge, while the Charlestown, East Boston, and Chelsea waterfronts within a 700-yard radius were soon ablaze from the heat. Buildings shook, windows shattered, and people in the vicinity were thrown to the ground when the LNG fire ignited the nearby jet fuel storage tanks that serviced Logan airport. Mayor Menino found himself living out his worst nightmare. The initial estimates were that more than 10,000 people were dead or seriously injured, mostly with burns. Boston's world-class hospitals were completely overwhelmed by the casualties. In addition to the hundreds of homes and buildings along the city's waterfront, "Old Ironsides" and the Coast Guard's largest base in New England had been lost in the fire. The asphalt roadway on the Tobin Bridge had melted, and the Massport engineers reported that the entire bridge might have to be demolished. Logan airport was effectively shut down for all but emergency aircraft because there was no fuel for the planes. Because of a prevailing northerly wind and effective firefighting, the Everett facility miraculously escaped complete destruction, but it would be out of commission for some time as repairs were made. The Mystic Station power plant, which depended upon it for fuel, had been shut down, leaving more than a million New Englanders without electricity.

In Long Beach, the tanker was so large that the initial explosion from the EFP was barely felt on the bridge of the ship. However, a member of the crew immediately reported that it appeared that it had been struck by a small boat. The harbor pilot acted quickly, directing the chief engineer to stop the engines, ordering that the anchor be released, and radioing a Mayday. Thousands of gallons of crude oil were pouring out of the rupture in the hull, and the *Mercury Glory* was on fire. But the quick action of the pilot prevented the ship from getting too close to the entrance of the middle harbor, where it would have blocked the main channel to the oil terminal. It would take three days to douse the fire, but the ship never sank. Tugs were able to nudge the vessel to the side of the channel so that shipping traffic could move again, but the oil spill was the worst maritime environmental disaster to hit the United States since the grounding of the *Exxon Valdez* in 1989.

The attacks on Boston and Los Angeles soon had national and global reverberations. Energy prices surged on global markets, rising to more than $100 per barrel. All of the nation's ports were put on their highest alert, effectively closing them to all inbound traffic. Given the absence of spare refinery capacity and the limited supplies of available refined fuels, gasoline prices quickly rose above $6 a gallon. The container ships that crisscross the Pacific Ocean and Atlantic Ocean with the supplies that support the global manufacturing and retailing sectors began to fill the anchorages on the West and East coasts. Many could not be rerouted, since they are too big to transit through the Panama Canal and only a handful of megaports can accommodate them. Since 60 percent of the world's container fleet is at sea at any given time, the port closure generated a domino effect. With so many vessels unable to discharge their cargo, overseas terminals recognized that they must not compound the problem and stopped loading ships destined for the United States. Since those terminals had no place to accommodate the scheduled deliveries of arriving cargo, they closed their gates to incoming trucks and trains and stopped servicing inbound feeder vessels. These conveyances become stranded outside the terminals, weighted down with shipments they could not deliver. Around the world, goods started piling up at factories and warehouses as the global transportation system became gridlocked.

Terrorist attacks do not come with the warning of a major hurricane. Even when they are over, no one really knows whether follow-on attacks may be in the offing and where they are likely to be directed. This is an important difference from natural disasters. While an earthquake or tsunami may come with little to no warning, it has a clear beginning and end. But an act of catastrophic terrorism inevitably generates a wider and more enduring sense of vulnerability. Should the next attack on the United States look something like the scenario outlined above, mayors and everyday citizens of port cities will ask themselves, If it could happen to Boston and Long Beach, why couldn't it happen to us?

Sadly, despite the passage of time since the 9/11 attacks, Washington is unlikely to provide a satisfying answer. As it has barely gone through the motions of improving protective measures on the home front, especially within ports and at facilities that handle dangerous substances, there is not much to point to that can reassure local elected officials or the general public. Further, the persistent problems that continue to afflict U.S. intelligence efforts, both abroad and at home, do not bode well for early detection and interception of terrorist operations. The challenge is compounded by the fact that terrorists can come from friendly countries that make it easy to fly to and from the

United States. They may have backgrounds like Khalid's that are not likely to earn them a place on a watch list. And they can align themselves with what appears to be a growing number of American citizens who are willing to be radicalized out of a sense of shared grievance with Muslims in the Middle East.

Outside of the Middle East, in the five years since 9/11, there have been terrorist attacks carried out in Bali, Mumbai, Casablanca, Madrid, and London. As evidenced by the June 2006 arrests in Toronto and the August 2006 arrests in London, the formal links with al-Qaeda have become increasingly tenuous, yet the pool of radical jihadists is growing. We *will* be attacked again, despite our overseas exertions. It is as inevitable as a hurricane, earthquake, or major flood. And as with those recognized disasters, there are things we can be doing right now to make us a more resilient nation.

THREE

INVITING DISASTER

O N AN UNSEASONABLY WARM EVENING in November 1872, a fire broke out in the basement of a commercial building on the corner of Kingston and Summer streets in downtown Boston. It took several minutes for the fire to be detected and for the alarm to be raised. At that time, the prosperous citizens of Boston were bankrolling one of the world's premier fire departments, under the leadership of an extraordinary chief, John Damrell. But despite the state-of-the-art pumping equipment and the firefighters' superb training, the response to the fire was delayed by a fateful calamity of a different sort: Boston was experiencing an epidemic of equestrian distemper that had started several weeks earlier in Toronto and spread along the East Coast. As a result, the workhorses that pulled the fire pumps were too ill to leave their stalls. The firefighters had to do the backbreaking work of pulling the pumps along the cobblestone streets by hand in order to reach the fire.

The flammable goods routinely stored in the lofts of the buildings along Summer Street fed the fire, and within an hour, the conflagration had consumed a city block. Because there were no pumps powerful enough to produce the water pressure to reach the top of the buildings, the fire began to leap to rooftops across the street. Chief Damrell arrived at the blaze within eight minutes of the first alarm. The year before, after Chicago had been destroyed by fire, Damrell had traveled to that ruined city to learn what he could about how to avoid a similar fate in Boston. As he assessed his own situation that November evening, he saw in play all the ingredients for replicating the Chicago disaster and decided to do something never done before: he sent out a request for assistance to every neighboring fire department within fifty miles of Boston.

What had destroyed Chicago in 1871 was a phenomenon known as a firestorm: a fire that had become so powerful that its appetite for air and fuel had created hurricane-force winds that sucked in everything in its path. Damrell worried that Boston was facing a similar fate. Throughout that evening, in an era without any of the tools a fire chief would have today, such as command centers or radios (the alarm sent to neighboring communities was transmitted by telegraph), Damrell organized his teams of firefighters into a line of defense around the perimeter of the commercial district and along the waterfront. His plan was to husband his resources to prevent the fire from spreading to the residential neighborhoods, to the docks and moored ships, and to historic Boston landmarks such as the Old South Church, the Old State House, and City Hall. The strategy appeared to be working, but by early morning, his men were at the end of their endurance. Just when exhaustion was about to overtake them completely, pumper cars and firefighters from four states began arriving by rail. Only nine hours after Damrell's call for help went out, he had reinforcements from as far away as New Haven, Connecticut, and Biddeford, Maine, to hold the line.

In the end, hundreds of commercial buildings lay in charred ruins. But thanks to the actions of Damrell, his Boston firefighters, and the speedy support of communities throughout the region, the majority of the city was still standing. The Great Boston Fire of 1872 became the first urban firestorm ever to be successfully contained.

Thirty-four years later, on America's opposite coast, the San Francisco earthquake struck at 5:12 A.M. on April 18, 1906, registering 8.25 on the Richter scale. The ground shook for a little over a minute, and the city of San Francisco lay in ruins. Simon Winchester's *A Crack in the Edge of the World* describes a quickly mobilized response, much like that in Boston. This time, help would come first from the U.S. military. Within two hours of the sudden shift along the San Andreas Fault, army troops were dispatched to the Hall of Justice Building, which was serving as the city's emergency headquarters. The troops' acting commander, Brigadier General Frederick Funston, did not wait for an official request from the city before offering assistance. The recipient of a Congressional Medal of Honor for his service in the Philippines, General Funston determined, on his own initiative, that all his available troops from the Presidio and Fort Mason could be put to good use in responding to the disaster. By 7:45 A.M., 153 minutes after the earth moved, Mayor Eugene Schmitz had scores of troops at his disposal, whom he directed to cordon off all burning areas and keep onlookers safely away.

With telegraph service throughout San Francisco lost, a boat was requisitioned and sent to Oakland to convey word of the catastrophe and wire for help. "San Francisco is in ruins," the cables read. "Our city needs help." By 11:00 P.M., a train from Los Angeles loaded with packaged food and medicine arrived in Berkeley in response to that request. The following day, William Howard Taft, the secretary of war, ordered that 200,000 rations be dispatched from Washington State and that trains from Army bases in Texas, Pennsylvania, Nebraska, Iowa, and Wyoming bring troops, tents, and other emergency supplies to San

Francisco. The largest hospital train ever assembled departed Virginia for the West Coast within thirty-six hours after the earthquake struck. Congress made all this legal by passing an emergency resolution shortly *after* Taft issued his orders. In the end, San Francisco was nearly completely destroyed: 490 city blocks were wrecked, 28,188 buildings lay in ruin, and 225,000 people from a population of about 400,000 were left homeless. The final death toll was estimated to be around 4,000.

The fire in the aftermath of the San Francisco Earthquake ranks first among the most destructive fires in U.S. history. The Boston fire of 1872 ranks fifth. The response to these two catastrophic events, 3,000 miles apart and more than a century ago, stands in stunning contrast to how the leaders of New Orleans, the state of Louisiana, and the federal government managed the aftermath of Hurricane Katrina. In New Orleans, 60,000 people needed to be rescued from rooftops and flooded homes, 25,000 of New Orleans' poorest citizens were stranded for days at the Superdome, and countless others were trapped on highway overpasses surrounded by water. Yet it would take six days for the 82nd Airborne—a military unit that is on call to respond within eighteen hours to any military contingency around the world—to be deployed to the Gulf Coast from its home base in Fort Bragg, North Carolina. As the Pentagon dithered for nearly a week, the rescue efforts were left to the perennially overstretched Coast Guard, a handful of Louisiana Wildlife and Fisheries boats, and a flotilla of volunteer sportsmen in flat-bottomed boats.

One conclusion to be drawn from these earlier catastrophes is that twenty-first-century Americans should reasonably be able to expect a far more nimble response to disasters when they happen. The speed at which assistance can be mobilized and deployed has more to do with political and bureaucratic will than the inherent constraints of getting outside emergency responders, equipment, and supplies to where they are needed. Logistics is something American companies like Federal

Express, Wal-Mart, and Target are very good at. There is no reason why our government can't be, particularly if it is willing to partner with the private sector.

During the initial stage of any large disaster, the needs tend to be generic. People who are trapped have to be rescued. The injured require medical care. Fires need to be extinguished. Food, water, and shelter have to be provided to those who are homeless. Some sense of order needs to be restored. From the standpoint of survivors, it matters little whether these basic needs are met by a local emergency responder, a military air rescue team from a faraway state, or Wal-Mart's distribution system. What is important is that there is an outstretched hand when they need it. The United States is the wealthiest and most powerful nation in the world. The only thing that is holding it back from providing immediate assistance to its citizens during times of grave emergencies is an unwillingness to hammer out the details in advance and a reluctance to invest in the capacity for doing so.

However, the more instructive lesson these past events provide for our times actually comes from what happened *after* the fires were extinguished in Boston and the troops returned to their barracks in San Francisco. Chief Damrell may have been one of the most skilled and heroic firefighters of his time, but his most lasting legacy is what he contributed to fire *prevention*. A year after the Boston fire he resigned as fire chief to become the city's chief building inspector. He went on to found a national association of building inspectors and mobilized and led an alliance of architects, builders, insurance underwriters, and fire chiefs to develop a model building code to make cities more fire resistant. By the early twentieth century, the code was widely adopted throughout the country.

Similarly, the San Francisco Earthquake ushered in new standards for constructing buildings so they could better survive the shocks of seismic events. These standards were rigorously enforced, so that when new commercial buildings went up in the city's downtown, they were built with steel framing, reinforced concrete supports, and fire protection systems. These efforts were not put to the test until eighty-three years later, when the Bay Area was hit by a 6.9-magnitude earthquake. Hardly any of the structures built in San Francisco after 1906 were damaged.

Damrell and his counterparts in San Francisco did not set out to eliminate risk. Instead, they sought to identify and pursue practical ways to make the places they inhabited more resilient, given these risks. Not every fire could be prevented, but it was possible to take measures that would protect the city from being consumed by a firestorm. Without warning, the ground could shift, but this did not mean that skyscrapers had to be reduced to rubble. The key was to acknowledge vulnerabilities when they were revealed and undertake reasonable measures to reduce them.

Sadly, if John Damrell were alive today, he would find himself hopelessly out of fashion. Increasingly, our preference seems to be to gamble that disasters won't actually happen and to make commercial and personal choices that only raise the stakes when they do. This willful disregard of risk, particularly when it comes to the forces of nature, is something that started to preoccupy me in the mid-1980s. At the time, I was serving as the commanding officer of a Coast Guard patrol boat based in Norfolk, Virginia. It is impossible not to develop a respect for the destructive power of a natural tempest when your primary mission is rescuing mariners off the Virginia Capes and the Outer Banks of North Carolina. Any delusions I may have had as a young twenty-four-year-old of my own relative invincibility were put to rest in early November 1985, when I responded to a distress call from the sailing vessel *Prelude*. The 45-foot yacht was manned by a crew of five very experienced ocean racers. It had been sailing back to the East Coast from Bermuda when it ran into a "no-name" storm nearly two hundred miles off the entrance to Chesapeake Bay. In hurricane-force winds, the vessel was knocked down and capsized four times. Miraculously, the yacht righted itself each time and the sailors survived the battering. However, two of the men were injured and the yacht's rigging was destroyed. Disabled and adrift, the skipper issued a Mayday call as the Gulf Stream pulled them further out to sea.

It would take fourteen hours for my 82-foot patrol boat to reach them. During the journey from Norfolk, we had three engineering casualties that nearly left us foundering. Each time, my seasick crew managed to make the necessary repairs, and we ultimately were able to locate the *Prelude* and place it under tow. It was another twelve hours before the storm weakened enough for us to make any real headway back to shore. Two days later we reached Ocean City, Maryland. After having a chance to talk with the *Prelude*'s crew, I remember thinking how narrow the line was between being the victim and the rescuer. The sea can destroy any vessel if it is in the wrong place at the wrong time. As I realized during that trip, this was true even for a Coast Guard vessel designed to sail into harm's way.

One cannot help but bring this bit of offshore sobriety back onshore. But I soon found that where I saw recklessness, most everyone else seemed to see only opportunity. For instance, I was struck by the dramatic contrast between the new construction furiously under way along the Virginia Beach and Norfolk waterfronts and the century-old quarters at Cape Henry, where I lived in the lighthouse keeper's house. Situated on a sandy peninsula at the entrance of Chesapeake Bay, my two-story keeper's house sat a respectful distance from the sea, behind a large sand dune. The nineteenth-century architect had constructed it with thick cinder-block walls that were faced with brick. It had been designed to ride out any storm. I wondered how those who had put so much care into building this small keeper's house would have reacted to the beachfront houses and condominiums flying up all around me.

I was particularly astonished by the hubris of developing every acre along a two-mile stretch of sand at the northernmost tip of Norfolk, known as Willoughby Spit. The land did not even exist in the first half of the eighteenth century! It was created as a result of the combined efforts of hurricanes in 1749 and 1806. Scientists speculate that the storms were probably centered just south of Norfolk, creating an influx of water into the Chesapeake Bay of up to fifteen feet above normal that shifted sand around to form the new strip of land. It occurred to me that what a hurricane could create, it could also take away. For a long time, this seemed to be the conventional wisdom, since for much of Willoughby Spit's history it was home to only a few summer cottages. But in modern times, realtors started throwing caution to the wind. In fact, in March 2006, developers began their most ambitious project yet. At the very tip of the spit, construction began on three towers containing 294 condominiums, 30 townhomes, and three loft apartment buildings, along with 22,000 square feet of retail space and a restaurant. Southern Virginia may be part of the Bible Belt, but the biblical admonition to be wary about houses built on sand clearly does not inform the deliberations of the Norfolk zoning board.

Of course, what I had observed happening along Virginia's beaches was not an isolated phenomenon. The years 1960 to 2000 were the quietest period of hurricane activity on record, and Americans, heartened by the lull, started migrating to the coast by the millions. The development boom was given a real boost with the creation of the National Flood Insurance Program (NFIP) in 1968. In theory, the NFIP was intended to encourage the adoption and enforcement of ordinances in flood-prone areas that would make homes less susceptible to flood damage. But in practice, the insurance often only ended up aiding and abetting development into areas where private insurers would never tread because flooding was such a sure thing. The combination of real estate interests, shortsighted local politicians, and complicit home owners translated into an effective lobbying force. The federal government has been pressured to keep the insurance priced so low that it has effectively subsidized people moving into extremely risky areas. Compounding the problem is the fact that few places are included in the "must-insure" category, so there are not nearly enough premiums coming from home owners facing a moderate risk of flooding to keep the program solvent.

Many experts recognized that what was happening was nothing short of madness. What would not be attractive about shifting the local economic risks of devastating storms onto the broad backs of American taxpayers? Certainly, builders in southern Florida and along the Gulf Coast like the new odds, which have led to a sustained boom in permanent development in vulnerable coastal regions, especially during the 1990s. For instance, from 1995 to 2000, nearly 90,000 people moved into Mississippi's three coastal counties and the three adjacent communities to the north. Hurricane Katrina would destroy 68,729 houses in the same area.

Even before Katrina struck, there were plenty of warnings that we were on a headlong path to disaster. The first serious indication of just how vulnerable all this new development was to a serious storm came in 1992 with Hurricane Andrew. Andrew made landfall south of Miami as a Category 5 storm, crossed into the Gulf of Mexico, and later roared into south-central Louisiana as a Category 3 storm. An automated weather station near Homestead, Florida, reported gusts of up to 177 mph before it too became a casualty of Andrew. The hurricane caused $26 billion in damage ($45 billion in 2005 dollars), most of it to poorly constructed housing and trailer parks in the Homestead area. If this was a wake-up call, it was one heard only locally, and it had to keep ringing for a very long time. It was not until 2002, a decade later, that the state of Florida established a new state building code, which the insurance industry estimates would have reduced Andrew's damage by $10 billion. However, this belated nudge in the right direction was more than offset by continued coastal development. Florida continues to be the fastest-growing coastal state and in 2004 had $2.4 trillion of

residential and commercial properties that were vulnerable to hurricanes. A computer simulation of a hurricane equivalent to Andrew hitting downtown Miami in 2002 estimated that it would have inflicted
double the overall economic losses of the 1992 storm.

Andrew turned out to be just a warm-up act for the Hurricane Katrina drama that played out in virtually every American living room in
late August and early September 2005. The storm and the destruction of
New Orleans have produced a torrent of "What went wrong?" hearings,
official reports, books, and media retrospectives. As a result, the basic elements of that narrative are now well established and widely known.

Louisiana's growing exposure to severe weather arose due not so
much to overdevelopment along its fragile coast but to the gradual
disappearance of that coast. Through the combined forces of coastal erosion and the unintended consequences of flood-control and navigable-
waterway engineering decisions, nearly one million acres of wetlands
south of New Orleans disappeared between 1930 and 2005. Historically,
those wetlands had served as a buffer for the city, which was located fifty-
five miles from the Gulf of Mexico, by both slowing down the movement of storms and absorbing some of the resulting storm surges. Now
storm surges that would have been reduced to ten to twelve feet fifty
years ago could arrive in New Orleans at eighteen to twenty feet.

Compounding New Orleans' exposure to storm-surge flooding is
the man-made seventy-six-mile-long Mississippi River Gulf Outlet
(MRGO) Canal, completed in 1968. The MRGO was constructed to
shorten the time and distance required for oceangoing vessels to reach
the city. During Katrina it also facilitated the flooding of New Orleans
by funneling the water that the Gulf of Mexico dumped into Lake
Borgne into this cement-sided waterway. As the hurricane came onshore, the water steamrolled down the MRGO on a collision course
with the Industrial Canal, causing an 800-foot breach. Many of the
communities to the east of New Orleans were victims of the overtop-
ping of the MRGO.

Of course, New Orleans' primary line of defense against the sea and the Mississippi River has long been its now-infamous levee and flood-wall system, which has changed little in the past fifty years. The city is like a fishbowl, with the water on the outside and a half a million homes on the inside. New Orleans has been sinking at a rate of three feet per century, so that it now lies an average of six feet below sea level, with some neighborhoods as low as eleven feet below. Without the levees and flood walls, much of the city would be a shallow lake.

With the majority of New Orleans resting below the level of the water that surrounds it, a routine challenge that the city faces is getting rid of the rainwater that every passing storm dumps on its streets. In the nineteenth century, three major canals were constructed to manage storm runoff. Pumps located at the city end of the canals collect the water and push it down the canals to Lake Pontchartrain. Unfortunately, canals designed to send water out of the city can also bring water back into the city if there is a storm surge. Since water always seeks its lowest level, when Lake Pontchartrain fills up with water blown in from the Gulf of Mexico, it empties back down the canals and into the city's center. Decades ago, the U.S. Army Corps of Engineers proposed constructing swinging floodgates on the lake side of the canals. These gates could then be closed when a hurricane drew near to keep the lake from backwashing into the city. They were never built.

The haphazard management of New Orleans' storm protection system is astonishing, given its importance. Invading floodwaters drown those who have been unable or unwilling to get to higher ground, paralyze basic infrastructure, including the city's drainage pumps, and create a toxic cauldron of debris that oozes out of the urban and industrial landscape. Yet throughout the 1990s, the federal funds that might have been used to repair and strengthen the levees and flood walls and protect the pumping stations were routinely bled off for other projects, such as widening the MRGO and deepening the water near docks to accommodate larger vessels. With the arrival of the new millennium, the funding of the U.S. Army Corps of Engineers district that is in charge of the levees was slashed by 44 percent over five years. In 2004, the Corps asked for $22.5 million for storm protection projects for New Orleans. The Bush administration cut that figure to $3.9 million, and Congress ended up appropriating $1.6 million more, for a total of $5.5 million. Undeterred, the next year the White House asked for only $3.0 million.

Despite the growing exposure of the Gulf Coast and New Orleans to major storms, the federal government, the state, and the city managed to amplify the risk further by not having in place a workable, comprehensive plan for dealing with the aftermath of a major hurricane. The problem wasn't actually the lack of a plan; it was that every parish and individual agency had one of its own and the sum of the parts didn't equal a whole. There was virtually no coordination between the state agencies and local governments even on issues such as when and how to evacuate.

After New Orleans' near-miss encounters with Hurricane Georges in 1998 and the powerful Hurricane Ivan in 2004, this complacency was shaken, but only enough to inspire some official hand-wringing. In June 2004, dozens of state and federal officials met for a weeklong simulation of a Category 3 hurricane strike on New Orleans sponsored by the Federal Emergency Management Agency (FEMA). The exercise, dubbed Hurricane Pam, had been built around comprehensive computer models developed at Louisiana State University, which predicted that a Category 3 storm would leave up to 500,000 residents stranded in ten feet of contaminated water due to flooding inside the levee systems. Follow-up sessions were scheduled, but FEMA canceled several of them in the first part of 2005 because it was unable to fund the $15,000 to cover the travel expenses of its people to attend.

As events in the wake of Hurricane Katrina would prove, the failure to develop a comprehensive plan for a foreseeable and well-understood disaster was an act of negligence that cost several hundred lives and tens of billions of dollars of damage. But in the ultimate act of arrogance, the reconstruction of New Orleans is proceeding without any serious effort to prevent a repeat of this catastrophe. Levees are being repaired to the same Category 3 standard they were supposed to have been at before they failed. There is no commitment by the federal government to fund the rebuilding of the coastal wetlands and barrier islands. At the local level, there are no comprehensive guidelines to inform the rebuilding of neighborhoods. The zoning rules are only being tweaked at the margins, so residents of the areas that suffered the most severe flooding are not being discouraged from rebuilding on the same spots and in virtually the same way as before Katrina struck. The FEMA guidelines released in April 2006 require only that new houses be built three feet off the ground, even though most neighborhoods experienced flooding of up to twenty feet. Houses can be built even in the areas that suffered the most severe flooding. Residents have been encouraged to rebuild on their own terms. According to Steven Bingler, the chief architect of the planning process, the goal is "to empower people to make decisions for themselves and their own communities." Unfortunately, this grassroots approach to recovery almost guarantees that there will be no serious effort to build a city that can survive the next "big one."

The aftermath of Hurricane Katrina brings into stark relief six overarching trends that practically ensure that future American disasters will end up being far more catastrophic than they should be. First, the natural environment is undergoing changes that are elevating the risk. While scientists and politicians can dispute just what the causes are, there is no debating the fact that we are entering a period of climate change. The "hundred-year storm" is becoming the "ten-year storm" and, by 2080, may be occurring every three years. Second, we have allowed the protective measures that earlier generations constructed to deal with catastrophic events to erode. Third, we have been embracing the kind of unfettered urban and coastal development, especially of residential housing, that exacerbates risk. Fourth, we have been unwilling to invest in appropriate mitigation measures or contingency planning to deal with a major disaster. This typically results from the growing reluctance of government at all levels to pick up the tab. However, in recent years, complex environmental issues have also come into play, making even repairs of existing infrastructure more and more contentious. Fifth, there are insufficient resources available to respond effectively when a disaster strikes. Last, when the dust clears, we go right back to "business as usual."

This lethal combination of natural and man-made factors suggests that the gravest source of danger for Americans derives not from acts of God or acts of terror; it is largely our own negligence that has placed us on the edge of disaster. The good news is that most of these trends can be reversed if we act with the same sense of national urgency that the threat requires. A failure to act will practically ensure future Katrina-scale disasters.

FOUR

DANGER ON THE DELTA

I N LATE JUNE 2006, I stood on a riverbank looking out at the deep-water channel that links the inland city of Stockton, California, with San Francisco Bay and the Pacific Ocean. My perch was atop an earthen embankment that encircled Twitchell Island, one of the fifty-seven leveed island tracts that belong to the Sacramento–San Joaquin River Delta. Behind me, tilled farmland rested nearly forty feet below the water that surrounded it. This fertile region, famous for its pears and asparagus, has been worked by farmers for more than a century while it has been sinking at a rate of three to four inches per year. Gazing at this bucolic setting, with birds gliding on a summer breeze, it was difficult to imagine that the vast cultivated fields spreading out across the horizon are only an earthquake away from becoming the bottom of a vast brackish lake.

When it comes to being in the crosshairs of disaster, California leads the nation. Earthquakes, wildfires, mud slides, floods, and tsunamis are perennially in the offing. Al-Qaeda has even held the nation's most populous state in its sights: on December 14, 1999, Ahmed Ressam, the "millennium terrorist," was heading for Los Angeles with a trunk full of explosives when he was apprehended in Port Angeles, Washington. His purported target was Los Angeles International Airport. While most Californians take the risk in stride, historically they have also taken their emergency planning seriously. But as in the rest of the nation, changing environmental conditions, aging infrastructure, unchecked development, shortsighted budget choices, and political intransigence, both in Washington, D.C., and in California, are combining to elevate the risk for Katrina-scale disasters. There are few places that better illustrate both California's and the United States' growing flirtation with home-grown catastrophe than the Sacramento–San Joaquin River Delta.

Located less than seventy-five miles east of San Francisco, the delta is a unique, critical, and dangerous bit of geography. A geological analysis of sediments drawn from the region has established that for more than six thousand years it has been a tidal freshwater marsh made up of channels, sloughs, and islands. Tucked between the Sierra Nevada mountains to the east and the Pacific Coast ranges to the west, the delta encompasses a 1,150-square-mile area that makes up the northern part of California's Central Valley. The majestic Sierra Nevada range includes the snowcapped Mount Whitney, the highest peak in the continental United States. The runoff from these mountains feeds the Sacramento and San Joaquin rivers.

Heavy winter and spring rains combined with the spring melting of mountain snows have made flooding a perennial issue in the region. Compounding that risk is the fact that California's Central Valley is as flat as a Midwest prairie. To protect the homes and fields of more than half a million Californians from this seasonal flooding, the region has nearly 2,400 miles of levees. Within the Sacramento–San Joaquin River Delta there are more than 600 miles of levees, many of which have the added duty of holding back the salt water of San Francisco Bay throughout the year. It is this critical function of keeping the freshwater fresh that makes the delta levees so important for the entire state.

Unfortunately, the delta sits along a number of active and suspected geological faults that will eventually trigger an earthquake. A major earthquake would cause the levees to vibrate, liquefying the mix of sand and peat soil they are composed of. A 6.5-magnitude earthquake at the western end of the delta would cause at least thirty levee breaches and the flooding of sixteen islands. Within a few days 300 billion gallons of salt water would flow from San Francisco Bay into the delta, contaminating the state's major water source. Under the most optimistic conditions, it would take more than a year to complete emergency repairs. In the interim, 45 percent of America's annual harvest of fruits and vegetables would wither under the sun, and many communities would run out of water.

The delta levee system was originally constructed around the turn of the twentieth century by Chinese laborers who had been enlisted in building the railways that connected the West to the rest of the United States. These workers did the backbreaking job of scraping muck from the brackish swamps of the region and mixing it with sand to protect the farmland from the surrounding channels and sloughs. Like the dikes made famous by the story of the Dutch boy and his finger, levees are earthen walls built to hold the water back by piling earth on a level surface. They start with a broad base and taper off as the embankment grows higher. From a sideward view, the final shape is trapezoidal, with a narrower flat top that often also does dual duty as a local road. The embankment wall exposed to the water tends to rise at a sharper angle than the inland side.

As the levees were essentially local self-help projects, the builders rarely had the benefit of input from professional engineers. Today these levees protect not just farmland but new tracts of suburban housing and strip malls. This is particularly true around Sacramento, whose population has been growing rapidly in recent years. The capital of California has the lowest level of flood protection of any major metropolitan area in the country, including New Orleans. Were the levees that protect the city to fail during a major storm, everything up to seventeen feet above street level would quickly end up under water. Three hundred thousand people would become refugees, and 140,000 buildings would be damaged or destroyed.

While crops still cover most of the Sacramento–San Joaquin River Delta, the area's biggest and most important export is water. Kenneth Kasprisin, the former deputy district engineer for the U.S. Army Corps of Engineers Sacramento District, describes California as moving water around the state like other regions move electricity. The arid sections of southern California are only made arable and livable by a complex web of rivers, canals, and aqueducts that bring water from the north and east to Los Angeles and San Diego. Balanced against the need for supply is the equally pressing need for flood control, and these two forces often find themselves in competition.

The delta region is the hub of the state's half-century-old water distribution system, providing water for nearly two thirds of the state's 37 million people. It also supplies water to irrigate millions of acres of the most productive agricultural land in the world. Nearly half the fruits and vegetables that Americans find on their grocery shelves were originally nourished by irrigation waters from the delta. This precious resource, which supports California's growing population and a state economy that ranks as the seventh largest in the world, depends on levees to protect it from being contaminated by the salt water of San Francisco Bay. The California Department of Water Resources estimates that if there were a catastrophic failure of the levee system, the disruption to the supply of delta water that would follow would cost more than $400 billion annually.

Even if there were not the serious risk of an earthquake, levee failures pose a major hazard for the region, because the state's flood protection system is rapidly deteriorating and becoming less stable. When the levees were first built, they protected land that was level with the water. Most of the embankments were only five feet high. But the soft ground behind them has settled and become more compact, while some of the topsoil oxidizes and basically evaporates every time the farmers till it. Over time, it has become necessary to add more and more earth to the inland side of the levee embankments to compensate for this gradual sinking. From the water side, the levee wall still appears to be five to ten feet high. However, on the inland side, the wall now descends thirty or more feet to the level of the field it is protecting. Some, like the one I visited on Twitchell Island, stand on fields that lie forty feet below the surrounding water level. As a result, whereas the levee walls once started out resembling something like a very thick book resting on a surface, where the water was at the same level as the land, now they are more like a book that has been stood on its end with the back cover facing the field while the water side applies pressure all along the front cover, threatening to tip it over.

But the danger does not stop here. Not only are the levees under a growing strain, which is likely to destabilize them, but their condition is rapidly deteriorating as well, as the powerful flow of water along the channel banks is eating away at the external levee walls. Meanwhile, on the interior side, small animals find the mix of peat and sand to make good burrowing material for constructing their homes. At the same time, the levees' foundations are becoming weaker. Most were built with not rock or even clay but a layer of peat soil. This material is porous and over time allows the surrounding water to seep in. This underseepage is very difficult to detect, allowing water to act like a cancer, eating away at the underbelly of the levee, until one day it will become so unstable that it collapses.

Between 1986 and 2003, the U.S. Army Corps of Engineers evaluated 1,059 miles of the levees throughout the Central Valley. They found that significant repairs needed to be undertaken along a total of 89 miles of the levees. In 2006, the Corps evaluated three hundred

Sacramento River flood-control system levee sites and found eighty-one of them to be "severely damaged."

But elected officials and Californians don't need technical assessments and white papers to enlighten them on the mounting danger. Flood disasters have occurred nearly every decade throughout the twentieth century. The year 1997 was a particularly bad one: rain-swollen rivers caused breaks in more than fifty levees, forcing the largest evacuation in California's history. In all, 120,000 people had to flee rising waters, which ultimately destroyed an estimated 30,000 residential and 2,000 business properties.

Past levee failures have highlighted the regional disruption that arises from a major breach. In 1972, the levee on the bay side of Brannan-Andrus Island broke, inundating the small towns of Rio Vista and Isleton. Highway 12, the main east-west thoroughfare that crosses the delta, was closed for a year. Salt water from San Francisco Bay entered the delta, dramatically increasing the salinity of the freshwater and leading to the loss of 400,000 acre-feet of water supplies.

The most recent levee breach occurred on June 3, 2004. It took place roughly eight miles west of Stockton and just four miles north of the Banks Pumping Plant and the Tracy Pumping Plant, which are the workhorses of the state's freshwater supply system. What made this failure particularly worrisome was that there was no clear cause. Officials later speculated that the likely source was animal burrowing. Regardless, within twenty-four hours of the levee breach, 12,000 acres of fields in an area called the Upper Jones Tract ended up submerged under ten feet of water. In addition, Highway 4, which runs from San Francisco to Stockton, had to be shut down because it was imperiled by the flooding. The tracks owned by Burlington Northern Santa Fe Railway, which are used by Amtrak and freight trains, were also endangered by the flooding, resulting in a disruption of rail service to the Bay Area. While the tract was awash, wind-driven waves pounded away at the now-exposed interior levee slopes, causing substantial erosion. Emergency crews worried that if they did not make the repairs quickly enough and pump out the floodwaters, there would soon be multiple breaches. It took twenty-three days to repair the original breach and six months of pumping to dry out the land.

The break in the Upper Jones Tract levee highlighted one of the central challenges of managing the delta's flood protection system: the fact that there is no single authority in charge. One of the more than fifty local levee or reclamation districts in the delta had the responsibility for routine maintenance, repairs, and upgrades of the Upper Jones Tract levee. But these farming communities have not been in a position to make the kind of investment now required to improve the levees. For one thing, the cost of repairs can run as high as $5,000 per linear foot, as opposed to an average of $300 per linear foot in the early 1980s. For another, local governments are often unable to offer much financial support to the local reclamation boards. Beginning in the 1970s, California has gone through a spate of property tax revolts, leading to two constitutional amendments that have basically crippled the ability of local governments to raise money to support new public works projects.

At the state level, California has a Reclamation Board that essentially plays a middleman role. The Reclamation Board administratively falls under the state's Department of Water Resources, but its members are appointed by the governor, and they are free to make decisions independent of the department. The board works with the 130 local levee or reclamation boards throughout the state and cooperates with the U.S. Army Corps of Engineers.

The Sacramento District of the Army Corps of Engineers is the lead federal agency involved with flood management within the Sacramento and San Joaquin Delta, but it operates with considerable deference to the state. This is a reflection of the fact that most of the levees started out as private property and many remain in private hands today. It is also a by-product of the Corps's dependency on Sacramento and local levee and reclamation districts to share in the financing of new flood-control projects and to take over the maintenance of the levees, reservoirs, and dams once a project has been completed. Typically, the Corps acts more like an architect than a builder: it designs the projects it undertakes but usually contracts out the actual construction. The Corps will help make repairs when there is an emergency, but it is allowed to restore a failed levee only to its previous condition. It is not authorized to fund improvements in the aftermath of a breach—that tab falls to the state or the local reclamation board or requires the submission and approval of a new project proposal, which is typically a multiyear process.

Across the country, many Corps projects authorized by Congress are never funded. The Corps currently has a backlog of more than five hundred projects that have been authorized but have never received appropriations to begin construction. Despite the critical nature of the delta, the process there is no different. For the $90 million Congress has authorized to spend on delta levee projects through 2010, the Corps received applications from fifty-four delta-area reclamation districts and other agencies, totaling over $1 billion in estimated project costs.

Up until 1996, the Corps of Engineers contributed 75 percent of the funding for flood-control projects. Congress then changed the formula, lowering the Corps's maximum contribution to 65 percent. The timing of this change was particularly bad for the state of California, which was experiencing serious fiscal problems, so that there was no slack in the state budget to bankroll levee improvements. Indeed, Sacramento began cutting the Department of Water Resources' budget for conducting even routine maintenance. The maintenance staff was reduced by one third between 1986 and 2005. Work to clear sediments that obstruct the flow of water, thereby contributing to erosion within the system, fell off by nearly 80 percent from the 1980s to the 1990s.

While California officials were busy cutting back on the maintenance of the levees, they turned a blind eye to local development projects expanding into the floodplain. According to the 2000 census, Sacramento County was among the ten fastest-growing counties in the United States. More than 150,000 new people flocked to the Sacramento area in the 1990s. The city of Elk Grove, which is almost completely dependent on levees to stay dry, grew at the second fastest rate in the nation in 2004. Local officials have authorized new construction based on decades-old flood maps that assume that the federal project levees automatically provide protection from hundred-year flood events, even though their experience with recent floods should tell them otherwise. As a result, land upon which celery, potato, and onion plants once grew now hosts new residential homes, which have sprung up by the thousands. The incentive for building behind levees got a boost in 2003, when a California Court of Appeals provided what amounts to a financial backstop should these new homes end up under water. In *Paterno v. State of California,* the court ruled that the state is ultimately liable for a failure in the structural integrity of the Linda Levee section of the Sacramento River Flood Control Project (SRFCP). Because California incorporated the levee into the flood-control project, which it administered, the state was ordered to pay for the damage to homes on floodplains behind the levees regardless of when, how, or by whom the levees had been constructed.

Compounding the risk for these new home owners is that the data used to establish the hundred-year flood baseline are almost certainly obsolete. California had five severe storms in the second half of the twentieth century that were greater than anything the state experienced before 1950, when the flood-control system was designed. Today the California Department of Water Resources estimates that during a typical thirty-year mortgage period a home owner residing in a neighborhood behind a levee has a 26 percent chance of experiencing a flood *greater* than a so-called hundred-year event. Further, when disaster strikes, the state will have a more difficult time responding. When there is a breach, the new development compounds the problem of moving heavy construction equipment and material to the site because the houses get in the way. Many are built right up to the ten-foot ease-ment that is required on the land side of the levee. Also, there are fewer full-time professionals available to help manage these events because the emergency response budget for fighting floods suffered along with the shrinking maintenance budget. In January 2005, a report prepared for the state warned that there might not even be enough staff to pro-vide twenty-four-hour coverage at its Flood Operations Center during a flood emergency. The stakes are enormous because there is a signifi-cant risk of additional breaches in the absence of a rapid response to a major levee failure.

The good news is that Hurricane Katrina was something of a wake-up call for Californians. In 2006, $300 million in funds for emer-gency repairs were approved, and a major bond issue is being sent to California voters for approval. On February 27, 2006, Governor Arnold Schwarzenegger sent a letter to President Bush outlining the danger associated with the serious deterioration of the state's levee system, as-serting that "this worsening situation creates conditions of extreme peril to the public and property protected by the levees, to the environ-ment, and to the very foundation of California's economy." Like an al-coholic contemplating recovery, California is now at least publicly admitting it has a serious flood management problem and taking the first steps toward addressing it. These first steps have included the in-evitable "blue ribbon commission" and the obligatory "vision" to sup-port the development of a "strategic plan." Governor Schwarzenegger signed Executive Order S-17-06 to establish a "Delta Vision" on Sep-tember 28, 2006.

Unfortunately, the state is still not addressing the vulnerability of the levees to seismic activity, nor is it pursuing a comprehensive effort to confront the nightmarish and likely event of a major earthquake on the delta. This is inexplicable, since the chilling consequences of such a disaster have been anticipated by the California Department of Water Resources and were presented by its director, Lester Snow, to the state senate on November 1, 2005. Drawing on research by Jeffrey Mount, a geology professor and director for the Center for Watershed Sciences at UC Davis, the Department of Water Resources believes that the state is facing the peril outlined below.

By 2050, an earthquake will almost certainly strike the delta region. The San Francisco Bay area is a seismically rich area that extends into the Sacramento–San Joaquin River Valley. Major faults, such as the San Andreas, the Hayward, and the Calaveras, lie within sixteen miles of the region. There are less active faults within nine miles and some smaller but still significant faults within the delta itself. No major earthquake has hit the area since the existing levees were built more than a century ago. That means that force has been building up over the entire course of that time. When the ground finally moves, there will be multiple levee failures that will produce a New Orleans–scale disaster with even farther-reaching consequences.

The core problem is that although it is possible to improve levees so that they can withstand seasonal flooding, none of the 2,400 miles of levees throughout the Central Valley is designed to ride out an earthquake. How they will hold up when put to the seismic test is an open question, as the region has been earthquake-free since the levees were first constructed. But an earthquake with a magnitude of 6.0 near the delta would shake the sandy soil that most levees are built with and turn many of them to liquid. Two to three dozen breaches are likely. Once the levees are knocked down and the islands flood, salt water from San Francisco Bay will surge into the delta.

If the earthquake were to take place along the faults just west of Twitchell Island, sixteen islands would be flooded and some 3,000 homes and 85,000 acres of farmland would immediately be destroyed. Highway 12 and Highway 160 also would be completely inundated. Many of the natural gas and oil pipelines that run through the delta would rupture. The energy infrastructure that survived would have to be taken out of service until its structural integrity could be confirmed. Rail traffic across the delta would cease. The deepwater shipping channel for the Port of Stockton would be closed as sediments from the neighboring levee embankments poured into the dredged channel.

After rescuing those stranded on rooftops, the emergency responders would need to quickly turn their attention to closing the breaches and limiting the inflow of seawater into the delta. This work would be complicated by the difficulty in getting access to the worst breaches, as roads and bridges would almost certainly be too badly damaged to support the movement of heavy construction equipment by truck. Emergency crews would be clamoring for barges with mounted cranes to move sand and rock to the work sites. The demand would vastly outpace the local supply, and additional barges would have to be towed in from Los Angeles and Seattle. There would also be the difficulty of obtaining enough rock to fill the breaches. Rock is not native to the region, so it would need to be imported from as far away as Vancouver. But this would generate its own logistical challenges, since there are so few ships that are capable of transporting rock as cargo.

Any delay in repairing the original breaches would raise the risk of domino-like failures of the surviving levees. Once an island was flooded, the water would wash up against the inboard side of the levee embankments, which are normally dry. Since there is usually no need for it, the land side is not armored with a rocky material known as riprap, which is generally used to prevent erosion, so the embankments would be compromised very quickly when exposed to the wave action of the floodwaters. Compounding the risk of additional breaches would be the fact that the earthquake would have weakened the foundation and embankment soil of any levee lying within two hundred miles of the epicenter.

All of this would be devastating for the people living and working in the delta. But the larger calamity would arise from the long-term impact on California's water supply. The Mokelumne Aqueduct, which supplies the urban areas on the east side of San Francisco Bay with water, would likely be severely damaged, if not completely destroyed. Even if the delta pumping stations escaped serious harm, the water authority would still have to shut them down immediately to avoid sending contaminated brackish water into the remaining operational elements of the state's water distribution system.

The first step in restoring the water supply system would be to concentrate repair efforts on the seven islands that are most critical to reestablishing the flow of freshwater to the pumping stations. The most optimistic projections suggest that it would take at least a year to accomplish the repairs. It would be slow and difficult work, including locating and off-loading 130,000 tons of rock to create the channel barriers needed to direct the water. In the interim, salt water from San Francisco Bay would seep into the delta unabated. Unfortunately, such contamination damage is something only time and lots of freshwater can repair. It would take several years for the spring mountain runoffs to clear the salt out of the watershed so that it could again be used for irrigation and drinking water.

During the first year, alternative water resources could probably be found to support approximately half of the state's population. The Bay Area, the Central Valley, and southern California could draw down their other water resources, but the overuse of groundwater supplies could result in the buildup of toxins restricting the use of these sources as well. At a reduced consumption rate, the city of Los Angeles, which gets much of its water from the Colorado River, could ride out this first year as well. Other communities would not be so fortunate. Ten million Californians left without water might be forced to evacuate until the water system could be restored.

In concluding his November 2005 presentation to the California state senate, Lester Snow warned that even with the most optimistic projections, it would take at least fifteen months to repair the effects of a 6.5 magnitude earthquake adjacent to the delta. "More realistically," he said, "the repairs will take much longer." He concluded his remarks by noting that his was a "plausible scenario," not a worst-case scenario. "We can work with seismologists and come up with something that is actually worse than this," he added. By way of comparison, Snow reminded the elected officials attending the hearing that the earthquake he had just described the effects of was a one-in-three-hundred-year event. He noted that Hurricane Katrina was also a one-in-three-hundred-year event.

The story of the Sacramento–San Joaquin River Delta has frightening parallels with the Katrina disaster. The threat has been long-standing and well documented. It is likely that changes in the natural environment will only elevate the danger over time. The infrastructure available for mitigating the disaster has been allowed to deteriorate. Local short-term decisions, such as allowing large housing developments to be constructed on the floodplains behind the levees, are compounding the risk. California is not prepared to respond to a major seismic event, and the spate of recent breaches and close calls has not produced any sign that there is a sense of urgency to fundamentally challenge the reckless status quo.

California has not yet even determined what earthquake-proof levees would cost. The state has estimated that bringing the delta levees up to FEMA flood-control standards would total about $1.3 billion. Washington has allocated a token $164 million in federal funds for

2007 to support this effort. But levees made of loose sand can be in compliance with FEMA standards even though they would liquefy, slump, and likely break following an earthquake. Les Harder, the deputy director of the Department of Water Resources, has concluded that to make the levees earthquake-proof would require starting over with a brand-new levee system. He argues that no amount of remediation is going to fix the current levees.

To prevent the direst consequence arising from an earthquake on the delta—the disruption to the state's water supply system—one option that Californians should probably be seriously contemplating is constructing a peripheral canal. The idea is straightforward, and it was originally a part of the design of its system: a canal that intercepts freshwater from the Sacramento River before it arrives into the levee-dependent delta. The canal would run along a more seismically stable path east of Sacramento and Stockton and end at the pumping stations that export the water to the rest of the state by way of aqueducts. The water supply for 22 million Californians would then be protected even after a devastating earthquake in the delta. It would cost an estimated $3 billion.

Constructing the Peripheral Canal was actually actively debated a quarter of a century ago, and funding for it was placed on a state ballot initiative in 1982. Ninety percent of northern Californians voted no. Consistent with the state's long-standing and, at times, adolescent-style regional rivalry, northerners complained that the canal was just a way for southern Californians to steal their water to fill their swimming pools and water their lawns. Meanwhile, residents of the delta area saw the canal proposal as endangering any hope they might have of the state providing adequate funding to repair the levees and to strengthen the local system for managing seasonal flooding.

Whether or not the Peripheral Canal should be built is undoubtedly a legitimate topic for debate. But what is outrageous is that there appears to be no serious debate under way about this or any other measure to deal with this predictable disaster. Why isn't new development in the floodplains being halted? Why is there not an aggressive schedule in effect to repair and upgrade the levees? Why isn't the region buying and prepositioning rock around the delta so that multiple breaches can be repaired? Especially given the example of New Orleans, why are the citizens not clamoring for something to be done to address the danger? Kenneth Kasprisin, the former Army Corps deputy district engineer for the Sacramento District, laments that the answer to all these questions is complacency.

The story of the Sacramento–San Joaquin River Delta underscores the fact that the seeds of disaster are more of our making than that of Mother Nature or our adversaries. It points to an almost adolescent sense of denial that our actions—or lack of action—have real consequences. If California were a country, its economy would rank seventh in the world. However, its taxpayers are unwilling to invest in the upkeep of the infrastructure that their lives and livelihoods depend on. Home to Silicon Valley, the San Francisco Bay area has the highest concentration of intelligent and innovative people on the planet, yet none of that intellectual capital is being applied to a challenge that, if left unattended, will turn their slice of paradise into a living hell. Meanwhile, California's elected officials show up for work in a state capitol building that relies on levees to stay dry when the waters rise, yet they are unable to find the political will to tackle an issue that is literally sitting on their doorstep.

What the nation witnessed with Hurricane Katrina was failures of institutional adaptiveness and competence. The story of the delta makes it clear that this is as much a West Coast issue as an East Coast one. As a nation we should be united in a collective effort to step back from the brink of disaster.

FIVE

AILING FOUNDATIONS

O N AUGUST 14, 2003, the lights went out across the northeastern United States and southern Canada. It was the largest electrical failure in North American history. At the time of the blackout, I was in a cab heading for Ronald Reagan Washington National Airport in Arlington County, Virginia, intent on catching the next shuttle flight back to New York. Fortunately, the driver had the radio turned on, so I knew right away that my trip home to Connecticut was not going to work out as planned. Suspecting the worst, I called a friend at the Department of Homeland Security (DHS) to see if he knew what was going on. It turned out he had just heard about the blackout from his boss, who was one of the top officials at the department—reporting directly to Tom Ridge, who was then the secretary. The senior DHS official had only a moment before found out about the outage. His source turned out to be his daughter, who had reached him by cell phone from a New York high-rise.

The cause of the massive blackout was not al-Qaeda or the kind of disaster the Department of Homeland Security was created to help protect us from. The subsequent investigation found that the trigger was some untrimmed trees in Ohio that had entangled themselves into three high-voltage power lines. The trees set off a chain of events that would lead to power plants being shut down from Ontario to New York. The final financial tally for the outage came to an estimated $6 billion to $10 billion.

Fifty million lives were disrupted. Some people were trapped in elevators. Others had to feel their way along dark subway tunnels to reach emergency exits. Hotel guests in New York ended up sleeping on the street. Local New Yorkers had to hike several miles to get home. I was one of the lucky ones. I told the cabdriver to take me directly to the airport car rental agency. I managed to get a jump on the crowd of other displaced passengers who were making a beeline for the rental counters. It was an eerie sight when I reached New York near midnight on my long drive home. The world's greatest city had plunged into complete darkness. I was seeing the night sky over Manhattan just as it would have appeared to the first Dutch settlers.

Power outages are the kind of thing that routinely bedevils the lives of people living in impoverished countries like Haiti or in war zones such as Baghdad. But why are we putting up with them here in the United States? If the great blackout of 2003 was a wake-up call, we seem to have hit the snooze button. Three summers later, in 2006, severe thunderstorms in the Saint Louis metropolitan area toppled trees on top of active power lines, and more than 700,000 homes and businesses found themselves without power during a heat wave. The power outage lasted several days, leaving many people to swelter inside their redbrick homes and causing real hardship for the poor and elderly, who quickly lost food and medications that required refrigeration. An investigation into a four-day blackout in 2004 had cited the local power utility, Ameren, for skimping on its tree-cutting budget.

Not trees but age and heavy use appear to be the source of a week-long power failure in the Queens borough of New York City in July 2006. Failures of ten of twenty-two aged underground power lines left more than 100,000 people in the dark, including many living in high-rise apartment buildings that depend on power to keep their elevators moving. The average age of the damaged transformers in the outage was thirty-one years. Reportedly, none of the power lines was operating above its emergency rating when the power went out. They failed anyway.

At nearly the same time, on the opposite coast, California authorities were poised to institute rolling blackouts to deal with triple-digit temperatures. The state utility established a plan that required businesses to cut or reduce their demand on the power grid. Despite the calls for conservation, demand peaked at 50 megawatts, a level 21 percent higher than what California had been using at the peak of the state's 2000–2001 energy crisis. When asked about the measures the state utility was undertaking to avert a power failure during the heat wave, an official from the California Independent System Operator, which transmits 80 percent of the state's electricity, said, "We've got to keep our fingers crossed that everything stays working."

"Keeping our fingers crossed" seems to be an apt metaphor for how America is dealing with its aging and increasingly ailing infrastructure. Chillingly, this applies to our emergency management and public health systems as well. Years of hospital cost cutting and parsimonious state public health care budgets have taken their toll. In a mass-casualty event, our health care sector will almost certainly fail us.

The September 11, 2001, attacks did not reveal how frail our emergency care capabilities have become for the tragic reason that virtually all the victims in the air and on the ground died before they could receive medical assistance. Emergency rooms that stood by on full alert had few admissions. But seventeen months later, a freak accident in West Warwick, Rhode Island, would expose just how poorly prepared the world's most expensive health care system is to handle a surge of patients with serious injuries.

On the night of February 21, 2003, the 1980s heavy metal band Great White was set to play in a packed house at the Station, a nightclub just outside Providence. The band opened its show with its signature pyrotechnics display. But this time something went terribly wrong. As soon as the fireworks went off, the wall behind the stage burst into flames that began to spread across the ceiling. As smoke filled the room, the concertgoers started to panic. The exit signs were obscured, and some exit doors were chained shut. In the ensuing struggle to escape the building, several people in attendance were trampled to death. Ninety-six people would perish in the fire that night, while more than 215 were injured.

Rhode Island's statewide emergency management system failed this real-world test. There was little communication between receiving hospitals and emergency responders who were on the scene at the nightclub. In many cases ambulances took patients to hospital emergency rooms unannounced. Adding to the confusion was the fact that the emergency transport units were often unaware of the capacities and capabilities of the hospitals to which they were taking patients. Even the bland wording of the official after-action report manages to convey how completely unprepared the state was to deal with this mass-casualty event: "Unfortunately, the deficiencies in statewide emergency response plans, interagency coordination, and regularly scheduled drills involving dispatch centers, EMS units, and hospital emergency departments were apparent on this occasion."

Among those with injuries, more than a hundred had second- and third-degree burns. Treating serious burns requires highly specialized medical training and facilities, which are expensive to maintain. As a result, over the past decade many U.S. hospitals have been trimming back on their burn care capacity as a cost-cutting measure. Nation-wide, sixteen burn centers were closed between 1991 and 2003, and many others (including the U.S. Army Burn Center) have been down-sized. This is a troubling trend since there were not that many burn beds to start with. The national total in 1991 was 1,966 beds. At the time of the Station fire, that number had crept down to 1,897 beds.

As with other aspects of specialized health care, hospital adminis-trators have been cutting back on the ability of their burn centers to deal with anything beyond the anticipated level of care. Today, it is not uncommon for a trauma center to have just a one-week supply of sil-ver sulfadiazine, which is used to prevent infections for people with second- and third-degree burns. A few years ago, several months' sup-ply would have been kept on hand. The trend toward cutting back on inventories of even emergency care medical supplies has been driven by a desire to reduce the cost of having to routinely replace expired medicines and other materials that often have a relatively short shelf life. As a result, the hospital industry has become as enthusiastic about "just-in-time" delivery as retailers like Wal-Mart. Arrangements are often in place for suppliers to deliver extra medical materials soon after they are ordered. This usually works out fine as long as the order is not too large and the transportation system is running smoothly. But dur-ing a major disaster the need for additional stock soars and transporta-tion is nearly always one of the first casualties.

In the case of the Station nightclub fire, the transportation system and the availability of medicines and supplies were not so much an issue as was the need to find hospitals that could care for the scores of victims. The nearest hospital to the nightclub, Kent Hospital, already had a full emergency room when the first burn patients began to ar-rive. Virtually every emergency medical helicopter in New England, as well as some from Long Island, New York, was mobilized to transport victims to a total of thirteen different facilities in Rhode Island and Massachusetts. Seventeen of the most severely burned patients were sent to Massachusetts General Hospital in Boston, which hosts the biggest burn unit in New England. This influx stressed the hospitals' medical staff to their limits.

The Station nightclub fire should give Boston-area emergency planners pause when they contemplate how they might cope with a terrorist attack on an LNG tanker within Boston Harbor. But there is another scenario that should have every American both anxious and angry about how badly this country's public health and emergency care system has been allowed to erode. That is the risk of a flu pandemic.

Laurie Garrett is one of the world's leading authorities on infectious diseases. In a recent essay entitled "The Next Pandemic?" which appeared in *Foreign Affairs,* she provides a very chilling picture of what may be in store for us should the H5N1 avian flu virus mutate and become capable of human-to-human transmission.

During a normal flu season, 200,000 Americans end up in the hospital and 38,000 do not survive their stay. The overall mortality rate is .008 percent, and the direct medical costs and loss of productivity to the U.S. economy are about $12 billion. Those numbers are sobering, but they pale against the nation's most recent experience with a virulent flu pandemic, which was back in 1918. During the Spanish flu outbreak, 675,000 Americans died, with the highest death toll being among young adults, ages twenty to thirty-five. The mortality rate for the overall infected population was estimated to be less than 1 percent.

What if H5N1 avian influenza should make the evolutionary leap that will allow it to spread among humans as it has among birds? Of the just over 100 documented human infections between 1997 and 2005, the mortality rate was 54 percent. So let us assume that the lethality of the virus goes down as it mutates and, conservatively, ends up with a 1 percent fatality rate. With a projected 80 million illnesses in the United States, 800,000 Americans would not survive the infection.

The millions in need of hospital care would find themselves largely out of luck; the entire inventory of staffed hospital beds within the United States is 970,000.

So how prepared are we for such a scenario? Maddeningly, the Station nightclub fire provides a hint. Our current situation can be described succinctly as ludicrous. The public health community is not adequately prepared to detect, isolate, and treat Americans at the start of a disease outbreak. Most states do not have the means to distribute vaccines and medicines to the general population in time for them to be helpful. And the emergency care system would effectively collapse under the strain.

While disease knows no borders, public health in the United States is run at the state level. Unfortunately, most states have not made public health a priority, particularly in their red-ink days following 9/11. A 2005 report by the nonprofit Trust for America's Health paints a very bleak picture. Each state was rated on ten key indicators of public health and emergency preparedness. Among the findings were that:

- Nearly half of states do not use national standards to track disease outbreak information.
- Only seven states and two cities have been recognized by the U.S. Centers for Disease Control and Prevention as adequately prepared to administer and distribute vaccines and antidotes in the event of an emergency.
- Hospitals in nearly one third of states and the District of Columbia are not sufficiently prepared, through planning or coordination with local health agencies, to care for a surge of extra patients by using nonhealth facilities, such as community centers, sports arenas, or hotels.
- Hospitals in only two states have sufficient plans, incentives, or provisions to encourage health care workers to continue to come to work during a major infectious disease outbreak.

- Hospitals in nearly one third of states lack sufficient capability to consistently and rapidly consult with infection control experts about possible or suspected disease outbreaks.
- Hospitals in nearly one third of states have not planned sufficiently for prioritizing distribution of vaccines or antiviral medications to hospital workers.
- Hospitals in more than 40 percent of states do not have sufficient backup supplies of medical equipment to meet surge capacity needs during a pandemic flu or other major infectious disease outbreaks.

As sobering as this assessment is, all the current trends suggest that the public health community remains in a state of precipitous decline. For one thing, the public health profession is aging and is about to lose nearly a majority of its most experienced people. Retirement rates are expected to be as high as 45 percent over the next five years. As those people go, they are likely to leave empty seats behind them. The current vacancy rate for public health positions is up to 20 percent in some states. Increasingly, those coming into the profession are deciding not to stay around. Public health employment turnover rates are at 14 percent in some parts of the country. The federal government has yet to enact a comprehensive plan to address this issue.

Hospital care capacity is shrinking as well. This is because most hospitals in the country are for-profit entities. As the situation after the Station fire highlighted, health care administrators have been hard at work trying to cut costs and streamline operations. From medical supplies to nurses, hospitals are run as just-in-time operations, trying to match supply with demand as directly as possible. Health maintenance organizations and hospital companies are often vilified as being more interested in the bottom line than providing adequate care for their patients. With the rare exception, the charge is an unfair one. Profits in the hospital industry are extremely thin, averaging about 1.9 percent. Thirty percent

of all hospitals are losing money, and with 45 million Americans unin-
sured, hospitals end up providing $25 billion in care that goes uncom-
pensated. Despite their financial struggles and efforts to keep costs
under control, most of the time hospitals are capable of delivering the
care we need when we need it. However, when disaster strikes, there is
a diminishing capacity to deal with a major surge in demand.

In 2005, half of the nation's 4,000 emergency departments were
routinely operating at or over capacity. Demand for emergency care
has been growing at twice the rate of the general population, with visits to emergency departments up by 26 percent between 1993 and
2003. Part of the reason for the rise is that 703 hospitals closed their
doors during that period. Nationwide, the number of emergency departments shrank by 425. Not surprisingly, 91 percent of emergency
departments reported overcrowding as a problem, with almost 40 percent reporting that overcrowding occurred daily. One major contribu-
tor to the overcrowding is that there are often no regular hospital beds
to send patients to. In 2001, 60 percent of hospitals were operating at
or over capacity. In the 1990s, 198,000 hospital beds were eliminated to
reduce overhead costs. As a result, patients are often held in the emergency department for forty-eight hours or more before an inpatient
bed becomes available. In 2004, patients in Los Angeles County who
needed medical assistance right away had seven fewer emergency departments to go to than six years earlier.

The increasingly chaotic conditions in emergency departments are
making it more difficult to attract high-quality professionals to work in
them. Three quarters of hospitals report having difficulty finding specialists to take emergency and trauma calls. Registered nurses are leaving the profession at a far faster pace than they are being replaced. As
of December 2005, hospitals had 118,000 registered nurse vacancies. In
New York City, the vacancy rate for registered nurses was 13 percent.
In 2005, the metropolitan Chicago area reported that it was short by

2,500 nurses, even though there are now far fewer hospitals needing them; since 1980, the number of Chicago-area hospitals has dropped from sixty-four to forty-two, leaving 10,000 fewer beds today, or less than half the 1990 level.

Even getting to a hospital is becoming more difficult and potentially life-threatening. On any given day in a major U.S. city, ambulance drivers are forced to search for an open emergency room that is accepting patients. When hospital emergency departments get overloaded, they direct ambulances to go elsewhere, which usually involves driving longer distances and may mean taking patients to less appropriate facilities. Patients in critical need of care now have to wait longer for it, elevating the risk that their conditions may become unstable before they get to a trauma center. Forty-five percent of hospital emergency departments reported turning ambulances away at some point in 2003, totaling 501,000 diversions nationally.

During a terrorist attack, a natural disaster, or a public health emergency, chances are that the ambulance personnel who arrive on scene will be unprepared for what they are confronted with. Only a tiny percentage of homeland security funding since 9/11 has been directed to support EMS training for mass-casualty events. Furthermore, EMS representation in disaster planning at the federal level has been extremely limited.

To summarize, our fraying public health workforce and shrinking emergency care system are operating at the breaking point. This should come as no surprise to anyone who has had to visit or been taken to an emergency room in recent years. Without drastic changes, there is simply no way the system will adequately respond to a local incident that involves more than 1,000 serious injuries. We are engaging in flights of fancy to pretend for a moment that our government and the health care system are remotely prepared to cope with a pandemic outbreak.

After the surge in media attention to avian flu in 2005, the federal government began to take the risk of a pandemic more seriously. However, what has consumed much of Washington's attention is the risk of a bioterrorism attack, even though no terrorist scenario poses anywhere near the danger of a virulent flu outbreak. Still, inspired by the anthrax mailings shortly after the September 11, 2001, attacks, the Department of Health and Human Services and the Department of Homeland Security have been trying to prepare communities for a sudden outbreak of disease. As a recent national exercise highlighted, the challenges associated with managing these kinds of events are enormous.

In April 2005, New Jersey, along with Connecticut, played host to TOPOFF 3, a biannual exercise mandated by Congress that is designed to test the capacity of the nation's top officials to response to a disaster. The exercise used a hypothetical scenario involving a bioterrorist attack. For the New Jersey component of the scenario, the simulated incident began with a group of terrorists who aborted a planned bioattack against New York City following a confrontation with an off-duty policeman at a New Jersey Turnpike rest stop. Believing their mission is compromised, the drivers of three sport-utility vehicles outfitted with biological dissemination devices release *Yersinia pestis,* the infectious agent for the bubonic plague, along the Garden State Parkway, U.S. Routes 1 and 9, New Jersey Route 18, and the New Jersey Turnpike. Exercise participants assumed that it would take two days before the attack was first detected.

The emergency care community is brought into the scenario when a fourteen-month-old baby is admitted to Robert Wood Johnson University Hospital with plague symptoms. Early on the following day, victims begin presenting themselves at hospitals in Middlesex and Union counties. At the same time that the hospitals are filling up, New Jersey authorities find an abandoned SUV with a dissemination device at Kean

University, arousing the concern of the law enforcement and intelligence communities that a bioterrorism attack may have been launched. By afternoon, casualties in Middlesex and Union counties rise dramatically. Later that evening, the New Jersey Department of Health and Senior Services announces the possibility of a plague outbreak.

By 3:00 P.M. that day, the New Jersey State Emergency Operations Center is fully staffed. At 6:00 P.M., Middlesex County applies to the state for a quarantine order. Later that evening, Union County identifies the presence of *Yersinia pestis*. Given that international travelers visiting New Jersey may have returned to their home countries infected with the bacterium, this information is communicated to the World Health Organization. By 8:15 P.M., New Jersey's governor declares a state of emergency and implements emergency powers. A presidential declaration for New Jersey is issued at 10:00 P.M.

New Jersey requests that the Centers for Disease Control and Prevention send the vaccines and medications from the Strategic National Stockpile. As the day draws to a close, local, state, and national resources have been rapidly mobilized and a massive response effort is under way. However, throughout the night there is cascading number of sick people seeking medical attention. By the middle of the next day, Union County opens the first point of dissemination (POD) to disperse medicines to the state's populations. As fatalities climb, soon every county is operating PODs.

The governors of Delaware, New York, and Pennsylvania order the bridges and roads into New Jersey closed. The transportation system breaks down as rail and truck transport unions refuse, at least initially, to operate in New Jersey. The Federal Aviation Administration imposes temporary flight restrictions over the state's airspace and closes its airports to civil and commercial aviation. The state becomes nearly completely isolated, undermining its ability to provide emergency care and services to its citizens. As a result, the most damaging travel restrictions are soon revoked.

Managing the incident is further complicated by serious staffing shortages at hospitals, public institutions, and emergency response agencies and in the workplace. Fear of infection leads many employees to stay home. The scenario has the public health crisis crest two days after the first sick child arrived at the Robert Wood Johnson University Hospital. While the number of sick continues to soar, the fatalities drop as medicines become widely available. Hospitals in twelve of New Jersey's twenty-one counties are receiving patients with pneumonic plague symptoms. In the end, the scenario assumes, there will be 9,500 fatalities and 29,000 ill.

Some experts criticized the TOPOFF 3 scenario for selecting *Yersinia pestis* as the bioterrorist agent used in the exercise, because it is unlikely to be as lethal as the scenario portrayed. Antibiotics, as opposed to vaccines, would provide a more timely and effective treatment for most people who become infected with the bubonic plague. However, there are two aspects of the exercise that proved to be very realistic. First, many of the government agencies involved had a difficult time communicating and working together. Second, the private sector was largely overlooked as an ally in managing the response to the emergency.

Of course, getting local, state, and federal officials to cooperate will always be a work in progress, but at least there is some progress. More worrisome is how much room there is for improvement when it comes to the public sector working with companies and business leaders to deal with a statewide or regional emergency. A week after the exercise was held, a group of private-sector companies and organizations that participated in TOPOFF 3 convened a roundtable meeting to prepare an after-action report. The meeting was organized by the New Jersey Business Force, an entity created by the Washington-based nonprofit Business Executives for National Security (BENS). The Business

Force is a nonprofit consortium of companies and institutions that have voluntarily come together to support New Jersey's homeland security efforts. It highlighted a number of issues that had not been adequately considered by the state's emergency response and recovery plans tested by the exercise scenario. Three of their major findings make clear how much of a gap there is between emergency-planning assumptions and reality.

First, the public sector did not have adequate means to keep business and industry leaders across the state in the information loop. When the incident began, business and industry leaders pointed out, they would be forced to rely on early news reporting, which would likely be inaccurate and incomplete. Part of the challenge of making good decisions based on these initial reports was that company executives had little in the way of advance information about the threats and hazards to evaluate those reports. This is because state law enforcement and homeland security officials were not sharing initial intelligence indicators with them. Throughout the event, the government had no means of rapidly communicating its intentions and decisions. As a result, the private sector was unable to quickly gauge the potential effects and consequences of those public decisions.

Second, the roles and responsibilities of private-sector companies, many of which provide critical services, had not been delineated in the state's emergency operations plan. This meant that the public sector was overlooking the ability of private companies to provide early detection and warning of a potential disease outbreak by reporting abnormal rates of absenteeism to the state (people tend to delay seeking medical attention for one to two days after feeling sick). In addition, many businesses would willingly contribute resources to support the state during a major emergency. But the state would need to know in advance what assets the private sector possesses.

Third, the state had no credentialing system in place to allow essential private-sector employees to travel during a quarantine. With so much of the society's critical infrastructure in private hands, this problem could undermine the ability of government officials to respond to and recover from an incident. This is because restricting the ability of employees who are essential to business operations to travel can affect essential maintenance and operation of utilities. In addition, draconian travel measures would disrupt the distribution of essential products, including medical supplies, and leave the general public without food and gasoline within just a few days.

To even a casual observer, the problems with the state's emergency response plans that the New Jersey Business Force identified should seem pretty basic. The fact that it had taken nearly four years after the 9/11 attacks and a major national exercise for them to get an airing is profoundly disturbing, particularly in light of the far more dangerous flu pandemic threat. To New Jersey's credit, it reached out to the private sector to include it in the exercise, and state public officials actively solicited feedback on the gaps in their plans. According to the nonprofit Trust for America's Health, the residents of New Jersey are far better off than those of most of the rest of the nation. In a report released in December 2005, New Jersey ranked among the top ten best-prepared states in the country in terms of preparedness. But the overall grade for the country was a D+.

As the recklessly dangerous condition of our public health and emergency preparedness systems highlight, Washington's ongoing failure to address our ailing infrastructure as a top national priority would seem to be inexcusable. After all, elected officials and policy makers in Washington are aware of virtually all the vulnerabilities and issues described in this book. I know this to be the case because the vast majority of my sources are official reports. But politicians and federal officials are often ready with an excuse for their lack of initiative. They argue that they are not responsible for stepping up to these challenges because the appropriate locus of response lies with state and local governments, the private sector, and individual citizens.

Still, such arguments grounded in small government orthodoxy ring hollow when even the electrical power needs of the National Security Agency are being neglected. The NSA is one the nation's premier intelligence agencies; it has the mission of high-tech eavesdropping and sifting through the massive volume of raw data that it receives twenty-four hours a day. Computers are the agency's lifeblood, and electrical power is the essential ingredient for keeping those computers running. But in August 2006, Siobhan Gorman of the Baltimore *Sun* reported that the NSA was unable to install two new supercomputers because the agency was afraid they would overload its power supply. The conservative estimate of how long the agency can stave off an electrical overload is two years. However, it would take from eighteen to thirty months to design and procure equipment, obtain permits, and build a new power substation. In the meantime, a power outage would cripple the NSA's ability to process information. Even power surges, which happen when the electrical infrastructure is stressed, could profoundly disrupt the agency's work by wiping out computer hard drives.

The fact that Washington's neglect of domestic infrastructure should extend to failing to ensure that there is enough electrical power to keep the lights on at one of its most important intelligence agencies is bewildering. It should have former president Dwight D. Eisenhower spinning in his grave. After all, it was Eisenhower who created the network of freeways throughout the United States that celebrated its fiftieth anniversary on June 29, 2006. The official name of our highway network is "The National System of Interstate and Defense Highways." One of the primary rationales for constructing the system as a federal project was that it could be used in military and civil defense operations within the United States. These included facilitating troop movements and even supporting the emergency evacuation of cities in the event of a nuclear war.

Fifty years after the interstate system was created, it is hard to imagine that there was a time when planners saw it as a way to help citizens get out of a city ahead of a nuclear attack. In October 2005, America watched in dismay as Houston-area drivers literally ran out of gas in twenty-hour traffic jams as they tried to flee the city in advance of Hurricane Rita. In 2003, the average commuter spent forty-seven hours idling on the nation's highways; 2.3 billion gallons of gasoline were burned in the process. The estimated cost of highway congestion is $63 billion a year.

Our transportation woes extend beyond commuters missing out on dinner with their families as they sit in traffic. One often underappreciated national asset is America's 12,000 miles of inland waterways. The system that runs from the Great Lakes through the Ohio and Mississippi river valleys serves as maritime highways for such cities as Memphis, Louisville, and Pittsburgh. Barges typically come in two sizes and can be loaded with up to 1,500 tons of goods or 420,000 gallons of petroleum products. Common cargoes include coal, ore, steel, petroleum, chemicals, and grain. A single barge can move the same amount of cargo as fifty-eight trucks at one tenth of the cost, saving shippers more than $7.8 billion in transportation costs annually. Typically, on the Ohio River a towing vessel moves up to fifteen barges at a time, averaging an overall combined length of 1,185 feet, or the equivalent of 225 railcars. On the Mississippi River, a single vessel may tow up to forty-nine barges, in seven rows of six to seven barges per row. Altogether, this towing arrangement is about the same size as a large oceangoing supertanker.

The U.S. Army Corps of Engineers operates the 257 locks along the interstate navigation systems. Thirty of these locks were built in the nineteenth century, and another ninety-two are more than sixty years old. Most have a planned life of fifty years.

Locks are like giant steps that allow vessels to move between points along the river that are at different elevations. The way these watery steps work is that a vessel enters a man-made basin with watertight gates at each end. Once the vessel is inside the lock, the gates are closed and water is either pumped in or drained out so that the ship or tug is raised or lowered to the water level it will be transiting to next. The gate to the adjacent canal is then opened, and the vessel continues on its voyage.

Along the Ohio River system there are fifty locks and dams that were constructed as part of a lengthy canalization project completed in 1929. As these systems have aged, inevitably the cost of maintaining them has grown. However, nearly two decades of federal belt-tightening has resulted in a $600 million backlog in maintenance projects. As a result, the total time that the locks are out of service throughout the year climbed by 110 percent between 1991 and 2004.

Fifty percent of the locks are now functionally obsolete. The congressionally chartered Inland Waterways Users Board has identified $5.4 billion of projects that should be completed to keep the system fully operational. But the commercial user fuel tax set by Congress to help pay for these projects brings in only $100 million per year. Every year that there is a delay in the funding for completing these projects, the average project cost climbs by $7.5 million to $9 million annually. Based on the current budget trajectory, by 2020, the number of functionally obsolete locks is expected to climb to 80 percent.

Just how fragile the system has become was highlighted in May 2004, when U.S. Army Corps of Engineers divers conducted a routine inspection and discovered cracks in the hinges of a 250-ton steel gate in the main chamber of one of the McAlpine Locks in Louisville, Kentucky. Major maintenance on the lock had been postponed for several years while an auxiliary lock built in 1921 was being replaced. However, cuts in congressional funding for the replacement project had extended what was a five-to-six-year timetable into a ten-year one. In the meantime, as the Corps divers discovered, the main lock, built in 1961, is deteriorating. The Corps engineers determined that emergency repairs would have to be conducted in order to avert a catastrophic failure of the gate that could close the river to barge traffic for up to forty-five days or more.

The McAlpine Locks allow vessels to transit through an area of the Ohio River where the water level drops twenty-six feet over a series of falls spread over a distance of two miles. By one estimate, it would take one truck moving on an interstate every 15 seconds, 24 hours a day, 365 days a year to match the cargo moving through the McAlpine Locks annually. One of the most important commodities that moves along the Ohio River each year is 17.4 million tons of coal, much of which feeds the voracious appetites of the steam turbines that generate the region's electricity. A single large power plant can consume one bargeful of coal every hour, or 30,000 pounds of coal every minute.

Large industrial plants in America's heartland are also dependent on the inland waterway system for a steady supply of their raw materials. For instance, the aluminum that finds its way into products ranging from aircraft to soda cans starts off as bauxite, which is imported from Jamaica and other overseas suppliers. The bauxite, or its processed and purified derivative, alumina, travels by barge up the Mississippi River to aluminum-smelting plants in the Tennessee and Ohio river valleys. These plants maintain only a limited inventory of bauxite, which would be exhausted should the river be closed for two weeks or more. Without new material to process, a smelting plant must be shut down, and it can be prohibitively expensive to restart.

Given the region's reliance on barge shipments, news of the Corps of Engineers' May 2004 discovery of cracks in the McAlpine Lock door generated considerable anxiety within the Ohio River Valley. During a May 27, 2004, meeting of industry representatives and waterway users, the Corps announced that it would have to schedule a two-week closure of the river that summer to conduct emergency repairs on the lock. One company executive warned that without at least two months' advance notice to stockpile extra material, the Century Aluminum

Plant in Rangeland, West Virginia, would have to be permanently shuttered, sending seven hundred workers to the unemployment office.

Another company manager pointed out that its manufacturing process for making polyurethane relied on weekly barge shipments of the highly toxic and flammable chemical propylene oxide. Because of its hazardous nature, the company kept only limited stocks of this chemical on site near its plant. The manager warned that an extended outage on the river could translate into a domino effect that would quickly be felt by the automotive industry, which depends on their product.

The most debilitating consequence of a lengthy closure of the waterway system would be its effect on power generation. Without the means to resupply power plants with coal, warned General Carl Strock, the Army Corps commander, the Northeast electrical grid would shut down. Strock went on to express his concern about the increasingly rickety state of the nation's waterway system more generally. One year before the post-Katrina levee failure in New Orleans, Strock ominously cautioned, "We have not yet had a catastrophic failure of a Corps of Engineers project, and that, for us, is the Holy Grail. But I'll tell you what, we are mighty close. We are running closer and closer to that risk every day."

Given the economic stakes, it makes no sense that Washington is skimping on maintaining this infrastructure. But there are security equities that are being overlooked as well. Some of the world's most dangerous chemicals are transported in vast quantities aboard barges, making these cargoes potentially highly destructive weapons. These hazardous materials pass along inland city waterfronts from Saint Louis to Minneapolis and transit through critical canal locks. By targeting these shipments, would-be terrorists could cause mass casualties and vast economic disruptions in America's heartland in much the way that al-Qaeda exploited domestic airliners on 9/11. However, while Washington has spent $20 billion on aviation security in the five years since 9/11, it has dedicated virtually no resources to the security of the inland waterway system.

From the Great Lakes to the Gulf of Mexico, and across the nation to the east and west, America's infrastructure is crumbling. Even the Sunbelt is not exempt. Home to one of the fastest-growing metropolitan areas in the country, Phoenix, Arizona, sits on a plain that faces a seasonal threat of flash flooding when summer and winter storms quickly convert dry rivers, washes, and channels into raging rivers. The flood-control system of dams, basins, and channels constructed to manage this threat was built thirty to fifty years ago for a much smaller population. And like those of the Sacramento River Valley and New Orleans, the system has not been well maintained.

One of the region's oldest flood-control structures is the McMicken Dam, located in Maricopa County's West Valley. The surrounding hills are made of loose, sandy topsoil. The dam holds back runoff that rushes down the slope after a heavy rainfall. Without this dam, two to three inches of rain could generate two to three feet of floodwaters in the valley. Originally constructed in the mid-1950s to protect the sparsely populated Luke Air Force Base, the McMicken Dam is a ten-mile-long earthen embankment that now stands sentry over the burgeoning community of Surprise, Arizona.

A small crack in the dam's foundation could place the entire structure at risk. In 2000, inspectors found a hairline crack running under the dam's southern flank and repaired it. The fissure is believed to be the result of basin soils that are settling as groundwater is withdrawn to satisfy the growing thirst of the neighboring population. As the water table is lowered, the basin soils consolidate.

Although more cracks and fissures are inevitable, there is still no approved plan to build a new dam or reinforce the existing structure. The county hopes to have a plan in place by the end of 2007 but still has not identified any source of funding to undertake it. Meanwhile, there are plans to construct new residential planned communities, subdivisions, and commercial and industrial developments within a quarter mile of each side of the dam property owned by the Flood Control District. These projects will add 13,000 homes and approximately 35,000 people to the area.

Along with the McMicken Dam, fifteen of the twenty-two flood-control dams in Maricopa County need to be rehabilitated or replaced. The county intends to seek federal funding assistance to complete this work over the next twenty-five years. Meanwhile, by 2020, the population of the county is expected to grow by 25 percent, to 4.5 million.

Jared Diamond, in his seminal book *Collapse: How Societies Choose to Fail or Succeed*, identifies four factors that contribute to why societies end up destroying themselves through disastrous decisions. First, a society may fail to anticipate a problem before it arises. Second, when the problem does arrive, the society may fail to perceive it. Third, after it perceives it, it may fail even to try to solve it. Last, the society may try to solve it but may not succeed.

When it comes to critical infrastructure, we would appear to fall into the third category, that of failing to solve a known problem. This neglect is happening despite the likelihood of catastrophic consequences as we look to a future marked by climate change, the rapid global spread of disease, and terrorism. Part of the problem may be that the wealthiest among us are increasingly isolated from the trials and tribulations of the average citizen. Their wealth is no longer derived from smokestack factories or railways or a fleet of ships. Software companies such as Microsoft and Google are run out of offices that look like small college campuses. So our business elites have little incentive to grab elected officials by the lapels and insist that power grids, roads, bridges, dams, or canal locks be put on the front burner. The rest of us seem resigned to be living in a society marked by a decaying industrial landscape.

The case for reinvesting in our critical foundations has certainly not been helped by the example of Boston's "Big Dig," the nation's largest public works project in recent times. The project to reroute the chief controlled-access highway through the heart of Boston into a 3.5-mile tunnel under the city was estimated at $2.5 billion in 1985. By 2006, the actual price tag stood at $14.6 billion. In addition to the meteoric cost overruns, the project has been afflicted with long delays, the use of substandard materials, botched workmanship, and a steady dose of political intrigue. Culminating with the collapse of a ceiling section in the Ted Williams Tunnel on July 10, 2006, that killed a woman riding in a car as a passenger, the Big Dig has fueled the impression that government construction projects are just cash cows for the corrupt and politically well connected.

But other parts of the world are taking on such projects and doing them well. Although we are seemingly oblivious to the decay that is around us, China has stepped out in the opposite direction. Outside Shanghai, the Chinese have built a new magnetic levitation (maglev) train to ferry passengers the eighteen miles from Pudong International Airport to the financial district. Maglevs levitate half an inch above the ground and can travel at more than 300 miles per hour. The train makes the trip in less than seven minutes, passing the interminable gridlock of the highways the trains parallel to. The Chinese are currently building a second line, from Shanghai to Hangzhou, set for completion in 2010, for approximately $4 billion. Tired of its frequent blackouts, China has set up the world's largest electrical grid, increasing its electrical generation capacity from 217,000 megawatts in 1995 to its current level of 508,000 megawatts.

According to the investment firm Morgan Stanley, in 2005 China invested an estimated $200 billion, or 9 percent of the country's gross domestic product, in infrastructure. I experienced firsthand the fruits of this investment on a recent trip from New York to Hong Kong. It took an agonizing ninety minutes in bumper-to-bumper traffic to travel the sixteen miles from my office in Manhattan to John F. Kennedy International Airport. Eighteen hours later, when I arrived at the Hong Kong International Airport in Chek Lap Kok, I noted the time when I was walking down the jetway into the terminal. I cleared immigration and customs within ten minutes, walked one hundred yards, and boarded the dedicated airport railway that transported me twenty-two miles into downtown Hong Kong. I then caught a cab to my hotel. When I stepped into my hotel room, I looked at my watch. From the time I got off the plane until I set my bags down in my room, only forty-seven minutes had elapsed.

While Asia is building high-speed rail and metro systems at a frantic rate, our own rail infrastructure is literally falling apart. The American Society of Civil Engineers estimates that our passenger rail systems will need an infusion of $60 billion by 2025. Our freight rail systems are in even worse shape, requiring an infusion of $175 billion over the next two decades. If we don't make these investments, the gridlock on America's roadways will continue to worsen. If rail freight had to be moved by truck, the costs to shippers would skyrocket by $69 billion annually and our roadways would only deteriorate all the more quickly.

Perhaps not surprisingly, our indifference to the need for constructing and maintaining resilient systems at the national level is becoming an extension of how we run our daily lives. Many of us live just-in-time lifestyles, running to ATMs when our wallets are cashless. For some of us, were it not for last night's leftovers from the Chinese takeout, our refrigerators would be bare. Sometimes living on the edge can be exhilarating. But it is always debilitating and often perilous when things we have grown accustomed to stop working.

SIX

THE BEST DEFENSE
IS A GOOD DEFENSE

Y OU HAVE TO REMEMBER that these terrorists are not super-men." It was September 2002, and I was on the receiving end of a call from Admiral William J. Crowe, Jr. As chairman of the Joint Chiefs of Staff from 1985 to 1989, Admiral Crowe had been the nation's top military officer during the final act of the Cold War. He was reacting to a draft I had prepared for a blue-ribbon task force that the Council on Foreign Relations had convened one year after 9/11. The title of our report was *America Still in Danger; Still Unprepared.*

At first I was not quite sure how to respond. As a man whose career spanned the entire post–World War II era, perhaps Admiral Crowe was too old-school to recognize the change in the strategic landscape that 9/11 represented. But Bill Crowe was no military dinosaur. Instead, his nearly five decades in uniform provided him with the ability to locate the al-Qaeda threat within a broader context. "These terrorists cannot destroy us," he went on to say. "We are a country of nearly three hundred million people with infrastructure spread across a nation that has the fourth largest landmass in the world. This is not thermonuclear war we are facing." Then he provided an insight that has shaped my thinking on this challenge ever since: "The real danger lies not with what the terrorists can do to us but what we can do to ourselves when we are spooked."

Admiral Crowe is right. The terrorist threat is not the epochal threat of our age. It involves nowhere near the stakes of the Cuban Missile Crisis, when the United States and the Soviet Union were on the brink of nuclear war. Instead, it occupies a place—albeit a prominent one—on a growing list of potential disasters that we will have to manage throughout the twenty-first century. Further, our ability to overreact can produce more harm to our way of life and quality of life than terrorists are able to inflict.

It is not the terrorists themselves that should be our top priority. Instead, we should doing our best to improve our ability to weather the age of terrorism—and the age of disasters of a natural sort. As I argued earlier, our chances of eliminating terrorism are about as good as those of eradicating the seasonal flu. What we can aspire to do is to keep it within reasonable bounds by preventing it when we can and minimizing the risk that terrorist acts will have cascading consequences when we can't.

We will have to live with terrorism because our current and future adversaries will make it their weapon of choice regardless of what we do to combat it. This is because they have no other alternative in challenging U.S. power. The United States spends more on conventional military capabilities than the rest of the world *combined*. Never in human history has so much military power been concentrated in the hands of a single power as the United States possesses today. Our current and future adversaries are not going to attempt to go toe-to-toe with our navy, air force, or ground forces. They must try to sidestep our overwhelming military might, and terrorist acts are their only means of doing so. So unless war itself becomes obsolete, terrorism is here to stay.

While terrorism will be our enemies' tactic of choice, it does not automatically follow that we need to rely primarily on our traditional offense-based military forces to fight back. Wars can also be success-fully waged with defensive measures when the adversary recognizes that his offensive efforts are likely to prove too costly or will fail to achieve the desired result.

However, when it comes to the war on terrorism, the Bush admin-istration has given defensive measures a decidedly bad rap. The White House and Pentagon point to the extreme ideology and the demon-strated willingness of radical jihadists to die for their cause, and argue that terrorist groups cannot be deterred. In light of this zeal for mar-tyrdom, they argue, America's only choice is to unleash the power of the U.S. military overseas to destroy terrorists before they strike here. Any serious effort to protect ourselves at home has been written off as largely futile because the menu of possible targets is almost limitless.

I agree that when there is specific intelligence to support it, going after terrorist groups before they strike makes sense. But there's the rub. As has been well documented by a number of blue-ribbon com-missions since 9/11, America's intelligence system is not firing on all cylinders. It will likely require another five to ten years both to work through all the kinks associated with the recent reforms that have been imposed on the intelligence community and to develop the kind of human intelligence capabilities needed to support ongoing counterter-rorism operations. In the interim, the United States will be operating partially in the blind.

Though the Bush administration has insisted that the only way to confront the terrorist threat is to "take the battle to the enemy," there is mounting evidence that those efforts are not achieving the intended result. In September 2006, the White House released an updated version of its counterterrorism plan that acknowledges as much. It documents the growth of small-scale extremist groups around the globe over the past three years. The report also acknowledges that the war in Iraq has been a "rallying cry" that terrorists have used to expand recruitment. Further, this recruitment is not limited to Iraq but is taking place among first- and second-generation Muslim immigrants in western Europe and Canada, where they are clearly outside the reach of the U.S. military.

But the war in Iraq is doing more than producing the angst that expands the ranks of jihadists. It is also becoming a proving ground where the skills of planning and conducting an attack within a modern urban setting are proliferating. Indeed, in some ways the situation in Iraq is analogous to what happened during the decade-long Afghan conflict from 1980 to 1989 against the Soviet occupation. The foreign participants who joined the mujahideen became the hardened foot soldiers who would ultimately transform themselves into al-Qaeda. But unlike Afghanistan, where the combatants waged war in a premodern society, in Iraq insurgents are refining the skills to sabotage critical infrastructures such as pipelines, refineries, and the electrical grid. Between January 2004 and March 2006, insurgents carried out attacks on oil and gas pipelines that cost Iraq more than $16 billion in lost oil revenue. Successful attacks on the electrical grid have kept Iraq's average daily output at 5 to 10 percent below the prewar level despite the $1.2 billion the United States has spent to improve the country's electrical production. The terrorist skills acquired are being catalogued and shared in Internet chat rooms. In addition, when foreign insurgents return to their native lands, they do so with the experience of successfully targeting the kinds of complex systems that support economic and daily life within advanced societies.

Finally, there is the toll the war is taking in terms of both blood and treasure. As of September 1, 2006, 2,654 U.S. servicemen and women had lost their lives in the conflict and the number of wounded stood at nearly 20,000. American taxpayers contributed $316 billion, or $250 million per day, to pay for the war effort during its first three years.

Persisting with this costly campaign despite its clear limits and unintended consequences might be an unpleasant necessity if there were no alternative. But it turns out there is. The conventional wisdom is wrong: terrorists can be deterred, and there are pragmatic and affordable things that can be done right now to make the United States a far less attractive target.

As a starting point, it is important to recognize that terrorist groups have their own constraints. First, their objective is not simply to engage in random acts of violence. Today's terrorist masterminds know that the main benefit of attacks is the economic costs they can generate. Certainly this lesson has not been lost on Osama bin Laden. In a videotape broadcast on Aljazeera on November 1, 2004, bin Laden claimed, "For example, al-Qaeda spent $500,000 on the event, while America, in the incident and its aftermath, lost—according to the lowest estimate—more than $500 billion. Meaning that every dollar of al-Qaeda defeated a million dollars by the permission of Allah, besides the loss of a huge number of jobs." From al-Qaeda's perspective, therefore, not all targets are equal. The most attractive ones are those that have the potential to create the biggest bang for the terrorist buck.

Second, the stated objective of al-Qaeda leaders is for the next attack on the United States to be bigger than 9/11. By raising the bar, it also adds considerable complexity to the enterprise. Success will depend on careful planning, good organization and logistics, and effective leadership. This includes locating safe houses, providing identity documents, and recruiting accomplices who can blend into the civilian population. They can draw on only a limited pool of operatives who have the requisite combination of motivation and capabilities to participate in a major terrorist operation within the United States. Assembling a cadre of these individuals, who will be able to go undetected by neighbors or local law enforcement for potentially extended periods of time, is tricky business.

For instance, recruiting and sheltering a suicide bomber is difficult. The radicalization process that produces a dependable operative who is willing to die for the jihadist cause typically requires at least two years. The individual must also be capable of operating in a Western country without drawing undue attention to himself. A poor Punjabi who has spent his life memorizing the Koran in a remote madrassa in northern Pakistan might be a willing recruit. However, he is likely to stick out should he travel to the United States.

This leads to the third significant constraint that a terrorist group must deal with: that it will likely have only one bite at the apple. Any attempt at a terrorist attack will be like unleashing the hounds at the start of a fox hunt. Law enforcement will descend in force. Investigators will pick up the forensic trail that any attempted or successful operation always leaves. The organization will have to flee, go to ground, or almost certainly be apprehended. In other words, a group planning a terrorist operation really has only one round in the chamber. If it uses it, it loses it.

As a consequence, a radical jihadist group must conduct extensive surveillance of its attempted target and carefully rehearse the operation in advance. Suicide bombers are not willing to throw their lives away for nothing. They want to be reasonably confident that their sacrifice will contribute to the success of a meaningful attack on their avowed enemy. This is good news for terrorism prevention. Throughout this preparation time they are at risk of being observed and intercepted. The more ambitious the operation, the more up-front effort is required to pull it off. Along the way they risk doing something that will set off an alarm.

All this translates into two core realities about the terrorism threat that have been largely overlooked since 9/11. First, terrorists are interested in carrying out attacks where they have near-certain odds of gen-

erating the maximum consequences. We are not talking about an un-
bounded problem. There are a finite number of meaningful targets
that our enemies would find worth attacking. Second, adopting measures to protect those likely targets has value. The harder the potential
target is, the more planning, surveillance, and rehearsals are required
to attack it. Outside expertise may have to be found. This raises the operation's risk of detection. Alternatively, if the target is a soft one, the
group can be smaller and the planning cycle shorter. The window for
detecting and intercepting the operation also will be constrained as a
result.

From an adversary's perspective, however, going after lesser targets
is not likely to be worth it. It will still involve the time-consuming effort of putting into place the organization to carry the plan out. But attacking a shopping center, a school yard, or a sports event is unlikely to
have any lasting impact. Such attacks will certainly draw media attention. But they also spawn enforcement efforts that make them almost
impossible to replicate. Since they cannot be sustained over time, their
long-term economic consequences are likely to be negligible.

Therefore, defending the targets that would be most appealing to
terrorists is worth doing. Accordingly, we need to identify what those
targets are and invest adequate resources in safeguarding them. Un-
believably, given that more than five years have passed since September 11, 2001, no such national list exists. Congress demanded one
when it passed the Department of Homeland Security Act of 2002,
but to no avail. As recently as June 2006, the federal government's
National Infrastructure Protection Plan lays out only the *process* by
which priorities should be developed and provides a suggested action
plan for how to better secure these potential targets. What those priorities should be still hasn't been determined.

This is not rocket science. Chemical facilities near urban population centers have the potential to inflict the greatest casualties; attacks
on the electric grid, oil and gas facilities, major ports, and the food sup-

ply system have the potential to create the greatest cascading economic effects. For help in constructing this list, Washington could turn to the congressionally chartered National Academy of Sciences, the National Academy of Engineering, the Institute of Medicine, and the National Research Council. The national academies bring together scientists, engineers, and other experts who are on call to provide free expert advice to the federal government.

Once we identify the things we need to protect, the process of protecting them will not be as arduous as it might first appear. There are essentially four ways of protecting critical infrastructure, only one of which involves physical defenses like the cement barricades, or Jersey barriers, that increasingly dominate our post-9/11 landscape. Hardening a potential target is the only option when a critical facility cannot be moved or replaced. The Hoover Dam, the White House, and national monuments such as the Statue of Liberty fall under this category.

However, some critical systems can be protected simply by investing in redundancy. For instance, attacking a computer server is not attractive if there is a remote server that can automatically kick in if the main server goes down. Similarly, a high-voltage line is a good target only if an attack against it will result in a major and lengthy outage. If the power can be rerouted through other lines serviced by other power generators, the attack will result in only a temporary disruption of service to a few customers. Given the absence of any carnage caused by or lasting effect of such an attack, the incident would probably not survive more than a single news cycle.

Sometimes the best way to protect something is simply to be prepared to fix it should it break or be targeted. For instance, it would be prohibitively expensive to provide physical security for the entire Trans-Alaskan Pipeline. Constructing a spare pipeline to provide redundancy is also a nonstarter. But a terrorist attack on the pipeline would not be attractive if the process, equipment, and people were in place to repair any section damaged. This might require positioning spare pipe every few miles and maintaining surveillance cameras or other sensors so that a breach in the pipe can be detected quickly. It would also require an emergency response team that could be mobilized on short notice to perform the repairs. Often this response capability already exists as a result of safety and environmental protection mandates.

The fourth way to protect critical infrastructure is to make it less dangerous by reengineering its processes so as to make them less potentially hazardous, or in some cases to physically relocate a facility to a more remote area. For instance, public water filtration plants are among the top three consumers of chemicals, including chlorine. Chlorine was one of the poison gases used as a weapon along the western front during World War I. If released into the air, it would be lethal for anyone caught downwind. It is often transported under pressure in liquid form by tanker trucks, which must drive through city streets to reach the treatment facilities. There, it is stored in tanks adjacent to the plants that may be close to residential neighborhoods, potentially placing tens of thousands of people at risk. This risk can be alleviated by replacing chlorine with sodium hypochlorite, the active ingredient in household bleach. However, many facilities have resisted doing so since it involves additional costs.

Alternatively, it may make sense to move an inherently dangerous facility out of a congested urban location, thereby making it a much less appealing target. That is what Houghton Chemical Corporation decided to do with the contents of several large tanks next to a major hotel on Boston's Charles River. The tank farm stored highly flammable liquid vinyl acetate and was on the list of 121 U.S. chemical facilities that the Environmental Protection Agency said could potentially put more than a million people in jeopardy in the event of an accident. After September 11, 2001, company executives decided that the risk of a miles-long toxic cloud over the Boston skyline was not something they wanted to live with, so they quietly removed these deadly substances.

With this menu of options in mind, let us revisit the sobering terrorist scenario outlined in Chapter 2. Earlier I traced how a small cell of terrorists with expertise in constructing an improvised explosive device could launch a small-boat attack on an LNG tanker as the tanker transited Boston Harbor. The subsequent explosion would incinerate everything within a 700-yard radius on the Charlestown, East Boston, and Chelsea waterfronts. There would be thousands of casualties, including many who would be badly burned, completely overwhelming the hospital and emergency care systems throughout New England. Hundreds of homes and buildings along the city's waterfront, the USS *Constitution,* and the Coast Guard's regional base would be destroyed in the fire. The transportation and energy systems of the greater Boston area would be crippled, possibly for years. How could such a hypothetical catastrophe be prevented?

The most straightforward solution would be to construct a replacement LNG facility on a remote location near the harbor's entrance or to place it further offshore. If an LNG tanker did not need to transit within one mile of a densely populated area, it would cease to be an attractive target. Though the fire would be spectacular, the consequences would not. Ships can be replaced, and most of the fuel would be burned off in the fire, limiting the environmental damage.

Is this unreasonable and impractical? It depends on the timeline. It certainly could be done in two years if Washington treated the issue with the same vigor with which it has approached trying to restart the energy industry in Iraq. Too expensive? The energy sector has ample resources to move the facility if it were required to do so. In 1990, a year after the tanker *Exxon Valdez* spilled 11 million gallons of oil into Alaska's Prince William Sound, Congress mandated that all oil tankers be changed to a double-hull design so as to add a safety gap between the oil tanks and the external hull of the ship. This required the reconstruction and replacement of much of the world's tanker fleet. The industry absorbed the enormous expense of doing so with no measurable effect on the price of oil. If we could insist on such an industrywide change to better protect the environment in 1990, we can do the same to protect the city of Boston seventeen years later.

Apart from moving the Distrigas LNG facility, there are other steps that could be taken in the near term to address this scenario. One measure that would likely have the biggest return on a very small investment is a strong outreach effort by the Coast Guard and local police to the people who live, work, and play on Boston's waterfront. Since it would be very difficult for terrorists preparing to conduct this kind of attack to remain inconspicuous, the idea would be to educate people who might witness a dry run or actual event. They should be told about the threat and provided with some basic indicators for spotting a small-boat attack. Typically, there are plenty of potential eyes and ears around a city marina that could detect a boat behaving erratically. Many boat owners spend a good bit of their free time doing maintenance or simply relaxing on their boats while they are tied to the pier. Some people even live on their vessels. Yacht clubs and marinas are minicommunities where the locals tend to know one another well. They have a good feel for the rhythm of the waterfront and can recognize when something is out of sync. A citizen report, particularly during a terrorist dry run, could be indispensable to foiling this kind of attack.

Captain Peter Boynton, the Coast Guard's sector commander for Long Island Sound, headquartered in New Haven, Connecticut, is a big believer in these kinds of efforts. His conversion came in 1987, when he was commanding a patrol boat based out of San Juan, Puerto Rico. As a result of a citizen tip-off of a vessel operating "strangely," he ended up making a two-ton cocaine drug bust that for seven years held the record as the largest maritime cocaine seizure. Based on some specific law enforcement intelligence, Boynton had been patrolling the area for three days, looking for this smuggler's vessel. He doubts that he would ever have spotted it without the local help.

The Coast Guard has an ideal asset to assist with this kind of outreach effort: the Coast Guard Auxiliary. Since its creation by Congress in 1939, the Auxiliary has served as a volunteer civilian component of the agency. In 2006, there were 30,000 members from more than 2,000 cities and towns throughout the United States. Auxiliarists are typically well known and well liked within their communities since they help boaters in distress, conduct courtesy safety examinations of recreational vessels, and offer free boating and water safety courses. The Auxiliary could be tapped to include information on the small-boat threat in the courses they conduct, as well as to fan out across the waterfront and take the word to other mariners and local residents.

Another relatively modest step that could be taken to help trip up a small-boat assault involves providing local authorities with better tools for monitoring the waterfront. A very basic need is to have a better feel for who actually belongs to the boating public. There are an estimated eighteen million recreational boats in the United States—it's an estimate because no one in Washington really keeps track of boats. There is no national registry or national system for licensing operators for recreational vessels. Thirteen million small boats are registered by states; roughly 5 million are not registered at all. Boats are not toys, particularly in this age, but at present anyone who has the cash can own and operate one in U.S. waters. Training is optional. This needs to change.

Another helpful tool would be surveillance cameras installed in places like boating ramps and other strategic places in the harbor. The kind of small boat used in my scenario would have to be launched relatively near to Boston Harbor and close to the time when the ship was due to arrive. A small boat cannot carry very much fuel, and its passengers are exposed to the elements. As a result, these cameras would not have to be monitored by Coast Guard officials all the time; they could simply add some extra watch standers to keep an eye on them at an appropriate window in advance of an LNG ship's arrival. Such cameras have their limits, but they can be programmed with software that allows them to detect abnormalities, such as a boat remaining in the same place for a long period of time. Then an alarm could be activated and a watch officer could direct a security team to investigate.

At present, the Coast Guard is unable to routinely maintain security patrols even in America's busiest harbors, and most local port police forces are tiny. With just 39,000 active-duty officers and enlisted men and women, the Coast Guard is about the same size as the New York City police department. But the service is responsible for patrolling 3.36 million square miles of water and 95,000 miles of coastline. The Coast Guard should have more people and more boats to maintain active patrols in America's city harbors. If there are regular "cops on the beat," terrorists are far less likely to risk carrying out a waterborne attack.

However, an attack on an LNG or oil tanker is only one potential way in which terrorists could carry out a major attack on the United States. There are other, potentially higher-probability, scenarios, such as attacks on chemical facilities, whose consequences could be on a similar scale. But all these scenarios require a considerable amount of planning. All require surveillance and practice runs if they are likely to succeed. All would have to be done by a very small number of terrorists operating inside the United States. In other words, all are susceptible to being detected by local law enforcement that engages in strong community policing.

The model for the nation on how to do this right is the New York Police Department. New York Police Commissioner Ray Kelly has leveraged a police force of nearly 40,000 officers, drawn from every ethnic group in the city (and therefore much of the world), to develop the most effective counterterrorism program in the United States. As NYPD Deputy Commissioner Richard Falkenrath maintains, New York cops bring "grit, creativity, and street smarts" to the job of preventing terrorism in what remains al-Qaeda's number one American target. The heart of the program has been to maintain a highly visible and dynamic police presence throughout the city and to pursue a community policing initiative that makes the general public and the private sector allies in detecting terrorist activities.

Shortly after returning to the job of police commissioner in 2002 (he had previously held the post from 1992 to 1994), Ray Kelly decided that the NYPD would need its own autonomous intelligence capacity. To create it, he hired David Cohen, a veteran CIA officer, to become the department's deputy commissioner of intelligence. The idea was to have a tailored understanding of the ongoing terrorist threat so that the NYPD could make the best use of its resources.

Collecting intelligence to support counterterrorism operations required an important cultural shift. Traditionally, law enforcement agencies have had a very tactical and utilitarian approach to intelligence. Their goal was to gather just enough of it to build a case to support arrests and prosecutions. But confronting the terrorism risk requires more patience and a greater emphasis on building a strategic understanding of the rapidly evolving terrorist threat. Cohen has hired civilian analysts who can work alongside seasoned detectives to try to help identify trends that may warrant an adjustment in tactics. The intelligence division also helps to support the department's outreach effort by providing tailored and current information that can be shared with corporate security officers and business owners to make them aware of activities they might come across that suggest terrorist operations.

Training traffic cops and uniformed patrolmen to spot potential terrorism indicators is another important effort the NYPD has undertaken. This includes educating police officers on what chemicals they encounter that point to bomb making. The department also provides an ongoing training program for its senior officers, including seminars with top international terrorism experts.

The NYPD has created a specific program to deal with the challenge of protecting New York's critical infrastructure. The Threat Reduction and Infrastructure Protection Section, or TRIPS, works with the private sector by providing public and private entities with security advice and helping to develop threat assessments for potential terrorist targets. It is broken into five teams: (1) key facilities, (2) transportation and maritime, (3) utilities, (4) chemical, biological, radiological, and nuclear, or CBRN, and (5) explosives.

One of the department's best-known initiatives is a program called Hercules. Each day the NYPD assembles a large number of well-armed uniformed officers and sends them off to a subway station or near a city landmark to conduct security sweeps. The timing and locations are always varied so as to create uncertainty for potential terrorist operatives. This lack of predictability is a very effective counterterrorism tool, since terrorist organizations have a low tolerance for failure.

What New York is doing is impressive. It has turned its police force from serving as first responders to acts of terrorism into what the counterterrorism expert R. P. Eddy has called "first preventers." These efforts are very expensive, costing the city more than $200 million annually. With the notable exception of Los Angeles, this price tag has scared other U.S. cities away from trying to emulate the NYPD programs, even on a far more modest scale. Most cities assign a couple of officers to the local FBI counterterrorism task force and then turn their attention back to their traditional crime-fighting activities. Given both the growing threat of homegrown terrorism as well as the indispensable role local law enforcement can play in detecting and preventing terrorist activities, more needs to be done to enlist them formally in the nation's counterterrorism efforts.

Maddeningly, the trend is moving in the wrong direction. Police departments are finding themselves stretched thinner as the Bush administration has cut back on the funding to support the Community Oriented Policing Services, or COPS, program, which put 100,000 new police officers onto America's streets during the Clinton administration. At the same time, the number of violent crimes crept up for the first time in nearly a decade in 2006. Police chiefs are understandably reluctant to invest in a new mission when they are treading water on their bread-and-butter one.

The federal government should undertake a COPS II program, with an emphasis on providing local police departments with the means to build counterterrorism and terrorism intelligence units that are smaller-scale versions of the NYPD's. To achieve this, the federal government should provide funding for hiring three entry-level police officers for each ten- to fifteen-year veteran detective the city assigns to the counterterrorism mission. Why should the federal government fund this? First, because there is no way the local knowledge possessed by an experienced detective can be replicated by a federal official. Second, it is about helping our communities to perform more of a national service than a local one.

There is no terrorist rule that says that a terrorist operation must be planned in the same city it will be carried out in. Though New York, Washington, or Los Angeles will be the targeted city of choice, terrorist organizations are likely to base their operations some distance away. This was the case with the train attacks in London on July 7, 2005. The bombs were actually constructed in an apartment in Leeds, 175 miles north of the British capital. It is unrealistic and unfair to expect that local communities will shoulder the cost of assigning experienced law enforcement officers to perform work that will probably end up protecting other large cities, potentially several states away. The federal government should provide the funding for such a national effort.

The medical field offers a compelling analogy for recalibrating the war on terrorism. Consider how doctors currently deal with patients infected with the human immunodeficiency virus (HIV), the retrovirus responsible for acquired immunodeficiency syndrome (AIDS). While every physician would welcome a cure for AIDS, the medical community has not been wagering everything on developing a vaccine that could clear the body of an HIV infection. It recognizes that the virus is incredibly complex and highly mutable.

Realizing that a vaccine is likely to remain out of reach for some time to come, researchers and doctors have had to devise other strategies to deal with those who have been infected with HIV. Since the mid-1990s, physicians have been prescribing a combination of medications known as antiretrovirals to keep HIV within acceptable limits so that the patient's immune system continues to function. The logic behind pursuing this course is straightforward: HIV becomes fatal only when it succeeds in destroying the immune system so the body no longer has the ability to ward off diseases such as pneumonia or tuberculosis that become the real killers. Since modern medications can help assist the body to keep its natural defense system intact, HIV has become a chronic illness. In other words, though new infections cannot be wholly prevented and there is still no cure, AIDS is now a treatable disease.

The radical jihadist threat has proven itself to be like a complicated and elusive virus. In confronting that threat, I believe, we should adjust our strategy in two ways that are analogous to how doctors are treating HIV infections. The first is to place far greater emphasis on the kinds of counterterrorism efforts we could be pursuing here within the United States, as opposed to expending so much of our blood and treasure on trying to win campaigns overseas. The second is to focus on ensuring that our national "immune system"—that is, our civil society and the economic and political foundations that support it—is in top form. Living with a chronic illness may not be ideal, but if it is treatable, a person can adjust to it and continue to have a fulfilling life.

The counterterrorism initiatives I have described here—strong local police work, hardening some vulnerable potential targets, adding redundancies to others, developing a capacity to respond nimbly when protective measures fail, and relocating or changing the processes at dangerous facilities—are much like antiretroviral drugs in the treatment of HIV. But unlike the HIV-therapy "cocktails," pursuing these initiatives will have few damaging side effects. Community policing efforts will help combat crime as well as improve our ability to detect and intercept terrorist organizations. The kinds of things we need to do to make critical infrastructure more durable so as to reduce its appeal as a terrorist target can simultaneously bolster its capacity to ride out both daily trials and natural disasters. Finally, none of these defensive measures will provide fodder to fuel the jihadists' claim that the United States is at war with Islam.

In short, just as we have accustomed ourselves to living with the chronic risk of natural disasters, so too must we learn to live with the threat of terrorism. Rather than myopically and futilely trying to cleanse the global system of this threat, Americans need to take a deep breath and recognize that terrorists cannot destroy us. However, if cooler heads do not prevail, what terrorism *can* do is lead us to attack our own immune system. We must not fall into a trap where, in a frantic effort to make ourselves "secure," we end up inflicting injuries on our civil society, the economy at large, and our constitutional system of checks and balances. Then we ourselves will be responsible for destroying what Abraham Lincoln famously called "the last best hope on Earth."

SEVEN

GETTING IT RIGHT

WASHINGTON IS WIRED WRONG to deal with the major challenges that confront us. The "homegrown" terrorist risk is growing, but the White House and Pentagon continue to treat the war on terrorism as an overseas military campaign. Though major natural disasters pose the most probable risk to the lives of everyday Americans, the federal government insists on maintaining an arm's-length approach to emergency response. Rather than preparing a comprehensive plan for addressing the eroding foundations of our modern society, members of Congress are content to treat funding for capital investments as so much pork to be divvied up among their districts. By one estimate, in 2006 the U.S. Senate blessed 6,371 pet projects tying up $25 billion in highway funding.

We need to make some changes. Our top national priority must be to ensure that our society and our infrastructure are resilient enough not to break under the strain of natural disasters or terrorist attacks.

This requires making a substantial investment in repairing and upgrading America's crumbling industrial landscape as well as bolstering the capacity of our emergency response institutions to help us when we need them. To achieve this, we must be willing to think large and act with dispatch. We must also be willing to rethink the authorities and capabilities of the federal government to support states and localities in managing disasters.

Let's begin by putting together a new process for identifying what needs to be done, establishing priorities, and marshaling the necessary funding. Taking a page from the Department of Defense's book, we should create a commission whose mission is to improve infrastructure resiliency, roughly modeled on the Base Closure and Realignment Commission (BRAC) that Congress created for deciding which domestic military installations would be closed or downsized. It should be called the Infrastructure Resiliency Commission.

BRAC provides an attractive model for undertaking the politically charged work of prioritizing and funding critical infrastructure projects because it was established by Congress for the expressed purpose of minimizing the risk that parochial interests would triumph over our national security needs. The commission is made up of distinguished individuals, mostly retired generals and admirals, former cabinet secretaries, and members of Congress. The process begins by assessing the current and anticipating the future national security environment. The commissioners then evaluate the force structure plan and basing requirements to meet ongoing and anticipated threats. Only then do they start to look at individual bases and weigh their relative importance against eight criteria established by Congress. The commissioners hold public hearings in the local communities to receive public feedback on a preliminary base closure recommendation. After completing this process, BRAC prepares its final list of bases for closure or realignment.

No base in the United States or its territories is off limits. Once the commission completes its work, it submits its report to the president, who must either forward it to Congress or return it to the commission for further evaluation. If the report is returned to BRAC, it must resubmit it within thirty days, after which the president must send it to Congress. Congress then has forty-five days to enact a joint resolution to reject the report in full. If it does not vote to reject it, the Pentagon must abide by the report's base closure recommendations.

Just as BRAC was set up to limit the role of parochial politics in making decisions that may affect the capacity to respond to national security threats, the purpose of the Infrastructure Resiliency Commission would be to identify the investments that need to be made most urgently, regardless of which congressional district a project will reside in. It would be made up of fifteen members nominated by a bipartisan committee of the House of Representatives and confirmed by a bipartisan committee of the Senate. The commissioners would have a permanent staff of individuals with expertise in each infrastructure sector.

Their work would be supported by the congressionally chartered national academies, which include the National Academy of Sciences, the National Academy of Engineering, the Institute of Medicine, and the National Research Council. The national academies draw on experts from around the country who volunteer their time "to address critical national issues and give advice to the federal government and the public." The National Academy of Public Administration (NAPA) would also be assigned a formal advisory role.

The national academies and NAPA would form permanent committees with rotating memberships to support the commission. These committees would identify vulnerabilities and establish criteria for evaluating the needs of the energy, transportation, information, and other sectors. In addition, they would form an advisory council made up of the chairman of each of the individual committees. The advisory council would examine the interdependence issues associated with all the sectors and assign relative weight to the recommendations provided by each sector.

Complementing the work of the national academies would be physical infrastructure committees organized by the American Society of Civil Engineers (ASCE). ASCE has 139,000 members drawn from both academia and the professional civil engineering community. In addition to the extensive survey of the nation's infrastructure needs that it prepares periodically, the ASCE supports disaster response by sending technical teams to assess the condition of infrastructure, identify failings, and provide recommendations for remediation.

The Infrastructure Resiliency Commission would include in its mission providing recommendations for properly funding the modernization of our public health services and expanding the capacity of our emergency medical system. This includes improving state and local public health agencies so that they can be full partners in fighting emerging disease outbreaks, whether natural or terrorist in nature. It will also require funding for hospital disaster preparedness and setting up metropolitan megaemergency departments capable of handling incidents that create mass victims. The Institute of Medicine and the Association of State and Territorial Health Officials would provide support for this work.

The staff of the Infrastructure Resiliency Commission would assemble the input from the American Society of Civil Engineers, the Association of State and Territorial Health Officials, and the national academies. When appropriate, the staff could commission additional studies by other outside experts as well. This information would then be presented to the commissioners in much the way that the governors of the Federal Reserve Board receive economic data to review prior to deciding where to set interest rates. In subgroups of three, the commissioners would then conduct regional hearings to receive additional public input on the proposed projects they are evaluating. After these hearings, they would prepare their final project recommendations along with a detailed budget proposal to support each. The budget proposals should accompany the commission's annual report on the condition of our infrastructure, modeled on the ASCE Report Card. The report would be presented each year to Congress and published in a format easily accessible to the public.

The true power of the commission would be the stature of its commissioners and its annual public report. The commission report should be something that is highly anticipated each year, both as an inventory of where we stand and as a projection of where we need to be and why we are not there. The report can be a powerful tool for the public, which would then have the information it needs to assess whether Congress is spending money only for things that truly need to be done. If a member of Congress tries to fund a project that is not on the commission's list, he or she would have to explain why.

In order to create the Infrastructure Resiliency Commission, the president would probably have to use his bully pulpit to cajole Congress into embracing it. This is because the charter of the commission differs from that of BRAC in an important way that is likely to be politically sensitive. In the case of BRAC, members of Congress widely agreed that U.S. defense infrastructure needed to be trimmed, but such cuts would inevitably anger constituents in districts where the cuts are made. BRAC deflects the blame for these cuts onto the commission as opposed to the politicians.

The Infrastructure Resiliency Commission would be less appealing to members of Congress, because it serves as a very public check on new government spending, thereby restricting their ability to work behind the scenes to negotiate pork-barrel projects to bring back to their home districts. But the creation of a commission would be essential for overcoming the reservations everyday Americans would have about dedicating billions of dollars of additional tax revenues to spending on public works. Sadly, the public's cynicism about the current appropriations process has been well earned.

Beyond its charge to recommend and prioritize critical infrastructure projects, the Infrastructure Resiliency Commission's mission would also include analyzing new privately funded projects, such as refineries, LNG terminals, waste disposal facilities, and nuclear power plants. The commissioners would have an advisory role to Congress, making recommendations for tax incentives or grant support for the projects it finds will address important safety, environmental, and security considerations.

The real value of the Infrastructure Resiliency Commission would be its ability to help Congress set priorities for new funding dedicated to making improvements in infrastructure. To this end, Congress should create a dedicated Infrastructure Resiliency Trust Fund. Investing in our infrastructure will strengthen our security and help keep our nation competitive in the global market place. But the costs of doing this will not be small. The American Society of Civil Engineers estimates that we need to invest $295 billion per year in restoring America's infrastructure. Another $12 billion is needed to restore local and state public health infrastructure.

Not all the funding for infrastructure should come out of public funds. Toll roads, rail lines, ports, and energy infrastructure can all be profitable investments for U.S. and foreign companies. In European countries, private investment in public infrastructure has taken off over the last decade. Recognizing that they have only a limited capacity to finance their infrastructure needs, European governments, as well as those of Australia and Canada, have embraced the concept and adapted their laws and regulations to support this trend.

The United States has been slower to respond to the growing interest by private investors in public infrastructure projects. One notable exception has been the new Chicago Skyway toll road. A Spanish company, Cintra, and an Australian private equity company, Macquarie Infrastructure Group, financed the construction of the road. Macquarie is extending its investments to other areas, including a water utility in Connecticut and a power company outside Pittsburgh. Recently, U.S. firms with very deep pockets, such as Goldman Sachs and the Carlyle

Group, are showing a serious interest in making multibillion-dollar investments in this sector.

Still, public funds will have to be found for the overwhelming majority of the funding to repair our highways, bridges, tunnels, dams, canals, water treatment and waste management facilities, navigable waterways, transit, and public buildings, as well as to bolster our public health capabilities. There are several potential sources for funding the Infrastructure Resiliency Trust Fund. The first might be the roughly $40 billion of estate taxes. President Bush and many members of Congress want to eliminate this tax. But those who accrued a great deal of wealth in their lifetimes did so in part because they were living in a secure, advanced society. A strong case could be made for reinvesting a portion of that wealth into the infrastructure that will make it possible for future generations to succeed as they did. The estate tax in its present form applies only to estates over $2 million. The current maximum rate for estates of any size is set at 46 percent. However, the estate tax is set to expire in 2010, take a year hiatus, and kick back in by 2011 at its much more controversial pre-2001 rates. Congress and the president should move beyond the polemics that have marked the debate about the future of this tax. One way to do this is to make the present estate tax formula permanent but dedicate it to the Infrastructure Resiliency Trust Fund. In this way, taxpayers will know that the dollars the federal government collects when they die will be used for a laudatory purpose.

The second source might involve returning to a tax structure that assigns a greater level of burden for bankrolling the cost of our government to the wealthiest wage earners. Since President Bush took office, Congress has cut the top tax rate twice, disproportionately benefiting the wealthiest Americans vis-à-vis middle-income and lower-income taxpayers. Tax rates for Americans making more than $200,000 per year could be returned to their 2001 levels. Additionally, the top rate for investment income could be restored to 39.6 percent for dividends and 20 percent for the sale of assets. This would generate approximately $45 billion per year that could be added to the trust fund.

The third source of revenue for the trust fund, and admittedly a politically contentious one, might be a gas tax of $1 a gallon. One way to make this new tax equitable would be to provide an offset for low-income taxpayers by reducing their payroll taxes. This recommendation has been proposed by N. Gregory Mankiw, the chairman of the White House Council of Economic Advisers from 2003 to 2005, as a way to advance a number of public goods, including national security. The tax would generate about $100 billion per year in revenue. For five years these proceeds would be used to fund road and transportation improvements. That amount would meet the estimate of the American Association of State Highway and Transportation Officials (AASHTO) of $92 billion per year for the capital outlays required by all levels of government to maintain the current level of roads, bridges, and rails. The AASHTO recommends that an additional $33.6 billion be allocated to make appropriate improvements to the transportation infrastructure. This extra amount could be provided by facilitating private investments and dipping into the revenue provided by the trust fund's other sources.

Instituting a gas tax to pay for these improvements would place much of the cost of maintaining and upgrading our roads on those individuals who take the greatest advantage of them. It could also provide an economic incentive for reducing our dependency on oil and lowering our carbon dioxide emissions by encouraging Americans to use smaller cars and hybrid vehicles.

The fourth source of funding might be the defense budget. The rationale would be that it is appropriate to reallocate some defense spending to support investments in resiliency, since that spending contributes tangibly to national security. Five billion dollars might be taken directly from the $16.4 billion that the Pentagon is receiving to pay for protecting its facilities and assets from terrorist attacks. Most of this money is being used to protect U.S. military bases on American soil, which has the perverse outcome of making our cities and critical infrastructure more attractive targets for our adversaries than our armed forces, whose core mission is to protect us. Former Reagan administration assistant secretary for defense Lawrence Korb has suggested that an additional $200 billion can be saved over the next five years by reducing or eliminating investments in big-ticket Cold War–era programs that are not relevant to the enemy we are facing today. His recommendations include cutting the funding for the missile defense program by $8 billion, as well as scaling back or eliminating high-priced weapons programs like the F/A-22 fighter and the Virginia class submarine for $28 billion, and cutting Pentagon bureaucracy and congressional appropriators' earmarks for another $5 billion. This would provide a total of $45 billion additional dollars that could be dedicated to the Infrastructure Resiliency Fund.

The final source of funding might be state and city governments, which would be asked to supply 15 to 20 percent of the funds for public work projects supported by the federal government within their jurisdictions. This would amount to $45 billion per year. Altogether, these five sources of public funding along with initiatives to actively promote $30 to $40 billion in annual private investment would generate over $300 billion per year. Some may think that investing this amount to renew and strengthen our national infrastructure is too extravagant. But that sum should be evaluated against the size of the U.S. economy, the economic costs associated with allowing the infrastructure to continue to fray, and the risk of having brittle infrastructure when we will continue to face acts of terrorism and catastrophic storms and disasters. To put my proposal into a global perspective, China, with an economy six times smaller than that of the United States, invested $200 billion in its physical infrastructure in 2005. The fact that these funds would be dispersed for projects that have been well vetted by an independent committee as opposed to congressional horse trading should make taxpayers more receptive to investing more of their tax dollars in this effort.

Renovating the United States' infrastructure so as to improve its condition while reducing its vulnerability should have two salutary outcomes. First, it would make it a less attractive target for our adversaries since they would not be able to achieve the "big bang for the buck" they desire. Second, should deterrence fail or a disaster strike, the consequences would be more manageable. But the incident would still have to be managed, and the federal government needs to be far better organized to assume a more constructive and proactive role in responding to and recovering from disasters.

By any measure, the Department of Homeland Security failed its first major test during Hurricane Katrina. Some commentators argued that this dismal performance was proof that the massive reorganization effort that created the department in 2003 had only made matters worse. Others suggested that it was too early to tell because change always comes slowly to bureaucracies. This latter group would often point to the creation of the Department of Defense as a cautionary tale. The DOD was established in 1947, but it took more than four decades for the Army, Navy, Marines, and Air Force to start acting like a joint military force. Indeed, it required the prodding of the Goldwater-Nichols Act of 1986 to get them across the finish line.

The trials and tribulations of reorganizing the U.S. military are instructive, but not because they tell us we must wait forty more years for the Department of Homeland Security to get its act together. Instead, we can skip ahead to the punch line and identify what it was about the Goldwater-Nichols Act that finally set things right. The key turned out to be streamlining the operational chain of command from the president to the secretary of defense to the unified commander. The unified commander is the senior military officer in charge of all military operations within a geographic area of the world. For instance, the Central Command handles the Middle East and the Southern Command is responsible for Latin America and the Caribbean.

The four-star general or admiral who is in charge reports not to his service chief but to the president through the secretary of defense. He has absolute control over all military assets and units in his regional area, no matter what service they belong to. Marine, Air Force, Navy, and Army officers on his staff take their orders from him and him alone. The principle is simple: to be effective at fighting wars, the lines of responsibility and command must be streamlined and clear.

One of the obvious things that marred Washington's response to Hurricane Katrina was the level of confusion across the federal government over who was supposed to do what and when. However, the Department of Homeland Security and FEMA's abysmal performance points to a problem that goes deeper than blurred jurisdictional issues. Unlike in the armed services, many of the people at the top of DHS and within FEMA are not made up of individuals who routinely work in the operational world and are trained for crisis action. FEMA has only 2,600 full-time employees, most of whom work in and around Washington. The remainder are sparsely spread across ten regions. For instance, FEMA's Region IV has only 115 full-time employees to cover Kentucky, Tennessee, and the hurricane-prone Carolinas, Georgia, Florida, Alabama, and Mississippi. That is about the size of a single rifle company in the U.S. Army.

FEMA's bureaucratic culture is legendary. It is illustrated by two stories separated by sixteen years. On September 22, 1989, Hurricane Hugo, a massive Category 4 storm, slammed ashore near Charleston, South Carolina. The FEMA team that arrived to assist did not even have the most basic supplies to take care of themselves, let alone to provide immediate assistance to the 100,000 people left homeless. Charleston's mayor, Joseph P. Riley, Jr., recalled turning to the FEMA official who was with him as Hugo's eye was passing over City Hall and asking him for advice. "You need to make sure you're accounting for all your expenses," the FEMA man said.

Fast-forward to October 24, 2005, just two months after Katrina had decimated New Orleans and the Gulf Coast. Hurricane Wilma had passed through Florida's Everglades as a Category 3 storm, knocking out power to millions. Water trucks were stranded in a FEMA staging area because the FEMA truck dispatcher was holding up deliveries of ice and water over some glitches with the paperwork. Florida's director of emergency management, Craig Fugate, helicoptered down to the staging area with FEMA's federal coordinating officer, Justin DeMello, to clear up the bottleneck. Fugate diagnosed the problem perfectly when he told the crestfallen federal worker after the man had been relieved of his job, "It's not your fault. You've been trained to serve bureaucracy, not victims."

The situation at FEMA is improving under the leadership of its current director, R. David Paulison. Director Paulison has extensive emergency management experience, and morale at the agency is on the mend. But contrast the mixed record of FEMA with that of another agency within the Department of Homeland Security. What follows is a description of the Coast Guard's rescue operations as reported in an internal agency message drafted by Captain David Callahan and Captain B. C. Jones, the commanding officers of the agency's air stations in Mobile, Alabama, and New Orleans, on September 12, 2005 (I have added to the original text in brackets only the meaning of the acronyms). Even though it is several pages in length, the message is worth reprinting in its entirety for two reasons. First, it starkly conveys that a nimble operational response by a federal agency is possible in the aftermath of a disaster. Second, it highlights the ingredients required to provide it.

SUBJECT: COAST GUARD HURRICANE KATRINA AVIATION RESCUE OPERATIONS

1. On 28 August 2005 aircraft from Airstas [Air Stations] New Orleans and Houston and ATC [Aviation Training Center] Mobile

descended on the devastated city of New Orleans and Mississippi coastal communities only to find the utter horror of great expanses under water up to rooftops or completely flattened by winds with burning gas mains and buildings and thousands of survivors clinging to rooftops adding to the unimaginable scene. In tropical storm conditions, every available helicopter immediately began hoisting survivors, reacting intuitively to the difficult task of triaging the neediest from among the throngs of victims, and delivering those recovered to the nearest dry land or overpass.

2. As the scope of the disaster became known, Airstas around the Coast Guard immediately began dispatching aircraft and aircrews to join the enormous rescue operation, staging out of both ATC Mobile and Airsta NOLA [New Orleans]. Each and every Coast Guard Air Station, without exception, contributed personnel and/or aircraft to this extraordinary effort. In addition, logistics and support personnel from units including PSU [Port Security Unit] 308, ISC [Integrated Support Command] St. Louis and New Orleans, MSU [Marine Safety Unit] Houma, SFOS [Sector Field Offices] Atlantic City and Grand Haven, CEU [Civil Engineering Unit] Miami, Atlantic Strike Team, MLC (K) [Medical Division of the Maintenance and Logistics Command], ESUs [Electronic Support Units] NOLA and Portsmouth [Virginia], and many others descended onto the severely degraded Airsta NOLA facility to help with watchstanding, aircraft dispatch, loading of equipment, aircraft maintenance, facility repairs and any other task required, making this operation the epitome of the "Team Coast Guard" concept.

3. All Airsta NOLA berthing and most shop spaces were rendered uninhabitable by flooding after Katrina's Cat 4 winds peeled back the hangar roof. Consequently, during the intense first four

days of the operation until temporary tent cities and other shelters began to arrive all aircrew and support personnel staging at CGAS NOLA [Coast Guard Air Station New Orleans] bunked head to toe on floors or on cots in the Airsta's crowded admin building. For much of this time the admin building/operations center was without power, air conditioning, running water, and all but one working cellular phone making the concept of "adequate crew rest" an impossibility. ATC Mobile encountered challenges with their own hangar roof, losing all of their operations spaces, Opcen [Operations Center], and many maintenance shops, along with a loss of basewide power and phone communications.

4. Despite these hardships, the extraordinary Coast Guard men and women who gathered from all over the Coast Guard to join the fight worked ceaselessly and cheerfully, allowing around the clock SAR [search and rescue] and maintenance operations to continue unabated and at an unprecedented level. The dogged determination, enthusiasm and eagerness to serve in any capacity exhibited by all members was awesome to behold. Many members of the embedded media commented frequently and with wonder at the superb quality, dedication and camaraderie of the entire crew.

5. In around the clock flight operations over a period of seven days, Coast Guard helicopters operating over New Orleans saved an astonishing 6,470 lives (4,731 by hoist) during 723 sorties and 1,507 flight hours. They also saved or assisted thousands of others by delivering tons of food and water to those who could not be moved immediately. These figures include all Coast Guard helicopter operations over the New Orleans metro area regardless of whether the flights originated at CGAS NOLA, CGAS Houston or ATC Mobile, and are almost certainly underreported as some sorties returned to their bases before overtaxed

flight operations personnel could collect their data. The numbers from coastal Mississippi are still being scrubbed, and will increase the total considerably.

6. Challenging each pilot and flight mechanic to his or her limits, most hoists were completed in obstacle-strewn environments, often on night vision goggles, over power lines and downed trees with daytime temperatures near 100 degrees, often in power-limited aircraft. The conditions encountered by rescue swimmers included flooded houses and buildings, steep, slippery roofs, foul and contaminated water, and the need to hack through attics with axes or break out windows to free survivors. Add to this the urgency felt by all crew to continue rescuing a seemingly endless supply of increasingly desperate survivors as the hot days wore on. Aircrew returned from missions with dozens of rescues on a single sortie. One ATC HH-60J [Jayhawk medium-range helicopter based out of the Aviation Training Center Mobile] crew completed its day's work with 150 lives saved. One CGAS Houston HH-65B ["Dolphin" short-range recovery helicopter] crew saved 110. Another crew returned to base almost dejected, having saved "only" 15 lives. The stories of heroism and initiative these courageous professionals from all over the Coast Guard have to tell are remarkable.

7. That these extraordinary operational accomplishments, often achieved by mixed crews and aircraft from across the nation flying together for the first time, were accompanied by no significant personnel injury or major aircraft mishap is simply remarkable. The operation's superb safety record is a testament to the leadership, professionalism and skills of each individual participant, and also to the Coast Guard's aviation training, safety and standardization programs we have relied upon for years.

8. The Coast Guard's superb aircraft mechanics and aircraft maintenance program were a key enabler of the operation's success.

Aircrew from every unit commented on the quality and speed of aircraft turnarounds and maintenance. Again, Coast Guard aviation's outstanding training, safety and standardization programs in place at CGHQ [Coast Guard Headquarters], ATTC [Aircraft Technical Training Center] and AR&SC [Aircraft Repair and Supply Center] and at each individual Air Station enabled maintainers from across the country to instantly form effective teams at ATC Mobile and at CGAS NOLA and keep aircraft flying to save lives.

9. ATC Mobile served as the major staging area, force provider and maintenance depot for aircraft and crews cycling continuously to and from New Orleans, while simultaneously conducting major SAR and post-hurricane operations in its own AOR [area of responsibility]. At times ATC had no less than 37 USCG aircraft on its ramp and in its hangar. As helicopters operating out of New Orleans approached major maintenance cycles, both ATC and Airsta Houston accepted these aircraft and provided fresh mission capable aircraft and crews in return.

10. The support and logistics chain worked around the clock to return the hurricane-scarred CGAS NOLA and ATC facilities to life. Logisticians here and up the chain determined how best to meet our vital needs, and where they could not be met quickly using existing administrative procedures and requirements, steps were taken to procure needed equipment and supplies by whatever means possible. There are many "Radar O'Reilly's" in the Coast Guard and God bless them. Not a single life was lost due to Coast Guard red tape.

11. The generous and unwavering support of our fixed-wing shipmates in ferrying vital equipment, supplies and many generous care packages, often paid for with personal funds donated by unit civilian and military personnel, was essential to the continued operation at CGAS NOLA and greatly appreciated. It is hard to de-

scribe the gratitude felt by those working for days without air conditioning or showers upon the arrival of crates of new underwear, deodorant, toothpaste and other amenities. Staggered rotation of all personnel out of theater for rest was an essential component of the success of this operation and we are grateful to the Falcon and Hercules communities for their continued support.

12. The dedicated volunteers of the Coast Guard Air Auxiliary, as always, stepped up to the plate and provided outstanding support to the operation. Their commitment allowed SAR aircraft to stay focused on SAR while still accomplishing necessary logistics missions.

13. To each and every Commanding Officer who sent personnel to serve in theater, your men and women were without exception superb and your leadership is apparent. Thank you. We ask that your returning personnel have the opportunity to meet with CISM [crisis] counselors (opportunities have already been provided in theater).

14. That this complex operation could be so overwhelmingly successful despite a nearly complete loss of connectivity between Airsta NOLA and the outside world and chain of command for extended periods of time is a testament to the value of our Principles of Operations (reference Pub One). Particularly, the principles of Clear Objective; Unity of Effort; Effective Presence; On-scene Initiative; and Flexibility. If you turn highly trained and properly equipped Coasties loose on an objective, they will tackle it, and let you know when it is done.

15. The New Orleans and Mississippi air rescue operation is but one part of a much larger story of the Coast Guard's response to Katrina. For example, 300 Coast Guard men and women from 20 different units quickly coalesced at Station New Orleans and rescued or assisted in the rescue of an estimated 22,000 people over ten days with surface assets, in horrendous conditions and with

amazing displays of bravery and perseverance. Many of these shipmates lost everything in the flooding. Their stories remain to be told.

16. To those hundreds of devoted Coast Guard men and women who toiled to and beyond the point of exhaustion to keep helicopters flying, CGAS NOLA's and ATC's facilities functional and to save lives, you have more than upheld the traditions of your predecessors. You embodied our core values of Honor, Respect, and Devotion to Duty. You have earned your place in history. Be proud of your extraordinary accomplishments.

17. After several days of cover from various other H[H]65 units staging out of ATC Mobile, CGAS NOLA resumes its own B-0 [airborne within ten minutes of notification] and B-1 [airborne within one hour of notification] SAR response requirement today and continues to find its "new normalcy." ATC Mobile will return to its business of Coast Guard aviation training next week. We will continue to rely on the generosity of the operational and logistics communities in providing personnel and services, so that our own personnel can take care of the many issues to be dealt with in the aftermath of family dislocations and hurricane damage. CGAS NOLA will be both home and workplace for almost all of its crew while they wait for the city to be reopened for occupancy, children's schooling and spousal employment. The expressions of concern and offers for assistance from outside the command are overwhelming, and we are deeply grateful.

18. God bless our incomparable Coast Guard men and women. Semper Paratus!

19. Signed, CAPT B. C. JONES and CAPT D. R. CALLAHAN.

The story that Captain Callahan and Captain Jones relayed in this message is the polar opposite of what Americans saw played out by

FEMA and the Department of Homeland Security on their televisions after Hurricane Katrina came ashore. It shatters the stereotypical view of government employees as lazy and incompetent. Instead, it demonstrates what highly motivated and well-trained people are willing and able to do in the service of their fellow citizens. It also suggests that the Coast Guard's organizational competencies would serve as an ideal foundation for constructing a federal domestic disaster response capability.

The Coast Guard has admirals in charge of a total of nine districts or regions, seven within the continental United States and one each in Hawaii and Alaska. FEMA is divided into regions along similar lines. I propose that rather than trying to turn FEMA into a responsive operational agency that neither its small size nor its bureaucratic culture permits, we should follow the Department of Defense model of unified commands by forming Domestic Incident Management Commands headed by the Coast Guard's district commanders. The FEMA regional director would be assigned to the district commander as a deputy. The district commander would have a one-star Coast Guard admiral as another deputy who would assume the daily oversight of managing the Coast Guard's operational units. This would free the district commander to focus on the broader responsibility of preparing the federal government's response and recovery efforts. Modeled after the Defense Department's unified commands, during a presidentially declared emergency, the district commander would report directly to the president through the secretary of homeland security.

Every Coast Guard District Office currently has an Operations Center operating twenty-four hours a day to support Coast Guard missions. FEMA maintains Regional Operations Centers that sit empty and idle until the president declares an emergency. A better approach would be for the Regional Operations Centers to be colocated with and anchored by the Coast Guard's Operations Centers. The centers should also maintain formal links to the state Emergency Operations Center and metropolitan operations centers.

FEMA, the Army Corps of Engineers, National Guard units, the Centers for Disease Control and Prevention, and the Environmental Protection Agency should assign permanent liaisons at the regional level to work as a part of the district commander's staff. During a federally declared emergency, the district commander would assume operational control over all federal assets within his district and direct them so as to optimize the federal response.

The case for having the Coast Guard play the federal leadership role, no matter what the disaster, would capitalize on several of the service's unique capabilities. First, it recognizes that the most valuable skill the Coast Guard possesses is not its ability to work in the maritime environment, but its ability to manage complex, life-threatening, and time-sensitive events that often require close coordination with many other entities. This skill is not something that can be developed on the fly by periodically participating in national emergency response. It must be honed by daily experience over the course of a career. Coast Guard officers get that kind of experience.

Next, as a uniformed armed service, the Coast Guard understands and knows how to work with the U.S. military. It frequently operates with the U.S. Navy and has liaisons assigned to many military commands. In fact, Coast Guard admirals serve as the senior officers of two joint interservice military commands on the East and West coasts to support drug interdiction operations. The Coast Guard plays this role because it has law enforcement authorities that the other armed services within the Department of Defense do not possess. Coast Guard officers have the power to conduct searches and to make arrests. The agency's experience working so closely with the other armed services makes it ideal for coordinating the support of the active-duty elements of the Defense Department during major disasters.

The Coast Guard also works regularly with state and local authorities. This arises primarily from the service's "Captain of the Port" responsibility. The Captain of the Port is essentially the "mayor" of the waterfront. He has the authority to open or close the port, direct traffic, and enforce all federal laws related to maritime safety and security. This inevitably involves frequent interaction with local and state law enforcement and regulatory officials.

Finally, the Coast Guard works closely with the private sector in its capacity as the primary regulatory agency for the maritime industry. The Captain of the Port sits as the chair of Area Maritime Security Committees, which bring together representatives ranging from marine terminal operators, passenger ferries, and cruise lines to tour boats. Getting these often diverse and competing interests to cooperate on safety and security issues requires considerable diplomacy.

The role of the FEMA regional director would be to do the thing for which FEMA is best suited: to lead the planning effort by states and communities to prepare for emergencies. In addition, it would champion the federal programs that aim to mitigate potential hazards. In the aftermath of a disaster, FEMA would coordinate the administration of federal relief assistance.

Placing FEMA in charge of emergency preparedness, mitigation, and relief assistance is consistent with the administrative posture the agency maintains during most of its workweeks. Assigning the Coast Guard the lead responsibility for directing the federal government's efforts to help states to respond and recover from disasters is consistent with the service's year-round operational culture. For a relatively modest additional annual investment of about $1 billion per year, the nation would get a federal agency that is trained and experienced at responding professionally and compassionately to help those who are in need. While bringing many of the strengths of a military organization, the Coast Guard could play a domestic federal incident commander role without arousing the constitutional concerns associated with federalizing the active-duty military.

After looking back on the federal response to the 1906 San Francisco Earthquake, I suggested that twenty-first-century Americans should reasonably expect a far more nimble response from the federal government when disasters happen. As both the U.S. Army's quick action in that event and the Coast Guard's response during Hurricane Katrina made clear, the speed at which federal assistance can be mobilized and deployed has more to do with political and bureaucratic will than with the constraints inherent in getting outside emergency responders, equipment, and supplies to where they are needed. Given the certainty that we will face major disasters, it is imperative that we find the will to ensure that the U.S. government is poised to respond quickly and effectively to emergencies when they happen.

Looking back on our nation's history offers another important lesson when contemplating the proposed Infrastructure Resiliency Commission and trust fund. From the locks that line the upper Mississippi Valley to the levees that stand sentry over the floodplains of Sacramento and the highways that crisscross the expanse of this nation and link all of our major cities, the federal government has played a vitally important role in building the infrastructure of this country. That infrastructure is now at or, in many cases, beyond its expected life span. If future generations are to benefit as much from this inheritance as we have, we must commit ourselves as a nation to building on this remarkable legacy.

EIGHT

TAPPING THE PRIVATE SECTOR

S INGAPORE NOW TOPS THE LIST of the world's busiest container ports, handling three times as many containers than the United States' biggest port, Los Angeles. In September 2004, I was invited to this tiny city-state, famous for its technological prowess, entrepreneurship, and fastidiousness. I was asked to speak at a meeting of the largest ocean shipping companies in the world. Gathered at the venue were the chief executives who together were responsible for moving roughly 80 percent of all the maritime containers on the planet. I was struck by the fact that they had put the issue of security at the top of their annual agenda. I also suspected that this might be a tough audience, for when the group was called to order and I looked around the conference room, I realized that I was the only American there.

I had been asked to provide an analysis of the terrorist threat, an assessment of the post-9/11 maritime security initiatives being advanced to respond to it, and recommendations for improving on those initiatives. During my presentation, I pointed out that the maritime threat had less to do with the destruction that any terrorist attack would likely reap; the real problem would arise from how the U.S. government was likely to handle the response to this attack if it took place in a domestic seaport. I then provided a snapshot of what an extensive port closure within the United States would likely mean for the international transportation system.

I reminded these executives that nearly two thirds of their container fleets were at sea on any given day. Prior to a terrorist incident, these vessels would have left under the normal security alert level, which involves an examination of less than 1 percent of their cargoes. But after a major security breach, particularly if it involved something on the scale of a dirty bomb, there would be enormous pressure to examine all cargo closely prior to permitting its entry into the United States. Depending on the scale of the attack, other seaports around the world might follow suit.

Inspecting containers that were already at sea would be an impossible task. Unlike in the immediate aftermath of the 9/11 attacks, when U.S. officials could examine the entire grounded passenger aviation fleet over the course of three days, it would be impossible to even gain access to all the cargo loaded aboard a modern container ship. This is because the containers are stacked atop one another like giant Lego blocks with often only eight to ten inches of space separating them. Newer container ships can carry more than five thousand 40-foot boxes, each carrying freight that can weigh more than 32 tons.

The only way to confirm the safety of a container is to remove it from the ship to inspect it. But therein lies the Catch-22: U.S. port authorities would be unwilling to allow containers to be off-loaded until they were inspected. Dozens of ships would start piling up in anchorages. Potentially, they would have to turn around and return to the ports where they came from so the containers could be examined there. But the port of origin might not let them back in. Even if some overseas ports were willing, it would take ten or more days to transit back across the Pacific Ocean. The schedules for global shipping lines would be completely upended, causing chaos for global logistics and generating huge losses for the shipping lines.

I recommended that the best way to address this scenario would be for private marine terminal operators to invest in the means to routinely scan the contents of each container before it is loaded on a ship. This could be done using "nonintrusive" inspection technology that works much like driving through a tollbooth that is equipped with an electronic toll collection system. Instead of a booth, a container would drive through two portals that collect an electronic image of a container's cargo and record the level of radioactivity within the shipment. A photograph of the top and sides of the container would capture the container number using "optical character recognition" technology. The files would then automatically be associated with that number and stored in a database, where they could be accessed remotely.

These files could be used for two purposes that would directly benefit the maritime transportation industry. First, they could help lower the cost and disruption associated with government inspections of outbound containers. On its face, inspecting a container before it is loaded instead of after it arrives should be no big deal. After all, airports routinely examine passenger baggage before it is loaded onto a flight. However, in a seaport, the process is considerably more cumbersome. In selecting the tiny percentage of U.S.-bound containers to be inspected overseas, U.S. customs authorities rely on the notification they receive at least twenty-four hours before the container is to be stowed on a ship. They assess the potential risk each container might pose by checking the notification information against any specific intelligence they might have and by using an algorithm known as the Automated Targeting System. When a shipment sets off an alarm, U.S. customs authorities contact their foreign counterparts in the port of origin and ask that the shipment be examined. The local customs authorities then notify the container yard holding the container to deliver it by truck to the government inspection facility. If the local inspectors find that there is no problem, which is most often the case, the truck takes the container back to the yard. This extra handling can cost several hundred dollars per container and is disruptive to the operations of the marine terminal. It also creates a considerable risk that the container may not make it back in time for its scheduled voyage. Missing a voyage can cause real havoc for importers who rely on just-in-time deliveries to keep their assembly lines running or their store shelves stocked.

However, by automatically collecting each container's image as it arrives in the yard, customs authorities would be in a good position to decide whether an inspection at the government facility is even warranted. Before they order a container to be removed from a marine terminal, they could look at its scanned images. Most of the time, they would be able to determine that everything appears to be in order. Customs officials could check as many containers as they liked and it would not slow down the loading process. Everyone would benefit from a system that allowed for closer scrutiny of worrisome shipments that did not simultaneously disrupt the loading process.

The second purpose the files could serve is to help prevent the post–terrorist attack meltdown I outlined in my scenario. By having an archive of images, customs authorities would be in a position to conduct a retroactive inspection when the circumstances required. For instance, these images could serve as a valuable forensic tool, allowing investigators to isolate the likely place where a container shipment involved in a terrorist incident was compromised. The response then could be more tailored than a wholesale port closure because officials would be in a position analogous to the one that British authorities were in after the London subway bombings in July 2005. In that incident, surveillance cameras did not stop the suicide backpack bombers from getting on the Underground. However, the surveillance tapes supported the investigation. Additionally, as the tapes were quickly re-leased to the public, the attackers were no longer faceless. Riders were able to return to the transit system quickly with a sense of the limited scope of the terrorist operation and some confidence that authorities were on the case.

In a similar fashion, by having databases at marine terminals around the world containing images of all containers before they were loaded, authorities would be in a stronger position to reopen a seaport to container traffic after a terrorist event. This is because inspectors could use the files to conduct a virtual inspection of the tens of thou-sands of containers that were already at sea when the terrorist incident took place. They would then be in a position to reassure local port au-thorities and elected officials that the inbound cargo could be safely off-loaded. In other words, by having such a capacity in place, they would be in a position to tame the fear of the unknown that tends to be more disabling that the actual terrorist attack.

In short, I made a business case for their investing in security. Since these were foreign executives and not U.S. ones, I knew that a pitch built on safeguarding American lives and property might have evoked some sympathy but little in the way of action. There had to be a bottom-line interest for these executives for them to institute a system that would cost their industry well over a billion dollars to deploy.

After digesting the case I had made, one shipping line president spoke up and said, "Look, as long as it actually enhances security, I would be willing to pay more for container security. Also, I would want to know that everyone around this table has to pay the same amount." Then another executive weighed in and said, "The U.S. government should mandate it, and then everyone will have to take it seriously."

I took two things away from the meeting. First, it is possible to make a case for the private sector to make a substantial investment in security, as long as it is tied to its long-term financial interests. Second, without assertive leadership by the U.S. government, it would be impossible to implement the kind of industrywide changes that I was recommending.

Why can't the private sector go it alone? Because securing critical infrastructure is as much about looking out for the public's well-being as about safeguarding private interests. This means that companies that pursue their own security initiatives always face the risk of having the rug pulled out from under them in the aftermath of a major security incident. The more spectacular the event, the greater the pressure on Congress and the White House to pass new laws to address the perceived or real vulnerability.

For instance, imagine that a security-conscious CEO who operates a global container-leasing company decided to deploy a radiation sensor in his entire fleet of containers. Let's suppose the company had 100,000 containers and that each sensor costs $100, requiring a total investment of $10 million. Then, six months later, a dirty bomb goes off in the United States involving a competitor's container that did not have a detection device. Predictably, Congress would rush into law a host of new requirements to secure containers. Odds are that the legislated "solution" would be different from what the company that had exercised good corporate citizenship had invested in, and its $10 million investment would end up on the trash heap. Faced with this kind of scenario, most CEOs would understandably adopt a wait-and-see posture.

But there are other understandable reasons why the private sector resists making security investments when the government is out of the picture. One significant barrier is the difficulty of obtaining information about the threats they are trying to secure themselves from. Government agencies collect this kind of information, but they don't like to share it. This leaves CEOs in a tough spot. Without a clear sense of both the probability and character of potential threats, making practical decisions about investing in countermeasures becomes little better than guesswork.

Companies also worry about placing themselves at a competitive disadvantage by voluntarily embracing new security measures. This is why the shipping executive at my Singapore meeting said he would want assurances from his industry colleagues that they would all match the same level of investment for any new security measure he instituted. This makes sense. Security is not free, and private-sector executives have a fiduciary responsibility to maximize the profitability of their companies. Should one company incur costs that its competitors choose to forgo, they must either pass along those costs to their customers or take them out of their profits. Raising their prices would increase their risk of losing customers; absorbing the costs would increase their risk of losing shareholders.

Then there is the "weakest-link" dilemma. No one company owns all of a critical infrastructure. When one company incurs the costs of adding safeguards to the part of the infrastructure it operates and another company does not, the result is to displace the terrorist threat to where the security controls are weakest. But this has only a nominal benefit for the more conscientious company because of the integrated nature of these infrastructures. As illustrated by my dirty-bomb-in-a-port scenario, a successful attack in any part of the sector is likely to adversely affect the entire sector. Another example of this phenomenon was the discovery of E. coli–tainted spinach in September 2006. Practically overnight, Americans stopped eating their spinach. As a result, New Jersey farmers ended up suffering right alongside their West Coast counterparts, even though the contaminant originated in California.

All this suggests that everyone would benefit from the federal government using all the tools at its disposal to overcome these constraints on private initiative. U.S. officials should be actively working to share information about threats and vulnerabilities with private-sector leaders. Federal agencies should be rolling up their sleeves and working to identify appropriate safety, security, and continuity-of-operations standards for each critical infrastructure sector. Then Washington should marshal all the carrots and sticks it can to secure early adoption of the standards while working to ensure that there are no slackers. And industry leaders should be able to count on the federal government's not assuming a Dr.-Jekyll-and-Mr.-Hyde persona. Having the federal government as an active partner in developing a security regime would offer some insurance against a flurry of new government-imposed requirements when things go wrong. It would become harder for the federal government to throw the baby out with the bathwater if it is one of the parents.

However, when it comes to protecting critical infrastructure, the White House has expressed little interest in becoming a copartner with the private sector. The National Strategy for Homeland Security, issued with little fanfare in July 2002, establishes "broad principles that should guide the allocation of funding for homeland security [and] help determine who should bear the financial burdens." In creating that division of labor, the strategy concludes that "the government should only address those activities that the market does not adequately provide—for example, national defense and border security." What about the other elements of homeland security, such as safeguarding infrastructure? The strategy declares that "sufficient incentives exist in the private market to supply protection. In those cases we should rely on the private sector."

As 85 percent of the critical infrastructure within the United States is in private hands, the White House strategy ends up delegating virtually the entire job of protecting the modern foundations of our lives to the companies that own and operate them. Further, as is the case with the maritime transportation community, it ends up relying heavily on foreign-owned companies. Of the 11 million cargo containers that arrived in U.S. ports in 2005, 98 percent reached our shores on a foreign-flagged vessel. And as the Dubai Ports World controversy brought to light in March 2006, more than 60 percent of the marine terminals operating in the United States are leased to companies whose home offices are overseas.

The line between domestic and international is very blurry for our energy industry sector as well. Most of the energy that feeds the power generation plants on the West Coast is piped from natural gas fields in the western provinces of Canada. A growing percentage of the electricity that keeps the lights on in the northeastern United States is generated in Quebec. The parent company of the Boston Harbor LNG facility featured earlier in this book is the French energy giant Suez. While this interdependency on foreign infrastructure may be unsettling to some Americans, we derive enormous economic benefits from it. Foreign firms are spending billions of dollars of their own capital to construct and operate the foundations that our quality of life depends upon. But, contrary to the White House's operating premise, U.S. and foreign companies have raised their investment in security only marginally since 9/11.

The fact that private actions are not now adequately reducing public vulnerability does not mean that the pendulum should swing to having bureaucrats take over the job. That kind of approach practically guarantees that the mark will be missed. There are few people in government who have an intimate understanding of the design and operation of our increasingly complex infrastructures or who are capable of recognizing the real versus the perceived issues. Nor are government officials familiar with the business constraints that face these industries. And since federal, state, and local agencies rarely work well together, if they are left to their own devices, the result is bound to be a mix of unacknowledged gaps and misguided or redundant requirements.

The trade associations that the private sector relies on to represent its interest in Washington have not been helping matters. These associations are typically made up of government insiders who understand the ways of Congress and the federal bureaucracy far better than they understand the industries that they are hired to represent. Organizations such as the U.S. Chamber of Commerce, the International Mass Retail Association, and the American Chemistry Council see their core mission as preventing the federal government from adopting any measure that would raise bottom-line costs. The 9/11 attacks did not alter this stance. In many instances, trade associations successfully fought back efforts by Congress and by federal agencies to develop new security requirements. If they could not defeat legislative initiatives outright, as the American Chemistry Council was able to do between 2001 and 2005, they worked diligently behind the scenes to water down the final bill language to effectively neuter it.

So the problem boils down to this: the design, ownership, and day-to-day operational knowledge of many of the nation's most essential systems rest almost exclusively with the private sector, both foreign and domestic. But security and safety are public goods whose provision is a core responsibility of government at all levels. The government is unable to protect things about which it has only a peripheral understanding and over which it has limited jurisdiction, and the market, left on its own, is unlikely to provide the socially desirable level of security and dependability. Private companies will pursue investments that make sense for their core businesses and offer greater returns. Even when companies do make additional security investments in the interest of good corporate citizenship, these efforts may not be sufficient. Predictably, such efforts will not be sustained if they produce a cost disadvantage for a company that finds that its competitors have not chosen to make a similar investment.

In the end the federal government must abandon its essentially passive support role. Instead it should be leading a truly collaborative national effort that taps extensive private-sector capabilities and assets in the face of the ongoing risk of disasters. This should not be a top-down approach. For instance, when it comes to emergency preparedness and response, the private sector should be encouraged to support local, state, and metropolitan initiatives. At the national level, the federal government should be actively seeking out experts and industry for advice on what the optimal standards should be. The job of the government is not to independently craft and dictate standards from on high but to use its power to ensure that agreed-upon requirements are rapidly and uniformly adopted.

The most straightforward way to get the market to change its behavior is to pay for it. For instance, the federal government could provide a tax break to chemical companies that relocate dangerous chemicals away from densely populated areas or that convert to safer substitutes. Another possible candidate for tax credits would be private utilities that buy spare electrical transformers. Transformers play a critical middleman role between the high-capacity feeder lines that come from power plants and the smaller distribution lines that connect to homes and businesses. These units are expensive, and the time between order and delivery can be more than one year. If they are destroyed by an act of terror or an act of God, the result would be lengthy blackouts within the affected area. However, if a utility company has plenty of spares on hand, it can speed the recovery time. Having a spare also helps makes a power system substation a less appealing target for terrorists since they would know that a damaged unit could be replaced quickly.

Another form of financial incentive would be subsidies for companies that agree up front to build and maintain capacities that the government could call upon during an emergency. A good candidate for this would be the mobile satellite transmission trucks used in the media business. Most news organizations rely on independent camera crews that own vehicles with a full complement of audio-video and communications capabilities. These crews could enter into a contract to support emergency command posts in the aftermath of a disaster. A government contract would help to reduce their overhead cost, which would be attractive to them. It would also reduce the need for smaller communities to purchase, maintain, and train people to operate these kinds of units.

The city of Los Angeles has been exploring forming a particularly innovative partnership with major retailers, which would enter into an agreement to serve as emergency shelters. Residents are very familiar with the location of their local Wal-Mart, Target, Home Depot, or Loew's. These stores have large parking lots that can host many people in temporary outdoor shelters. They also keep in stock many of the supplies in greatest demand during an emergency. The parent companies have sophisticated logistics systems that can quickly reroute additional supplies to stores within a disaster zone. FEMA could enter into a contract that would pay large retailers to store extra stock of items such as generators, batteries, diapers, baby formula, first-aid supplies, and bottled water. The retailers could rotate these items through their store's inventory before their expiration date. This would reduce the overhead cost, making it a far less expensive approach than the traditional one, in which emergency agencies purchase these items outright and put them into storage at conventional shelters, such as public schools. Such a program could be quickly deployed around the country if the federal government provided the funding and exercised the leadership.

There is a well-established model for this kind of initiative. The Department of Defense has long relied on commercial airliners to lend it their passenger and cargo planes when needed. Under the Civil Reserve Air Fleet program, or CRAF, U.S. airlines pledge some of their aircraft and flight crews to support the Pentagon when its airlift requirements outpace what its military aircraft can provide. This includes quickly converting civilian Boeing 767s into air ambulances by taking out the passenger seats and replacing them with litters. The airlines store conversion kits in their hangars so that their planes can quickly be retrofitted to help evacuate casualties from war zones. The way the military provides an incentive for airlines to make this commitment is to award them sizable peacetime airlift contracts for routine flights for servicemen and military cargos.

Another example of a way to encourage private investment in something that addresses a public vulnerability is for government to actively support "distributed energy." The idea is to encourage medical centers, factories, financial institutions, and other entities that provide critical services to purchase "micro" power plants. These plants could independently support the facilities' energy needs while being able to send their surplus electrical power back to the power grid, particularly at times of peak demand. The electrical utility would pay for this surplus power generation when it needs it, effectively subsidizing the cost of companies that own and operate the micro plants. Everyone wins: companies that install these miniplants can be confident that they will always have access to their own power source should the grid go down. At the same time, they would provide extra capacity that would help reduce the odds that a surge in the demand for power will lead to a blackout. Where does the government come in? Many states have regulations that are designed to protect the monopolistic position of public utility companies. These regulations undermine the widespread adoption of distributed energy. Public officials need to roll up their sleeves and determine how to remove these barriers.

Still another way to provide incentives for private enterprises to invest in security and resiliency measures is by leveraging insurance. In much the same way as insurers provide a family a break on its premiums if it installs a home alarm system, companies ideally could reduce their insurance bill if they adopted measures that lowered insurers' exposure in the event of a disaster. But making insurance companies allies in dealing with the risk of catastrophic events is trickier than it is for home owners' policies for three reasons. First, insurers tend to steer away from things that may involve ruinous losses and insolvency. Second, they want to have as broad a pool of policyholders as possible to diversify risk. Therefore they need to be confident that enough people will elect to buy their insurance product. Third, they need to be confident that the measures they would be subsidizing by way of reduced premiums would in fact mitigate risk and that their clients will actually adopt such measures.

The federal government could help lower or eliminate each of these barriers for insurers. For instance, it could cap the risk that insurance companies face by effectively becoming a reinsurer. That is, the government could establish a ceiling on the amount of losses a private insurance company would have to pay and agree to make up the difference to the policyholder if the losses exceed the cap. The government could also help ensure an adequate pool of customers for the insurance by mandating it as a condition for receiving a permit or license, or providing a tax break to businesses that pay the premiums. Finally, the government could establish and reinforce the standards against which the insurance incentive is set.

An example of how the federal government can leverage the insurance industry to reduce the risk of disaster is provided by Congress's approach to preventing major oil spills by the shipping industry. After the 1989 grounding of the supertanker *Exxon Valdez* in Prince William Sound, Alaska, Congress passed the Oil Pollution Act of 1990, which requires all oil tankers to provide evidence that they carry a minimal level of insurance, based on their size, to cover the costs associated with an oil spill should they have an accident. This evidence, in the form of a certificate of financial responsibility (COFR), must be on file with the U.S. Coast Guard as a condition of gaining entry into U.S. waters.

The *Exxon Valdez* case highlighted the fact that the damage associated with a major oil spill can run into billions of dollars. Since insurance companies are understandably reluctant to take on that kind of risk, Congress created an Oil Spill Liability Trust Fund, which covers losses above an established cap. This $1 billion fund was financed by imposing a fee of five dollars per barrel on both domestically produced and imported oil. Once the fund was financed to its authorized level, the fee was suspended. If the fund is drawn upon in the aftermath of a major oil spill, the fee can automatically be reactivated to replenish it. The fund, which grows with accumulated interest, can also be used by Congress to pay for various oil safety and pollution prevention initiatives.

Ideally, insurance companies verify that a tanker complies with the minimum safety standards before issuing a policy documented in the certificate of financial responsibility. To give them an extra incentive for doing so, the Oil Pollution Act includes a clause that removes the liability ceiling if there is evidence of gross negligence, willful misconduct, or violation of federal regulations. Since insurers are always interested in reducing their exposure to large claims, many carefully inspect vessels to ensure that shipowners are abiding by the prescribed standards and deny insurance coverage if a ship is not up to par. The Coast Guard provides an added inducement for them to do so by periodically checking insured vessels to make sure they are in compliance with the established standards. If the vessel fails an inspection, it is denied permission to off-load its cargo in a U.S. port until the deficiencies are corrected. Further, every other vessel carrying a policy issued by the same insurer may be denied entry into a U.S. port until a Coast Guard boarding team confirms that they are in compliance. These delays can cost shipping companies several hundreds of thousands of dollars each day, creating a powerful incentive to make sure that they buy insurance from a reputable company.

In short, when government and the insurance industry work together, they can create powerful inducements for markets to behave in ways that serve the public interest. However, care must be exercised to ensure that insurance does not actually become a mechanism that rewards risk-taking behavior. Unfortunately, this has largely been the case with flood insurance, the premiums for which are set much too low. This relatively low price vis-à-vis the likely potential for catastrophic losses translates into taxpayers' picking up the tab for individuals who build homes where they shouldn't.

Though financial incentives can go a long way toward promoting prevention and response investments within the marketplace, when it comes to information sharing between the private sector and public sector, the issues tend to be more cultural than economic. This is particularly true with regard to intelligence-based threat information. Government agencies typically are willing to share only heavily censored versions of what they know out of fear that it will be leaked or that intelligence sources and methods will be compromised. Most company executives rightfully believe they would be better informed by just reading the newspaper. At the same time, companies worry about possible liability issues or being placed at a competitive disadvantage should information they disclose to government authorities not be properly protected. The consensus among corporate security officers I have met with since 9/11 is that information sharing with federal law enforcement is too often a one-way street: the companies provide specific information when asked but receive little information of value in return.

An exception to this rule and a model for what could be adopted nationally is the New York Police Department's Shield program. Each day small teams of police officers fan out across the city and visit with business owners to provide them with tailored information that might point to terrorist activities. This can range from briefings with garage operators on how to look out for car bombs to training visits in emergency rooms, where they provide information about injuries associated with someone who has mishandled explosives. Often the real benefit from these visits is the relationships they create within the community. By putting faces to its toll-free number, the NYPD is making people more comfortable with reaching out to local authorities if they come across something that worries them. But this program is very manpower-intensive. The federal government could help out by providing funding that would allow metropolitan police departments to staff these kinds of outreach efforts.

Sharing information that is not sensitive from a security standpoint but can be helpful in mobilizing a community to respond to an emergency presents fewer bureaucratic barriers. However, the mechanics of supporting communications among agencies, organizations, and companies that don't routinely talk to one another can be messy. One innovative program designed to address this issue is the Regional Alliances for Infrastructure and Network Security, or RAINS. Based in the metropolitan Portland area, RAINS links 250 users in nine Oregon counties. Among the network's participants are the Portland mayor's office, public school principals, hotel managers, heads of private security firms, and law enforcement chiefs. The system collects incident alerts from 911 call centers, law enforcement, transportation agencies, and other sources. Then it reformats them into a digital message that is sent to users via the Internet, cell phones, and pagers. In this way, everyone receives essentially the same information at the same time so that they can better coordinate the community's response to an emergency or a public safety incident.

An excellent example of a community-based initiative that fosters greater preparedness is under way in America's heartland. Inspired by the painful example of Hurricane Katrina, the city of Eden Prairie, Minnesota, launched a Partnership for Emergency Readiness in August 2006. The program's goal is to develop contacts, build trust, and coordinate planning so as to bolster the community's ability to respond to and quickly recover from a disaster. This includes creating an inventory of assets that businesses would be willing to make available to assist during an emergency. The city's information technology department has created a secure website to enable the partnership's participants to share information before, during, and after an event. All companies with more than 250 people are being encouraged to develop business continuity plans, with larger companies assisting smaller ones by sharing their plans as templates. Businesses participating in the partnership also agree to provide annual awareness training on security and emergency preparedness for their employees and to develop a preplan for emergency situations together with the city's police and fire officials.

There are a number of other examples of efforts to better link the capabilities of the private sector with those of the public one. For example, the nonprofit Business Executives for National Security (BENS) has mobilized companies into joining "Business Force" organizations with bases in New Jersey, Georgia, Missouri, and the San Francisco Bay area. These initiatives all depend on individuals who have the leadership skills and perseverance to forge these often unnatural alliances. What has been missing is any serious effort at the federal level to provide meaningful incentives for these model efforts to expand to other communities and regions. As a result, many of these programs are in danger of withering on the vine.

The bottom line is that the biggest barrier to tapping the enormous capacity of the private sector to assist in building a more resilient society is Washington's slavish adherence to free-market and small-government orthodoxy. Virtually all the major public policy challenges of our time do not lend themselves to atomistic decision making. This is especially the case when it comes to dealing with the nation's ailing infrastructure and our ongoing exposure to major disasters. There are ample past examples where federal leadership played a constructive role in addressing messy problems in market-friendly, non-big-government ways. We should be capitalizing on those experiences.

On April 1, 2006, Department of Homeland Security secretary Michael Chertoff visited Hong Kong International Terminal to witness a demonstration of a container inspection project that had been up and running for more than a year. The project was purely a private-sector initiative. It set out to see if it was possible to do what I had recommended be done at the meeting in Singapore—to routinely collect images of the contents and radioactivity levels of containers as they entered into two of the busiest marine terminals in the world. Standing in a control room overlooking the main entry gain to the terminal,

Secretary Chertoff saw the results of that effort. At a speed of 10 mph, or three hundred containers per hour, trucks were passing through the scanning portals, and images were collected and stored in a database that could be accessed from anywhere in the world.

The visit was cohosted by John Meredith, the group managing director of Hutchison Port Holdings, and Sean Kelly, the managing director of Modern Terminals. Hutchison is the world's largest container terminal operator, handling 53 million containers in forty ports around the globe in 2005. Hong Kong International Terminal is its flagship facility. Sean Kelly ran Hong Kong's second largest terminal. Eighteen months previously, these two company executives agreed to accept the risk that by volunteering to participate in this pioneering project, they might disrupt their operations. They willingly embraced the project out of a sense of enlightened self-interest. First, they were worried that they were but a single terrorist incident away from catastrophic failure of a system that they had invested billions of dollars in to construct and their customers depended upon. Second, they recognized that it was in their best interest to help design a security system that they could live with, rather than having one imposed on them.

I was there as Meredith and Kelly recommended to Secretary Chertoff that Washington require this inspection system be deployed at ports around the world. They said that if the U.S. government did so, they would purchase the systems and deploy them, charging a fee of about $15 to $25 per container to cover their costs. They said they were confident that their global competitors would follow suit. They also told him that after four years, it was long past the time for Washington to stop studying the problem and choose a path forward. Secretary Chertoff praised them for their initiative. Six months later, President Bush signed new port security legislation that included a section on screening containers in overseas ports. It called for three more field studies.

NINE

PREPARING FOR THE WORST

O VER THE PAST FIVE YEARS, I have visited nearly every major U.S. city and have spoken on the homeland security issue to audiences ranging from Rotary Clubs to corporate security officers, college students, and shock radio talk-show hosts. Initially I had some queasiness about undertaking these public events. I knew my message was a sobering one: Washington's post-9/11 assurances were simply untrue. Not everything that could be done was being done to make the nation safe. As a result, America remained dangerously unprepared to prevent and respond to catastrophic attacks on U.S. soil.

I expected thin crowds, wary expressions of disbelief, or even the occasional accusation that I was being an alarmist. Instead I discovered that Americans from across the political spectrum intuitively knew that we remain a vulnerable nation. I also found a wellspring of desire to make a meaningful contribution toward addressing our shortcomings. People would unfailingly ask whom they could contact or what they could do to help.

I have come away from my travels convinced that a sense of civic duty is alive and well in this country. We saw it displayed amply by the extraordinary generosity in the aftermath of Hurricane Katrina. Sadly, part of the motivation for this national outpouring arose from our collective sense of horror at how badly our government had stumbled in providing timely assistance to our fellow citizens who were in such peril. The vast majority of Americans are prepared to pitch in, but Washington has not given them much encouragement to do so.

A big part of the problem is that our national leaders have shown a decided preference for dealing with our vulnerabilities behind closed doors. The standard rationale for this is both that it would be imprudent to potentially advertise our weaknesses to our enemies and that care must be exercised not to frighten the public unduly. This reasoning should be dismissed as specious and self-defeating for three reasons. First, our softest spots are already in plain view for any determined terrorist to identify and exploit. Second, problems that lie outside the public eye invariably end up being pushed to the back burner. For elected officials, solving problems that constituents are not aware of offers few rewards, especially when there are always other issues in the headlines to attend to. Third, it underrates what can be accomplished quickly by harnessing the ingenuity and civic-mindedness of the American people.

When faced with disasters, Americans do not act like extras in the panicked mob scenes on a *Godzilla* movie set. On September 11, 2001, for example, I witnessed calm resoluteness combined with a genuine outpouring of compassion in New York City. As traumatic as the events of that day were, several million people safely evacuated Manhattan in just a few hours. Everywhere, people spontaneously extended a helping hand to perfect strangers. Restaurants gave away potable water to people walking uptown. Stores handed out clothing off their racks for the survivors who were caked in dust. That evening, hundreds of construction workers spontaneously showed up with their welding torches and heavy equipment to assist in the rescue effort. I spent the night in a hotel in midtown Manhattan and recall walking the twenty blocks to my office early the next morning. There were no cars on the streets except for the occasional emergency vehicle. But on the sidewalks I found pedestrians heading to work, intent on keeping to their daily routines as if to will normalcy back into the life of the badly battered city.

What many of our politicians are generally reluctant to publicly acknowledge, we already know intuitively. The uncomfortable truth about security and safety is that it is not just about preventing bad things from happening; it is also about mitigating the consequences when things inevitably go wrong.

Life always involves risk, as everyone who drives a car is well aware. More than 40,000 Americans are killed in and around automobiles each year. Sliding behind the wheel of a one-to-two-ton metal object that travels at high speeds in close proximity to perfect strangers all possessing varied levels of driving experience is inherently dangerous. Yet we freely undertake this activity because we value the benefit it provides—mobility—and because most of us undertake reasonable measures to reduce the odds that we will get hurt should the unexpected happen.

A safety measure that most Americans freely embrace is putting on a seat belt. The data are conclusive that seat belts are lifesavers for those involved in collisions. Since we all accept that accidents can happen despite our best efforts or wishes to the contrary, we buckle up.

However, there remain some people who see donning a seat belt as an inconvenience. Still others argue that mandatory seat belt laws are an infringement on their individual liberties. But most of us do not find these kinds of arguments persuasive. Not only is it reckless for these drivers and their passengers not to take this basic step to protect themselves, but their failure to do so can have consequences for the rest of us as well. Medical workers tied up with crash victims may not be available to assist in other emergencies. Traffic can back up for miles due to the lane and road closures associated with bringing emergency vehicles to the scene and the lengthy follow-on investigation when there are fatalities involved. And we all pay with added insurance costs. So buckling up has become widely accepted.

A central message of this book is that when it comes to dealing with the risk of disaster, as a nation we should be thinking about it as we do seat belts. Identifying and embracing pragmatic measures that reduce the consequences of unexpected events is not a defeatist position. It is the smart thing to do. A resilient society is one that won't fall apart in the face of adversity. Protecting property and successfully evacuating populations that are potentially in harm's way lessen a natural disaster's destructive impact. Making infrastructures resilient makes them less attractive targets for terrorists. And preparing for the worst makes the worst less likely to happen.

On its face, it would seem that there is little need to dwell on making this case for preparedness. According to a survey conducted by the Department of Homeland Security, 91 percent of Americans believe that being prepared for emergencies is very important or at least somewhat important. That is the good news. Unfortunately, nearly half of those surveyed also indicated that they had taken no steps to act on that belief. Even these official numbers of complacency appear to be understated. In an August 2006 *Time* poll, about half of those surveyed said they had personally experienced a natural disaster or public emergency. But only 16 percent said they were "very well prepared" for the next one. Of the rest, about half explained their lack of preparedness by saying they don't live in a high-risk area. But 91 percent of Americans live in places at a moderate to high risk of earthquakes, volcanoes, tornadoes, wildfires, hurricanes, flooding, high-wind damage, or terrorism, according to an estimate calculated for *Time* by the Hazards and Vulnerability Research Institute at the University of South Carolina.

Obviously, many people need more convincing. I make my case for doing so based on three straightforward arguments. First, preparing ourselves for disasters is an act of good citizenship. Every community has serious limits on the amount of emergency resources available to help people in real need. In a major emergency there will likely not be enough to go around, at least initially. Some people will suffer or die as a result. If we do things to reduce the odds that we will be among those demanding those services, we may be making the potentially lifesaving contribution of freeing up overstrained services for someone else who is truly needy. In other words, one reason we should prepare is not to be part of the problem. The less people need basic services in the aftermath of a catastrophic event, the sooner the society as a whole can recover. In the case of terrorism, a quick recovery undermines the benefits our enemies seek to gain by engaging in these acts.

The focus on preparedness as an act of good citizenship can also make the topic more approachable for families. Admittedly, it is difficult for parents to bring their children together and talk about the family disaster plan. Particularly for parents of young children, the topic brings with it anxiety that they may be causing their sons and daughters to worry. We envision our homes as sanctuaries from a messier world that may lie beyond the fenced-in backyard. Therefore, parents have an instinctive desire to want to convey a sense of safety and security within their homes. But talking about making preparations as a way of helping your community at large is a message of civic virtue that most adults should be willing to embrace.

Another important reason for preparation is peace of mind. Think of a family camping trip. We wouldn't leave the house without having undertaken some basic precautions: checking that the tent is in working order; putting together a first-aid kit, including all necessary medications; packing extra potable water; making sure the flashlights work; and checking to see if we have enough life preservers for going on the water or helmets for mountain biking. These are all things our parents or scoutmasters taught us to do with the admonition that if you fail to make this kind of up-front effort, you will have to live with the painful consequences. No one wants to be stuck in the wilderness having forgotten something or not having a splint and tape available if someone breaks a finger or toe. If we are prepared for these eventualities, we worry less and enjoy ourselves more.

Given the growing risk that we face of having our lives disrupted by disaster, we must make the decision to approach staying at home and working at the office like a trip to the woods or an outing out on the water. The normal rhythm of modern life is going to be periodically disrupted. Sometimes it will be extreme temperatures that knock out the power. On occasion it may be a major natural disaster or an act of terrorism. Being prepared to cope with these eventualities allows us to breathe easier when storm warnings or alerts are raised. For instance, utility companies have arrangements where they draw on outside repair crews to help restore services after a major outage. But it often takes two to three days for these reinforcements to arrive. Accordingly, it would be comforting for you and your family to know that you can get by on your own in the interim.

Finally, individual preparation makes a difference. In the event of an oven fire, having a fully charged fire extinguisher in the kitchen and knowing how to operate it can make the difference between a ruined meal and a burned-down home. Similarly, having the basic tools on hand to cope with the kinds of disasters your region is likely to experience can translate into short-term discomfort versus life threatening consequences.

The bottom line is that preparedness pays off. Insurers know this empirically. They use catastrophe modeling to lower premiums on policies when the insured have taken measures to mitigate an event's impact. Economists calculate that every dollar spent on preparing for a natural disaster saves seven dollars in response. For the average citizen, preparation can make the difference between life and death, especially for the 19.3 percent of us over the age of five who have some form of disability.

If we can agree on the *why* of preparing for disasters, establishing the *what* and the *how* is relatively straightforward. As a stepping-off point, we need to recognize that our normal daily lives are increasingly pulling us in the wrong direction. The widespread availability in most metropolitan areas of cash, gas, food, and even medicines on a twenty-four-hour basis translates into many of us adopting a just-in-time lifestyle. Confident that there is always an ATM machine in the deli store or a pharmacy open nearby, we routinely get down to the last dollar or pill before we replenish the wallet or medicine cabinet. So the first step in preparedness is to wean ourselves off of a lifestyle where we wait until the last minute to replenish the necessities of life.

In terms of preparing for specific events, the preparation obviously should be tailored to where we live and what we can reasonably expect to have happen. We can leave it to the math theorists to argue over the probability calculations that any particular disaster will affect any particular person. Suffice it to say that the likelihood that the average citizen will be directly injured or killed by a terrorist attack is very, very small. However, the chance that the average citizen will be affected by a natural disaster or that our lives will be disrupted after a terrorist attack is common enough that we need to worry about it. But common sense needs to rule the day. In coastal New England, where I live, wildfires and earthquakes are things we learn about on CNN, but snow and ice storms that disrupt electrical power hit home on a regular basis. Don't try to prepare for everything. Prepare for what you already know you can expect to come.

A plethora of helpful information is available on how to prepare for a disaster, and it is easily accessible on the Internet. Some of the best sites are hosted by such familiar names in emergency response as the Red Cross. On its site at www.redcross.org, there is a well-organized, comprehensive how-to on basic disaster preparation. It includes a broad scope of issues, from preparing a disaster kit to food safety, financial recovery, and the explanation of emergency response terms such as "shelter-in-place" and "quarantine." It also breaks down preparation recommendations by type of disaster and provides links to and advice on how to find specific information for the community where you live.

The population density of the area we live in affects how we will need to prepare. The urban high-rise apartment dweller is not going to be able to fire up a generator when the power goes out, and evacuation procedures for heavily populated areas will be much different from those for rural settings. Most major cities have plenty of information available. For instance, www.nyredcross.org provides information tailored to an urban population and New York City, including postings of preparedness events taking place in individual neighborhoods. Another website, www.ready.gov, is useful not only for the emergency preparedness checklists it provides but also for its list, searchable by state and county, of local emergency management offices that can provide area-specific information.

There are also many websites that go past the basics. FEMA hosts a site, www.fema.gov/areyouready, that provides guidance for a long list of disasters. It includes information that hopefully most of us will never need, such as what to do if trapped in debris, and advice on handling stressful experiences that many of us may face, such as how to drive in flood conditions. The site also provides contacts and processing information for postevent government programs, such as the federal flood insurance program. For disaster preparedness information that focuses on the needs of families with children, the American Academy of Pediatrics' website, www.aap.org, is particularly helpful. The academy has put together advice on what to tell children in advance of a disaster and how to care for them during one. The site also provides guidance on preparedness kits and links and contact information for emergency response resources.

The sources mentioned here are just a few that can be found by spending a little time surfing the Internet. I highlight them because they are all easily accessible and user-friendly and provide most of the preparedness information that the majority of us will ever need. Using such sources to prepare is not being paranoid. Preparation is like a rainy-day fund: setting aside some time now will translate into the greater peace of mind that comes from knowing you can minimize the hardship for you and your family when the unexpected happens.

Once we have made ourselves and our families more resilient at home, it is important to think about doing the same in our workplaces and our communities. For local government, the rationale is clear: public safety is the foremost job of local officials. CEO and senior managers should consider committing some of their own time and energy to workplace preparedness as a sound investment. This is not only because it is the right and responsible thing to do, but it is also likely to help with the bottom line in these increasingly tumultuous times. Employees who can worry less about their own safety and that of their families make for more productive workers.

Every medium and large company should have an "all-hazards" operational plan. The emergency plan should detail the roles of each department and its senior personnel. Some employees should receive extra training so that they can play leadership roles during an incident. It is also important that managers go beyond including training on emergency procedures as a part of their new-employee orientation program. One innovative approach taken by a very large New York–based investment firm is to use fire drills as mini town meetings where managers solicit employees' concerns and respond to their questions about security and safety.

Companies should also prepare emergency kits that can be provided to employees if they have to shelter-in-place or evacuate in a disaster. Employers can also encourage their workers to prepare emergency kits for their homes by periodically offering to help with the purchase of the more essential items as a part of the company's bulk purchases. The finance office should maintain an emergency cash fund so that in the event of an emergency building evacuation it can help out workers who may have left their wallets or pocketbooks behind, lending them money to get transportation home or to buy basics like groceries and prescription medicines.

High-speed communications are often lost in a major incident. Analog phone lines should be in place as backups, so that at least limited phone service will be available should the main system go down. A company should also consider setting up a remote website to support emergency communications. This would allow employees and their family members to post messages, either publicly or privately, so that they can stay in touch if workers cannot leave the building during an emergency.

Building resiliency at the local, community, and business levels isn't a new idea, but sadly it seems to run in cycles. The more time that passes after an incident, the more difficult it is to sustain the focus. At the federal level, the problem is compounded by competing ideological views over the extent to which the federal government should support emergency planning at the local and state levels. For instance, a very successful federal program to support communities in preparing for disasters was undertaken in 1997 by the then–FEMA director, James Lee Witt. Project Impact provided small federal grants and guidance to local governments to aid them in preparing their communities for natural disasters through cooperative efforts with local businesses and nonprofit groups. The idea behind the program was to provide seed money that would encourage cities to make investments up front that would minimize the consequences of disasters when they happened. Witt sought to make it attractive for communities to embrace "disaster resistance" as opposed to simply spending time and money on response and recovery. There is considerable evidence that it worked.

What began as a pilot in seven cities in 1997 reached 250 municipalities and included 2,500 businesses by 2000. In Tulsa, Oklahoma, Project Impact, which included 400 individuals and businesses, promoted the building of tornado "safe rooms," and in Seattle, the program sponsored earthquake retrofitting for homes and businesses with insurance companies and banks providing incentives and discounted loans. In Florida, local officials hurricane-proofed buildings. However, when the Bush administration came into office in 2001 it immediately ended the federal funding for the program.

What should have been an adequate replacement for Project Impact was the Disaster Mitigation Act (DMA) of 2000. However, according to the congressional testimony of emergency management professionals, the DMA only made the process for communities seeking what little federal funding existed more complicated and at the same time lost one of the things that had made Project Impact successful: its focus on the local business community. Last year, in the wake of Hurricane Katrina, several lawmakers, including Senator Patty Murray from the state of Washington, called for reinstating the program. Senator Murray issued a press release in which she stated, "You can't cut emergency preparedness before a disaster, and then hope things will be fine after a disaster." I agree with her.

However, there is neither time nor reason to wait on the federal government to act. Seattle, Washington, is an example of a city that has not. Even in the absence of federal funding, Project Impact Seattle survives through a grant from the City of Seattle Emergency Management. Mayor Greg Nickels has championed the program as bolstering Seattle's ability to deal with both natural and man-made disasters: "We've strengthened infrastructure like bridges and fire stations; helped businesses and residents to retrofit; participated in national emergency exercises and made sure our plans include citizens who are vulnerable."

Part of Seattle's effort includes the Disaster Resistant Business

(DRB) Program, which was designed with feedback from businesses after the Nisqually Earthquake struck Washington State on February 28, 2001. Besides providing business-oriented information on issues such as SARS, radiation, and pandemic flu, the DRB Program provides guidance for assessing vulnerabilities and potential losses, writing disaster plans, and training employees. Moreover, Seattle's DRB Program has put together a Business Emergency Network (BEN), a communication system between the government and businesses. It is designed to help to disseminate information quickly and accurately when a disaster strikes, to help companies protect their people and property. Most important, BEN is designed to aid the local business community in predisaster preparation so as to minimize the impact of an event.

Project Impact and the Disaster Resistant Business Program are examples of real programs with measurable results. (For more information, see www.seattle.gov/projectimpact.) People around the country should refer to these initiatives in holding their own community leaders' and employers' feet to the fire on emergency preparedness. One of the main reasons why the country is less prepared than it should be is that there is not a vocal constituency to pressure officials to act. The only remedy for this is to organize. Represent your neighborhood group at the next city council meeting, tell the council members about your neighborhood plan, and ask them the tough questions. Talk with the president of the chamber of commerce, the fire chief, the city councilman or -woman, and the company human resources director or security manager, and ask questions about what they are doing to prepare. We all have good antennae for when we are getting fluff for a response. Demand to know specifics. For both government and business, a constituency with a plan and specific demands is both easier to work with and harder to ignore.

But there are other ways for everyday citizens to contribute. Launched as a national initiative in 2002, the Citizens Corps today has more than two thousand Citizen Corps Councils, located in all fifty states and six U.S. territories. Citizen Corps set up an umbrella organization for local community emergency response teams (CERTs), medical reserve corps, neighborhood watch groups, fire corps, and volunteers in police service. Through these councils, citizens are banding together with emergency responders to improve their knowledge, skills, and capability to support their communities when disasters strike or to deploy to other communities when there is a need.

Twenty-three hundred community emergency response teams around the country provide citizens with nearly twenty hours of training in providing basic medical aid, managing utilities and putting out small fires, organizing spontaneous volunteers to be effective, and collecting disaster intelligence to support the efforts of emergency responders. The program was first developed in Los Angeles in 1986 and was based on a Japanese model for earthquake emergency preparedness in which entire neighborhoods are organized into teams of individuals trained in fire suppression, light search-and-rescue operations, first aid, or evacuation.

The medical reserve corps are community-based teams of volunteer medical and public health professionals who donate their time and expertise to prepare for and respond to emergencies. Often they are retired or semiretired health care providers. These teams include physicians, nurses, pharmacists, dentists, veterinarians, and epidemiologists. Interpreters, chaplains, legal advisers, and office workers play a support role. There are 475 medical reserve corps programs nationwide, and members often volunteer to deploy outside their jurisdiction to supplement emergency and public health resources responding to major disasters. For instance, during Hurricane Katrina, more than six hundred volunteers traveled to the Gulf Coast to support American Red Cross disaster operations.

Neighborhood watch, fire corps, and volunteers in police service are community programs that support local law enforcement and fire departments. Neighborhood watch involves citizens' patrols and reporting suspicious activities to local police; fire corps and volunteers in police service involve citizens who provide back-office support so that firefighters, emergency medical responders, and police officers can focus on providing their frontline services.

There are other ways to help without formally enlisting in one of the affiliate organizations within Citizen Corps. Get the neighbors on the block together. Know who is a doctor or nurse; know who has a generator or a chain saw or a four-wheel-drive vehicle; know who has special needs. Make a plan.

Preparing for disaster is something individual Americans, our employers, and our local governments must embrace just as we do automobile safety. Getting people to buckle up did not happen overnight, but now it has become widely accepted. Just as highways have their inherent risk, so too do many of the daily systems we rely on and too often take for granted. By arming ourselves with a bit of knowledge and making elementary preparations, we can continue to embrace the many benefits of modernity without being crippled by anxiety when we hit the inevitable bumps in the road.

TEN

A RESILIENT SOCIETY

IN AUGUST 1992, I found myself in command of a three-decade-old vessel with a crew of thirty-five Coast Guardsmen. The ship was called the *Redwood,* and its mission was important but not glamorous. Our job was to maintain the lighthouses and sea buoys that sailors rely on to find their way around Long Island Sound. The sound is the back door for New York Harbor, where tugs and barges carrying heating oil and other commodities take advantage of its relatively sheltered waters to transit to and from New England. Long Island Sound is also a maritime playground, with one of the highest concentrations of recreational vessels anywhere on the planet.

Buoys are essentially floating road signs that tell those who leave the safety of land where a shipping channel starts and stops and where shoals lie. Even in our electronic age, vessels—especially larger commercial ones—count on buoys being where they are supposed to be. These aids to navigation help ships to meet other ships in a channel

without colliding and alert them to shallow water, where they risk running aground and spilling their potentially hazardous cargoes.

Many buoys are equipped with lights, bells, and horns so that
mariners can find their way in the dark or in the fog. This equipment
has to be maintained. In rough weather buoys can drag their moorings,
so it is important to check their positions regularly. Buoy tenders make
sure that these navigational aids are in the right place and operating
properly.

This may sound like a pretty simple job. But it is an extremely demanding one that involves considerable hazards for the crew. In my
case, I had to take a 525-ton vessel into waters where ships its size do
not belong—to the very edge of a channel or next to submerged rock
formations that the buoys mark. This required very careful maneuvering. The work of servicing a buoy involved plucking one of these multi-
ton steel objects out of the water with our onboard crane. Then a
half-dozen men would hover below the buoy as it was swung onto a
slippery deck, using lines and winches to try to prevent it from becoming an errant wrecking ball as the ship rolled with the sea. Lines, cables, and chains occasionally parted, and the hydraulic systems that
operated the crane periodically broke down. When this happened, life-
threatening injuries and even fatalities were always a risk. Once the
buoy was serviced, the dangerous job of picking it up, hoisting it over
the side, and maneuvering the ship back into the hazardous waters followed, and the process began all over again.

The *Redwood* was the oldest ship in its class of buoy tenders, and it
had not aged gracefully. During an inspection of my new command, I
found problems such as cracked, asbestos-laden walls in my crew's
sleeping quarters, leaky hydraulic seals on my crane, and a ship's pro-
peller that would, on its own volition, violently change its pitch during
maneuvering. The ship had badly corroded hull frames, and the buoy
deck had so many holes from wear and tear that the crew used buckets
in the compartment below to catch the water when it rained. In total,

I documented more than two dozen engineering deficiencies that warranted emergency repairs because they threatened the safety of the vessel and its crew. None of these items was frivolous. If *Redwood* had been a commercial merchant marine vessel, it would not have passed a standard Coast Guard inspection.

Armed with my list of woes, I visited the maintenance command responsible for overseeing repairs. I was anticipating a chilly reception, and I got one. The Coast Guard had been limping along for much of its two-hundred-plus-year history always with more missions than resources. But the 1990s was a particularly brutal time for the agency's budget. Congress and the Clinton administration consistently underfunded the growing maintenance needs of the service's aging—in some cases ancient—shore facilities, vessels, and aircraft. So I was not surprised when the Coast Guard engineers told me that they would be able to fund repairs for only five of my twenty-five critical casualties and the remainder of the work would have to be deferred. I pushed back, arguing that I was being asked to engage in a naval engineering version of Russian roulette. The response was essentially "Sorry, you can't get blood from a stone."

As I reflect back on that experience fourteen years later, it strikes me that I was on the receiving end of an ominous trend that has gathered considerable steam since. This take-it-or-leave-it approach to the funding of non-defense-related activities that the federal government performs has become nearly a permanent part of the budgetary landscape. Its effect has been pernicious. As a professional who is responsible for issues involving public safety, having your judgment consistently vetoed in the interest of fiscal expediency is demoralizing. This is especially the case when it violates established rules of engineering, standards of safety, and common sense. We are asking federal employees like the Army Corps of Engineers to maintain critical systems like the levees around New Orleans and the Sacramento River Valley and then tying both hands behind their backs. In 2004 and 2005, the Army Corps documented the need for emergency repair projects for the storm protection system for New Orleans, which went largely unfunded. The Corps was faced with the same kind of Russian roulette scenario that I was confronted with as a junior Coast Guard officer. But as events the following year would show, far more lives and property were at stake.

As a nation, we can afford to maintain and improve critical infrastructures like our waterways. We can bankroll basic government functions like public health. It is inexcusable that we don't. Not all government is pork. Not all civil servants are incompetent, and we should not be treating them much as we did returning Vietnam War veterans. Many are motivated by a sense that quality public service matters and that their jobs are important, even if largely unappreciated, as my buoy-tender job was.

If the United States is to prosper in the twenty-first century, we must change our ways. We cannot live in an advanced society without being mindful of what made it advanced in the first place. We would do well to recall that what sealed the fate of the Roman Empire was not attacks from without but rot from within.

Disasters cannot always be averted, but we can anticipate and take pragmatic steps to prevent the cascading consequences that are likely to flow from them. In the end, this book is both a call to arms and a primer for living and prospering in the face of that reality. The tragic events of 9/11 and Hurricane Katrina should have given rise to considerable societal and political introspection. The preceding pages have attempted to inspire just that by documenting the fraying of America's infrastructure, public institutions, and the basic social contract and recommending appropriate corrective actions. Some of the major findings are as follows:

1) **Americans must insist that Washington make building national resiliency from within as important a public policy imperative as confronting dangers from without.**

While only the smallest percentage of us are likely to find ourselves victims of a terrorist act, at some point nearly all of us will see
our lives or property endangered by a natural disaster. Those odds only
climb as we continue to allow our nation to become more brittle by
neglecting critical infrastructure, avoiding actions on a personal and
societal level that could reduce our vulnerabilities, and forgoing investments in the frontline professionals we are expecting to respond to our
calls for help.

Historically, the issues of war and peace have fallen to the federal
government, while the issues of public safety have been state and local
matters. The decisions associated with mitigating the dangers and bolstering the durability of critical infrastructure are often shared by the
private and public sectors, but with Washington typically adopting an
arm's-length role. This division of labor has served us reasonably well
in the past, but it needs to be recalibrated, particularly when it comes
to how we are spending our tax dollars.

The Pentagon's budget and the war in Iraq are costing U.S. taxpayers more than half a trillion dollars annually. That amount represents
approximately one half of all federal discretionary spending for 2007.
It is illogical to invest so much in confronting the terrorist threat beyond our shores while being so parsimonious when it comes to protecting ourselves from acts of terror or catastrophic events here at
home. Nowhere in Washington is there someone asking if a tax dollar
that is now being spent to buy a new stealth jet fighter might be better
used as a tax incentive to nudge a domestic oil refinery into converting
to safer chemicals. Nor is anyone questioning whether we would be
better off investing more money on community policing than building
a futuristic navy destroyer. Conventional national security has been allowed to trump all other federal budget priorities. As the wealthiest nation in the world, we can afford both a second-to-none military and
pragmatic investments that will make us a more resilient society. It is
self-defeating to pursue the former at the cost of the latter.

2) Terrorism is only one of growing list of potentially catastrophic events that threatens the public.

Climate change will place the lives and properties of a growing
number of Americans at risk. Most coastal development decisions and
building codes have been premised on historic hundred-year-storm
data. But major storms can now be expected to arrive at more frequent
intervals, and when the sea level rises, so does the likelihood of flooding. Hotter summers will elevate the risk of drought and forest fires
and place a greater strain on an already rickety electrical grid.

Even without the added risk of a changing global climate, the
northeast is overdue for a major hurricane; the ground will eventually
crack open on the West Coast; and microbes will find new ways to
combine into lethal forms. When your life hangs in the balance, it matters little whether your survival is threatened by a radical jihadist, rising floodwaters, or a contagious disease. We should expect that our
government will be able to take timely steps to assist us when we are
unable to assist ourselves. Taxpayers are currently bankrolling a rapid-
reaction military force that is able to deploy to any part of the globe
within eighteen hours. But as a general rule, the White House has
been telling communities that they should not count on receiving
emergency federal assistance for at least seventy-two hours. We can
and must do better than that.

3) Living with ailing infrastructure is foolish and dangerous

A hallmark of a healthy economy is the efficiency and reliability of
its transportation and energy infrastructure. But America no longer
has a world-class transportation system, and we face blackouts whenever the weather gets very hot. Poor road conditions cost U.S. drivers
$54 billion annually in repairs and operating costs. Around the nation,
160,000 bridges are structurally deficient or functionally obsolete. Air

traffic control towers rely on decades-old technology. Antiquated railroad systems lose money and cut services along the nation's busiest intercity commuter corridor. Our ports will need to double in size by the year 2020 to handle the projected rise in trade, but there is no national plan to ensure that will happen.

Peak electric demand is expected to rise by 19 percent by 2016, but new transmission capacity is expected to increase by less than 7 percent. An unreliable electrical grid results in lost productivity and added overhead for companies that have to purchase and maintain backup power to support their operations during outages. There is always a human toll as well. Some elderly people end up dying when left to the mercy of the natural elements, and the poor must struggle to replace food or medications spoiled by the loss of refrigeration when the power goes out.

America's gross domestic product in 2005 was $12.5 trillion. This country sends men into space, moves military forces around the globe on little notice, and spawns extraordinary medical and technological breakthroughs almost daily. We don't have to live with second- and third-rate infrastructure, and doing so is both irrational and reckless.

The problem has a solution: proper planning and investment. In the end, it is about setting priorities, marshaling resources, and restoring a sense of public trust and confidence in pursuing public works projects. It is important to create favorable conditions to encourage private investment in infrastructure projects as well. The bottom line is that there is no economic, societal, or security benefit to letting the critical foundations that underpin our lives fall apart.

4) Our greatest untapped asset is the American people.

The biggest failing since 9/11 and one that was highlighted in the response to Hurricane Katrina is a failure of leadership. These two traumas drew the nation together with a sense of community and purpose. People were prepared to be called to service, but the call never came. It has been extraordinarily shortsighted not to capitalize on the patriotism, the sense of civic duty, the ingenuity, and the resources of the American people.

The federal government needs to replace the current climate of secrecy and suspicion associated with the war on terrorism with a climate of openness, candor, and inclusiveness. We *will* be attacked by terrorists again. Natural disasters *will* happen. Increasingly, our well-being will be tied to the measures we take in advance to mitigate the risk and consequences of a disaster. This will require the active participation of every American. In order to secure that participation, government needs to be candid about the risks we face, provide useful information and direction about what we can do to deal with it, and marshal the appropriate incentives so that we don't slide back into a state of complacency.

5) We are failing to adequately tap the ingenuity and resources of the private sector.

We have allowed America's age-old love affair with the idea of *laissez-faire* to trump common sense. A slavish adherence to the view that markets will automatically take care of themselves and the rest of us is misguided for three reasons. First, with 85 percent of the nation's critical infrastructure in the hands of the private sector, much of our public vulnerability is inextricably linked to the decisions of private actors. Second, we are depriving ourselves of the ingenuity and resources of the private sector at a time when we desperately need both. Third, the private sector is largely willing to partner with the public sector in addressing our collective vulnerabilities. However, it needs the federal government to be a competent partner and to take the lead by providing the necessary incentives.

The federal government needs to streamline the process by which it shares terrorism- and disaster-related information with major corporations. Also, federal emergency response and security officials must reach out to the private sector to incorporate their needs and capabilities into emergency planning in advance. They need to include the business community in disaster preparedness training exercises and create a private-sector liaison desk at emergency operations centers to help in the management of actual events. When disaster strikes, it should not be left to corporations to reach out on their initiative to offer assistance to government officials who are too overwhelmed to accept those offers.

Too often I have heard complaints from CEOs of major American corporations about how hard it is to help the federal government. Whether inspired by a sense of patriotism or an understandable concern about the risk disasters pose for their own enterprises, most business leaders in this country are prepared to help out when things go wrong. However, they won't do so if they think their efforts will be rebuffed or become mired in bureaucratic red tape. Companies still need to make money regardless of whether there has been a terrorist attack or a natural disaster. We all benefit from their not losing sight of this bottom-line imperative, since we need them to prosper so that we can continue to prosper as well. Washington needs to create and fund programs that encourage meaningful public-private partnerships as opposed to rhetorical ones.

6) We should not underestimate the value of individual preparedness.

Preparation is not about being paranoid. It is about being smart. But too many Americans are acting dumb. In surveys, the vast majority of us say that we believe preparedness is important but most of us are doing nothing concrete to act on that belief. Most Americans pay so little attention to their surroundings that they are unaware they are living in areas that are at high risk for a disaster, when in fact 91 percent of us are. What makes this behavior so inexplicable is that most of the things that we can do at the individual level to safeguard ourselves, our families, and our employees are relatively easy and can make a real difference when disaster strikes. The cumulative effect of personal preparation would be invaluable. Any disaster is going to strain emergency response systems, and Americans should see personal preparation as their civic duty. The more self-sufficient we are as individuals, the less stress there will be on emergency responders who need to attend to the real casualties. The better prepared we are, the less likely we are to be traumatized when things go wrong and the quicker we can get back up on our feet and resume a normal life.

7) Let's not pretend that a pandemic won't happen.

We know a flu pandemic is coming and we know how bad it can be. The influenza pandemic of 1918 circled the globe three times in eighteen months and killed 50 million people, in an era without commercial air traffic. Now, each flu season, new strains arise and spread around the world in a matter of days. Untold deaths and a global recession need not be the inevitable consequence of a pandemic. But medical experts agree that without adequate preparation, the prognosis is grim.

Yet the United States lacks the capacity to obtain enough vaccine and antibiotics and distribute them to the general population quickly in the event of a pandemic outbreak. The lack of vaccine arises from the fact that it is not profitable for major medical companies to invest in the industrial capacity to make vaccines for low-probability events. The problems with rapid distribution stem from a lack of adequate planning at the local level.

The public sector needs to step up with incentives, both positive and negative, to ensure that our society is prepared to manage an outbreak. Funding the creation of an adequate capability to produce and provide the appropriate medicines and medical equipment, properly preparing major metropolitan health systems to detect, communicate, and manage outbreaks with the active support of the private sector, and stepping up our international outreach efforts are basic and reasonable measures that need to be undertaken immediately.

8) Don't encourage construction along vulnerable coastlines and in flood-prone areas.

It makes no sense to encourage construction along vulnerable coastlines and within floodplains and then rebuild in the same spots after devastating storms. Nor does it make any sense to leave a major city like Sacramento exposed to the risk of tragedy like New Orleans faced in August 2005. According to a recent report by the National Institute of Building Sciences, every dollar spent on basic mitigation by society saves an average of four dollars on the cleanup and rebuilding. But even in the face of such compelling economic logic, Mississippi, where Hurricane Katrina destroyed nearly 69,000 homes, still has no statewide building code.

When it comes to reckless development in disaster-prone areas, we have no one to blame but ourselves. It is irresponsible to allow a willfully blind construction industry to facilitate the American migration to our coasts just as the storm cycles are growing more powerful and unpredictable. We should not be subsidizing such risk taking through low-cost insurance and lax or nonexistent building codes and zoning laws. We need to ask ourselves why we are letting this happen and impose commonsense rules to guide community development in high-risk areas.

9) Dedicate adequate resources to our local police and emergency responders.

Local police departments are increasingly our counterterrorism first line of defense. Well-trained police officers who have earned the trust of their communities are likely to be the first preventers, especially when dealing with the homegrown terrorism threat. At the same time, good community policing pays off in lower crime rates and a better quality of life. Yet federal funding support for community policing has been declining in recent years. Nor has there been adequate funding for improving the capacity for emergency responders to manage large-scale events. As a result, long-standing problems persist. For instance, most major metropolitan areas still do not have integrated communications systems that allow police officers and firefighters to communicate with one another directly. Neighboring cities, counties, and states frequently lack coordinated response plans and agreements to share specially trained personnel and expensive equipment. Nor are there sufficient resources available to support metropolitan-area training.

As citizens we need to insist that our elected officials provide adequate resources to those we turn to when we need help. We should insist that there be national standards for minimum emergency response preparedness. We also need to volunteer our time and expertise to supporting this critical mission.

10) Promote the concept of resiliency as a global imperative.

International networks of finance, communications, energy, manufacturing, and transportation and logistics have become deeply integrated. As a result, any major disruption to these networks invariably cascades across national borders. For instance, should a major accident disable a natural gas pipeline in western Canada, it can affect power generation across the Pacific Northwest. Should the federal government close all U.S. ports for two weeks in the aftermath of a serious terrorist incident, it will cause supply-chain chaos around the globe. If avian flu became highly contagious among humans, the resultant pandemic could take tens of millions of lives, and the World Bank estimates that the world gross domestic product would slow by 2 percent over one year, at a cost of around $800 billion.

Given this interdependency, we must assign a much greater priority to working with our trade partners and global industries leaders in developing and implementing common protocols and standards for managing the risk associated with transnational threats and large-scale disasters. These efforts should be collaborative in nature, for two reasons. First, the United States does not have a monopoly on insight and ingenuity. When it comes to preparedness for natural disasters at the local level, no one does it better than the Japanese, who have had to endure many devastating earthquakes. With so much of their country below sea level, the Dutch are the world's authorities on flood control. Switzerland has preserved its neutrality throughout its history by developing a civil defense system that is second to none. There is much that Americans can learn from others' experiences.

Second, the more inclusive the process for developing resilient global networks, the better the prospects that it will enjoy meaningful support by all the participants. International standards bodies should be invigorated, multinational compliance teams should be assembled, and international training and incident management exercises should be routinely conducted. Partnerships with global industry leaders among and across the infrastructure sectors will be essential to ensuring a rapid recovery of systems when they are disrupted.

The common thread running through this list is that Washington has been both underestimating America's growing fragility and failing to tap the long-standing sources of our national strength. A major part of the problem has been an unwillingness to challenge the conventional wisdom that our prosperity is tied to limiting the role of the federal government in all matters other than national defense. Imbued with a dogged faith in individual initiative, the market, and local and state governments, we have discounted the role of national leadership in organizing a national effort for tackling national problems.

Early in the 1990s, the economist Robert Heilbroner argued that there was a qualitative difference between the capitalist economy about which Adam Smith wrote in the late eighteenth century and our contemporary global economy. The earlier version was like a giant dune made up of individual economic actors who each represent a grain of sand. However, the modern economy is like a giant skyscraper that relies on a girder system to achieve its soaring height. There is little question that the skyscraper is more impressive than the dune. However, if the office building is struck in the right place, the girder system will fail and the entire edifice will collapse. The dune, on the other hand, shifts with the wind but always retains its essential form.

In light of the attacks on the World Trade Center on September 11, 2001, Heilbroner's analogy is a particularly chilling one today. But it describes well the precarious position in which America finds itself. Over the course of more than two centuries, it has grown to become the wealthiest and most powerful society in the world. It has taken the construction of increasingly complex and interdependent systems to obtain this standing.

Now the critical foundations upon which our nation has been built are aging. At the same time, the risk of man-made and natural disasters is growing. This is a deadly combination. Ensuring that the edifice of the modern American nation continues to stand tall is a challenge that cannot be managed by the invisible hand of the market nor by the sum of local government efforts. The days of making nondefense federal departments and agencies political punching bags and starving them of resources must come to an end. We will not weather the storm that lies before us with incompetent and bankrupt public institutions. Markets left on their own will not be able to throw us a life ring with enough buoyancy to keep us afloat. Local and state governments simply lack the jurisdictional reach to tackle challenges that sprawl across state and even national lines.

While the anti-big-government and antitax pendulum has swung too far, the solution is not to swing back to the left but return toward the middle. The private sector will need to play a prominent role, but to do so it will need meaningful incentives ranging from tax incentives to outright grants and the occasional regulation. Local, municipal, and state governments are where the first preventers and emergency re-sponders optimally reside, but they will need help from the federal government if they are to play the increasingly demanding and critical roles we need them to play. At the same time, the scale of disasters we confront requires a federal government that is poised to support them on short notice.

All this will require new revenues, which we can collect if we re-turn our tax system to one where those who derive the greatest bene-fit from the stability and vitality of our society pay their fair share. We must also be willing to think creatively about applying taxes to achieve desired public benefits, such as raising the cost of gas to wean Ameri-cans off their addiction to oil. Finally, we need to take a hard look at Pentagon spending and redirect some of the funding being spent on futuristic weapon systems designed to confront an adversary we are unlikely to face.

We can take care that these additional revenues are well spent. In-stead of just plowing the money back into the federal Treasury, we could put it into an Infrastructure Resiliency Trust supported by an in-dependent commission, as I have proposed. The added resiliency we will be investing in will advance our prosperity while improving our safety.

On their face, our growing vulnerabilities, along with the threats we face, are alarming. But there is ample cause for optimism. Ameri-cans have always responded well to a challenge. The missing ingredient in our time has been the kind of leadership that reminds us of our better angels and imbues us with a sense of national purpose. Building a resilient society is not about caving in to our fears. Instead, it is about inventorying what is truly precious and ensuring its durability so that we can remain true to our ideals no matter what tempest the future may bring.

ACKNOWLEDGMENTS

Shortly after Hurricane Katrina left its biblical path of destruction across the Gulf Coast, I received a phone call from Susan Mercandetti at Random House. Susan was flummoxed and outraged by the fact that our post–9/11 nation proved to be barely able to rescue our most vulnerable citizens from a forecasted disaster. We agreed right away that what lies behind the 9/11 and Katrina stories is that Americans have grown much too complacent when it comes to confronting the ongoing risk of major disasters. Susan convinced me to take on a book project that would both try to make sense of this and also offer a plan of action for constructing a more resilient society. Happily, she also signed on as my editor. Together with her outstanding colleague Jonathan Jao, Susan patiently and sagely guided and cajoled this project to completion. I am indebted to her and Morton Janklow, America's most respected literary agent; together they made this book possible.

The writing of *The Edge of Disaster* involved making frequent forays into terrain that was less familiar to me than the national security and homeland security fields that have been the focus of much of my professional life. I would likely have lost my footing were it not for some extraordinary research support. Robert Knake was the research backbone for the writing of *America the Vulnerable,* and I was thrilled that he was willing to assist me with this project as well. There was no issue that intimidated him. He conquered every task I ask him to undertake without ever breaking a sweat. Rob is a gifted scholar and writer who is destined to leave his mark in the public policy arena.

At the Council on Foreign Relations, I have been extremely fortunate to have the very talented Andrea Walther as my full-time research associate. Andrea has unfailingly helped to manage the practical demands of serving as a senior fellow and has dedicated long hours to tracking down sources, mustering facts and figures, and carefully reviewing and commenting on drafts. She also played a leadership role in guiding a team of seven of the best and brightest undergraduate Columbia University students to undertake literature reviews and prepare summaries that informed the earliest stage of this project. Tiffany Bryant, Gabriel Peschiera, Charles Young, Stephan Stewart, Jonathan Hill, Benjamin Levitan, and Cecilia Wang all gave the precious gifts of their time and intellects to the project in the fall of 2005 and spring of 2006. I am particularly grateful to the support from Lavinia Lorch, who runs the Columbia Scholars program, and Ernest Drucker, who serves as a mentor to these young students. Additionally, I am indebted to Marcio Siwi and Daniel Dolgin, who worked with me as research associates from 2003 to 2005 on projects that have informed these pages.

The port-security scenarios have benefited from reviews and comments by Peter Boynton, John Holmes, and George Naccara, all of whom have had distinguished careers as senior Coast Guard officers. I am grateful to Council fellows Laurie Garrett and David Victor, who lent their expertise and critical eye to my ventures into the issues of global disease and the environment. Kenneth Kasprisin, formerly with the U.S. Army Corps of Engineers, looked over my work on the

Sacramento–San Joaquin River Delta. On the emergency preparedness issue, I am indebted to Walter Gramm, Maurice Suh, Barry Scanlon, Glen Woodbury, Michael Laden, George Esbensen, and Erin Kelly, who helped to inform me about many of the innovative initiatives being undertaken around the country to advance this important agenda.

An early draft profited from a discussion and critique by a group of interdisciplinary academics and experts who gathered for a day at the Center for Security and International Cooperation at Stanford University. CISAC director Scott Sagan graciously organized and hosted this event. I am particularly grateful to CISAC's resident expert on homeland security, Paul Stockton, and to Stanford Business School professor Lawrence Wein, who reviewed later drafts of the manuscript and provided very helpful suggestions for improving it. Christian Beckner, Dan Caldwell, Kiersten Todt Coon, Scott Gould, Ed Gilbert, Gary Gilbert, Robert Kelly, and Ira Lipman generously read the entire manuscript and suggested changes to improve its accuracy and clarity. Any remaining shortcomings are strictly due to my own limitations.

Over the past eight years, I have been extremely fortunate to have the opportunity to belong to the Studies Program at the Council on Foreign Relations. Since 2002, I have served as the inaugural Jeane J. Kirkpatrick Senior Fellow in National Security Studies. Sadly, December 7, 2006, marked the passing of Ambassador Kirkpatrick. She was a very special lady with a razor-sharp wit and intellect. Her example of intellectual leadership and integrity has been a source of inspiration for me and is a legacy to which I strive each day to be true.

Since 1999, I have worked under an extraordinary chairman, Peter Peterson, and two of the Council's most distinguished and capable presidents. Leslie Gelb hired me away from the Coast Guard, and I have been always able to count on him for offering unvarnished advice on how I could do or say something better. For the last three years, Richard Haass has continued to bolster the institution's reputation for providing compelling and practical policy guidance on confronting the risks and uncertainties of our world. He and James Lindsay, the former director of studies, provided the ideal work environment for conducting this project and gave freely of their time and high-octane minds, offering valuable feedback on each of my chapters. I am also fortunate to count Lisa Shields and Irina Faskianos as colleagues at the Council. Lisa has been an impeccable source of advice on how to manage the art of communicating with the media, and Irina has made it possible for me to reach out the national membership of the Council to inform and convey my call for advancing national resiliency.

My work also benefited from a Council-commissioned working group that I was privileged to co-lead with Daniel Prieto. Through a series of meetings with a nonpartisan group of business executives in 2005 and early 2006 and the preparation of a Council special report, I had the opportunity to tap the minds and real-world expertise of forty outstanding Americans who came together to discuss how the private sector could be mobilized to support homeland security.

I owe a particularly special expression of thanks to Sean Burke, with whom I have had the privilege to work and count on as a friend since 2000. I have yet to meet his equal in assessing where the line is best drawn between what *should* be done and what *can* be done toward managing so many of the great challenges of our time. This project would have been far poorer were it not for his willingness to serve as a sounding board and critic for all the conclusions and recommendations found between these two covers. There is no one whose judgment I respect more, and thanks to his gift of language and sharp editor's eye, it is a better-written book than might otherwise have been the case.

Finally, I am most deeply indebted to my wife, JoAnn, and daughter, Christina. Too often, my work has meant that I have missed the intimate and precious moments of daily family life. I am so very grateful for the warm and loving greeting they have always given me whenever I set my bags down in the entryway of our home. Their unwavering support has been my greatest source of strength and inspiration.

NOTES

INTRODUCTION

xiii *Nineteen U.S. servicemen:* U.S. District Court, Eastern District of Virginia, Alexandria Division, "USA v. Ahmed Al-Mughassil, et al.; Grand Jury Indictment: Conspiracy to Kill United States Nationals," June 2001, see http://www.pbs.org/newshour/updates/june01/khobar.pdf.

xiii *Commercial trucks have also been:* For a description of the 2002 attack on the Djerba synagogue, see MIPT Terrorism Knowledge Database, "Al-Qaeda Attacked Religious Figures/Institutions Target," April 11, 2002, http://tkb.org/Incident.jsp?incID=10218. On suicide bombings in Iraq, see "Report of the Independent Panel on the Safety and Security of the UN Personnel in Iraq," October 20, 2003, pp. 13–14, http://www.un.org/News/dh/iraq/safety-security-un-personnel-iraq.pdf.

xiii *Since he had no criminal record:* Transportation Security Administration,

"Hazmat Threat Assessment Program: Disqualifiers," Department of Homeland Security, see http://www.tsa.gov/what_we_do/layers /hazmat/editorial_multi_image_with_table_0228.shtm.

xiii   *When a gasoline tanker:* CBS Broadcasting, "FBI Steps Up Search for Missing Tanker," November 10, 2004, see http://www.truckingsolutions .com/stolentanker2.html.

xiii   *The younger cousin got a job:* City of Philadelphia, "Emergency Preparedness and Review Committee Report," June 30, 2006, pp. 114–15.

xiv   *The secondary explosions kill:* The expected consequences of this scenario are extracted from work done by the National Academies of Sciences' Committee on Assessing Vulnerabilities Related to the Nation's Chemical Infrastructure, *Terrorism and the Chemical Infrastructure: Protecting People and Reducing Vulnerabilities,* National Research Council (Washington, D.C.: National Academies, 2006), pp. 42–46, see http://fermat.nap.edu /books/0309097215/html.

xv   *Ultimately, many people fall into a coma:* National Institute for Occupational Safety and Health, "Hydrogen Fluoride," Pocket Guide to Chemical Hazards, Centers for Disease Control and Prevention, NIOSH Publication No. 2005-151, 2005, see http://www.cdc.gov/niosh/npg /npgd0334.html; "Occupational Health Guideline for Hydrogen Fluoride," 1978, see http://www.cdc.gov/niosh/pdfs/0334.pdf.

xvi   *Al-Qaeda has been acquiring experience:* The tactic of using multiple vehicles driven by suicide bombers so as to penetrate an oil facility was applied in the terrorist attack on Abqaig Oil Processing Facility in Saudi Arabia on February 24, 2006. Two vehicles containing improvised explosive devices and a third containing gunmen launched an attack on the gate of the Saudi refinery. The attackers fired on the guards at the gate, allowing the first vehicle-borne improvised explosive device (VBIED) to be detonated at the closed gate. The second VBIED passed through the destroyed gate into the next security zone. Reports about the second VBIED vary: some claim Saudi security forces fired on the vehicle and detonated the explosive, while others report that the vehicle, thwarted by the next layer of fence, drove around for several minutes looking for a suitable target before detonating the explosive device and causing minimal damage to a pipeline. The third vehicle, containing the gunmen, left the scene. Only the active intervention of a quick reaction force on site prevented the attack from being successful. See "Triton Quick Look Report: Suicide VBIED Attack on the Abqaiq Oil Processing Facility in Saudi Arabia, 24 February 2006," in *Triton Information & Analysis Report* (Hazard Management Solution: February 26, 2006).

For a discussion of how the Internet is being used to exchange information on bomb making and other tactics, see "E-Operations" in Daniel Benjamin and Steven Simon, *The Next Attack: The Failure of the War on Terror and a Strategy for Getting It Right* (New York: Owl Book, 2005), pp. 75–79.

xvi   *the dangers of hydrofluoric acid:* "A dermal exposure to 70 percent hydrofluoric acid over a 2.5 percent total body surface area resulted in death." Department of Environment, Health & Safety, "Hydrofluoric Acid Chemical Safety Information," University of North Carolina at Chapel Hill, see http://ehs.unc.edu/pdf/HydrofluoricAcid.pdf#search='Hydrofluoric%20Acid. During an industry-sponsored test conducted in a Nevada desert in 1986, a small accident was simulated by releasing one thousand gallons of the chemical into the atmosphere for two minutes. The experiment was done to gauge how far a deadly plume would travel. The test found that lethal concentrations of hydrofluoric acid aerosol were present up to five miles away. At 7.5 miles there were still concentrations of the vapor at levels "immediately dangerous to life and health" for people who breathe it in over a thirty-minute period. Gwen Shaffer, "Population Explosion," *Philadelphia Weekly,* April 20, 2005, see http://www.philadelphiaweekly.com/view.phd?id=9340.

xvi   *the vulnerability of the Sunoco facility:* Alexandra Marks, "A Push for Safer Chemical Sites," *The Christian Science Monitor,* December 13, 2005.

xvi   *We know that terrorists:* One long-standing problem is the abysmal state of intelligence sharing between federal agencies and local law enforcement. "While police departments from several big cities have representatives working full-time with DHS to glean sensitive intelligence information about terror threats, many police officials say they still are denied access to timely, relevant information about threats and terrorist activity." Robert Block, "Fighting Terrorism by Sharing Data: Homeland Security Plans to Improve Cooperation with Police Departments," *The Wall Street Journal,* October 16, 2006, A6.

xvii   *This neglect could be:* Stephen E. Flynn and Daniel B. Prieto, *Neglected Defense: Mobilizing the Private Sector to Support Homeland Security, a Council Special Report* (New York: Council on Foreign Relations, 2006), see http://www.cfr.org/content/publications/attachments/Neglected DefenseCSR.pdf.

xviii *Laurie is a Pulitzer Prize–winning writer:* Laurie Garrett, *The Coming Plague: Newly Emerging Diseases in a World Out of Balance* (New York: Penguin Group, 1994).

xviii *Laurie described how quickly:* Laurie Garrett, comments on Bioterrorism/Food Security at a working group meeting in New York on "The Role of the Private Sector in Homeland Security," Council on Foreign Relations, February 18, 2005.

xviii *The bad news is that viruses:* Laurie Garrett, "The Next Pandemic?" *Foreign Affairs,* July/August 2005.

xix   *The National Hurricane Center warned:* These figures are cited in NOAA's National Climatic Data Center, "Hurricane Katrina: A Climatological Perspective," Technical Report 2005-01, October 2005, p. 2, see http://www.ncdc.noaa.gov/oa/reports/tech-report-200501z.pdf.

xix *A series of articles:* John McQuaid and Mark Schleifstein, "Washing Away," New Orleans *Times-Picayune,* five-part series, June 23–27, 2002, see http://www.nola.com/hurricane/?/washingaway/.

xxi *Yossi Sheffi:* Yossi Sheffi, *The Resilient Enterprise: Overcoming Vulnerability for Competitive Advantage* (Cambridge, Mass.: MIT, 2006), p. ix.

xxi *Nearly 90 percent of Americans:* Amanda Ripley, "Time Poll: Not Ready for Disaster," *Time,* August 21, 2006. The estimate was calculated for *Time* by the Hazards and Vulnerability Research Institute at the University of South Carolina. See http://www.time.com/time/nation/article /0,8599,1254641,00.html. For more on the Hazards and Vulnerability Research Institute, see http://www.cas.sc.edu/geog/hrl/index.htm.

xxiv *Building flexibility, in turn:* Sheffi, *Resilient Enterprise,* pp. 279–83.

xxv *On the contrary:* Office of the Director of National Intelligence, "Declassified Key Judgments of the National Intelligence Estimate, 'Trends in Global Terrorism: Implications for the United States' dated April 2006," see http://www.dni.gov/press_releases/Declassified_NIE_Key _Judgments.pdf#search='National%20Intelligence%20Estimate %20Terrorism'. "The Iraq conflict has become the 'cause celebre' for jihadists, breeding a deep resentment of US involvement in the Muslim world and cultivating supporters for the global jihadist movement." Also "We judge that most jihadist groups—both well-known and newly formed—will use improvised explosive devices and suicide attacks focused primarily on soft targets to implement their asymmetric warfare strategy, and that they will attempt to conduct sustained terrorist attacks in urban environments. Fighters with experience in Iraq are a potential source of leadership for jihadists pursuing these tactics."

xxv *Lawrence Wein, a professor of management science:* Lawrence M. Wein, "Preventing Catastrophic Chemical Attacks," *Issues in Science and Technology,* Fall 2006, pp. 31–33.

xxvi   *Trees were defoliated:* Health and Safety Executive, "Release of Hydrofluoric acid from Marathon Petroleum Refinery, Texas, USA, October 30, 1987," Accident Report, Health and Safety Commission, see
http://www.hse.gov.uk/comah/sragtech/casemarathon87.htm.

xxviii *Shifting winds emptied:* Sarah Ovaska, Ryan Beckwith, and Bruce Siceloff,
"Apex Fire May Smolder until Dawn Saturday," *The News & Observer*
(North Carolina), October 6, 2006, see http://www.newsobserver
.com/102/story/495143.html; Chatherine Clabby, "Few Answers on
Hazards: Risks to Air, Water Quality Unknown," *The News & Observer,* October 7, 2006, see http://www.newsobserver.com/1360/story
/495519.html.

1. A BRITTLE NATION

4   *In many cities:* Bureau of Justice Statistics, *Local Police Departments 2003,*
Department of Justice, NCJ 210118, May 2006, see http://www.ojp
.usdoj.gov/bjs/pub/pdf/lpd03.pdf.

4   *Emergency room services:* Institute of Medicine of the National Acade-
mies, *Emergency Medical Services: At the Crossroads* and *Hospital-Based
Emergency Care: At the Breaking Point,* Committee on the Future of
Emergency Care in the United States Health System (Washington,
D.C.: National Academies, 2006).

4   *Federal agencies such as:* Admiral Thad Allen, "The Integrated Deepwater System," testimony before the Subcommittee on Coast Guard and
Maritime Transportation, U.S. House of Representatives, June 14,
2006, see http://www.uscg.mil/comdt/About_Commandant/14June
_Statement_DeepWater.pdf.

4   *The rallying cry:* George W. Bush, "Annual American Legion National
Convention," speech delivered at the Salt Palace Convention Center,
August 31, 2006, see http://www.whitehouse.gov/news/releases/2006
/08/20060831-1.html.

5   *Those two storms:* U.S. Government Accountability Office, *Better Plans and Exercises Needed to Guide the Military's Response to Catastrophic National Disasters,* GAO-06-643, May 2006, p. 10, see http://www.gao.gov /new.items/d06643.pdf. Hurricane Katrina destroyed 300,000 homes and impacted 93,000 square miles. The White House, "The Federal Response to Hurricane Katrina: Lessons Learned," February 23, 2006, see http://www.whitehouse.gov/reports/katrina-lessons-learned.pdf. Hurricane Rita impacted 85,729 square miles in Texas and Louisiana and damaged or destroyed approximately 60,000 homes. Daryl V. Burckel and Michael M. Kurth, "The Rita Report: A Summary of the Social and Economic Impact and Recovery of Southwest Louisiana One Year After Hurricane Rita," Louisiana Recovery Authority, 2006, see http://www .lra.louisiana.gov/assets/RitaReportFinal091806.pdf.

5   *The majority of plans:* U.S. Department of Homeland Security in cooperation with the Department of Transportation, Nationwide Plan Review Phase II Report, June 16, 2006, p. ix, see http://www.dhs.gov/xlibrary /assets/Prep_NationwidePlanReview.pdf.

7   *The use of sabotage:* Benjamin and Simon, *The Next Attack,* p. 37.

8   *The report also documents:* American Society of Civil Engineers, "Report Card for America's Infrastructure 2005," see http://www.asce.org /reportcard/2005/index.cfm.

8   *Half of the U.S. population:* National Oceanic and Atmospheric Administration, "Population Trends along the Coastal United States: 1980–2008," U.S. Department of Commerce, September 2004, see http://www.oceanservice.noaa.gov/programs/mb/pdfs/coastal_pop_ trends_complete.pdf.

8   *Just as scientists are predicting:* John C. Topping, Jr., "How Vulnerable Are Other U.S. Cities to Katrina-like Damage?" Climate Institute, see http://www.climate.org/topics/weather/katrina.shtml.

9   *A poll conducted on the eve:* Bonnie Erbe, "To the Contrary," *U.S. News &
      World Report,* August 29, 2006, see http://www.usnews.com/usnews
      /opinion/erbeblog/archive/060829/anniversaries_abound.htm; Michael
      Gross, "A Year After Katrina, Most Don't Believe the Nation Is Ready
      for Another Major Disaster," AP/Ipsos Poll, August 27, 2006, see http:
      //www.ipsos-na.com/news/client/act_dsp_pdf.cfm?name=mr060827
      -1tbrevised.pdf&id=3170.

9   *On the home front:* The "seventy-two-hour rule" has become part of
      emergency management policy across the nation. In San Francisco, the
      Office of Emergency Services has set up a website, 72hours.org, to give
      city residents advice on how to prepare for this three-day window before
      federal help can be expected to arrive after a major earthquake. The De-
      partment of Homeland Security inspector general has challenged
      whether this time frame is appropriate to meet the needs and expecta-
      tions of people affected by disasters. "Historically, FEMA has established
      a 72-hour time period as the maximum amount of time for emergency
      response teams to arrive on scene. However, it is unclear whether this is
      responsive to the needs of a state and the needs of disaster victims. What
      is clear is that a 72-hour response time does not meet public expecta-
      tions, as was vividly demonstrated by media accounts within 24 hours
      after landfall." He goes on to offer a brief set of policy initiatives that
      would allow FEMA and other federal agencies to get aid to victims of
      disasters in a timely manner. Department of Homeland Security, "A Per-
      formance Review of FEMA's Disaster Management Activities in Re-
      sponse to Hurricane Katrina," Office of Inspector General, OIG-06-32,
      March 2006, pp. 69–71, see http://www.dhs.gov/xoig/assets/mgmtrpts
      /OIG_06-32_Mar06.pdf.

10   *Within twenty-four hours:* "U.S. Coast Guard Fact File: Hurricane Ka-
      trina," see http://www.uscg.mil/hq/g-cp/comrel/factfile/index.htm.

10   *By the time the 82nd Airborne arrived:* The 82nd Airborne was actually

alerted for possible deployment on August 30, but the call did not come from the Pentagon until September 2. The 82nd Airborne commander, Major General Bill Caldwell, was quoted as saying, "We could have immediately responded within 18 hours. We could have come here [New Orleans] had we been asked, at any point." Julian E. Barnes, "Diary of a Mad Hurricane: The 82nd Airborne—A Waiting Game," *U.S. News & World Report,* September 17, 2005, see http://www.usnews.com/usnews/news/articles/050917/17airborne.htm?track=rss. Beginning on August 29, 2005, and continuing for about seventeen days, Coast Guard officials reported conducting 24,135 rescues of people by boat and helicopter and evacuating 9,409 people from hospitals as a result of Hurricane Katrina. By comparison, for all of 2004, the Coast Guard responded to more than 32,000 calls for rescue assistance and saved nearly 5,500 lives. From "Observations on the Preparation, Response, and Recovery Missions Related to Hurricane Katrina," GAO-06-903, July 2006, see http://www.gao.gov/new.items/d06903.pdf.

10   *In 2006, the defense budget:* Congressional Budget Office, "Baseline Projections of Discretionary Spending," *The Budget and Economic Outlook: An Update,* August 2006. Table 1–5, p. 14, see http://www.cbo.gov/ftpdocs/74xx/doc7492/08-17-BudgetUpdate.pdf.

10   *Not only are we spending:* Office of Budget and Management, "Appendix—Homeland Security Mission Funding by Agency and Budget Account: Department of Defense," Analytical Perspectives—Budget of the United States Government, Fiscal Year 2006, U.S. Government Printing Office, 2006.

10   *The Department of Defense is spending:* Department of Defense spending on force protection of $16.4 billion is roughly twenty-three times the $600 million in funding provided to America's largest metropolitan areas under the Urban Area Security Initiative. Department of Homeland Security, "Urban Area Security Initiative Allocation FY 2006, Grant Pro-

gram," see http://www.dhs.gov/xlibrary/assets/grants_st-local_fy06
.pdf.

11 *The U.S. Navy:* Author interview with Captain Stephen Metruck, Commander, Coast Guard Sector Seattle, July 18, 2006.

11 *Yet Washington sees no imbalance:* Department of Homeland Security, "Urban Area Security Initiative Allocation."

11 *"We are now in this war":* Franklin Delano Roosevelt, "On the War with Japan," Fireside Chat 19, December 9, 1941, see http://millercenter
.virginia.edu/scripps/diglibrary/prezspeeches/roosevelt/fdr_1941_1209
.html.

12 *The presidential scholar:* James MacGregor Burns, *Leadership* (New York: HarperCollins, 1978).

2. READY TO BLOW

13 *Among the fatalities:* An account of United 93 is contained in the 9/11 Commission report's recounting of the events, "The Battle for United 93," *9/11 Commission Report: The Final Report of the National Commission on Terrorist Attacks upon the United States* (New York: W. W. Norton, July 2004), pp. 10–14.

14 *"We have some planes":* Ibid., p. 149.

16 *The secretary of transportation, Norman Mineta:* In her testimony before the 9/11 Commission on May 22, 2003, FAA head Jane Garvey told the Commission that "FAA did not have any solid intelligence that indicated the type of attack we saw on Sept. 11 was planned, or even that it was possible within the United States." The next day, one of the commissioners, John F. Lehman, pressed Secretary of Transportation Norman Mineta for further details, focusing on how the FAA and DOT could have missed a scenario that was so prevalent in the popular culture. I quote the exchange in its entirety below:

MR. LEHMAN: Mr. Secretary, I have one question, and that is, we had testimony yesterday that there were many intelligence reports leading up to 9/11 and actual plots uncovered to use aircraft as missiles. Do you feel that the system set up to provide to you as secretary of transportation the latest intelligence bearing on your responsibilities, such as that subject, was adequate before 9/11? If not, have measures been taken to see that you are provided with the best possible product on a daily basis as to threats to the broad range of transportation assets under your purview? Could you comment on before and after?

MR. MINETA: Well, I do get a daily briefing, intelligence briefing. And I did during that time period, prior to the 11th of September and subsequent to the 11th of September. And there's no doubt that the nature of the intelligence data has improved. And so—but again, there was nothing in those intelligence reports that would have been specific to anything that happened on the 11th of September. There was nothing in the preceding time period about aircraft being used as a weapon or of any other terrorist types of activities of that nature. And so—but I do get briefings, and I think that since the 11th of September, 2001, the nature of the briefings have improved.

MR. LEHMAN: Just to follow up, Mr. Secretary, given the fact that there were, in the preceding couple of years, about half a dozen novels and movies about hijackings being used as weapons and the fact that there were reports floating around in the intelligence community, did you personally think that that was a possibility that it could have happened? Or when it happened, did it just take you totally by surprise? Because yesterday we had testimony from the former FAA administrator that, in effect, it never entered her mind.

MR. MINETA: Well, I would have to, again, say that I had no thought of the airplane being used as a weapon. I think our concentration was more on hijackings. And most of the hijackings, as they occur in an overseas setting, or the hijacking, if it were to be a domestic one, was for the person to take over the aircraft, to have that aircraft transport them to some other place. But I don't think we ever thought of an airplane being used as a missile.

MR. LEHMAN: Given that there was so much intelligence, not a specific plot, but of the possibility and the fact that some terrorists had, in fact, started planning, wouldn't you view it as a failure of our intelligence community not to tell the secretary of transportation that there was such a conceivable threat that the people like the Coast Guard and FAA should be thinking about?

MR. MINETA: We had no information of that nature at all. And as to whether that was a failure of the intelligence agencies, I think it would have been just even for them hard to imagine.

Jane Garvey, testimony before the 9/11 Commission on May 22, 2003.

17   *In the words of the 9/11 Commission:* 9/11 Commission Report, p. 14.

19   *What follows is a scenario:* The 2002 attack against the *Limburg* used a small boat with approximately one thousand pounds of explosives. The explosion tore a thirty-foot hole in the side of the tanker, penetrating both the inner and outer hull. Ninety thousand barrels of oil were lost. Jonathan Howard, "Hazardous Seas: Maritime Sector Vulnerable to Devastating Terrorist Attacks," *JINSA Online,* April 1, 2004, see http://www.jinsa.org/articles.htm/.

19   *the other on Iraq's Khor al-Amaya:* The attack on al-Basra is recounted in John C. K. Daly, "The Threat to Iraqi Oil," *Jamestown Monitor* 2, no. 12, June 17, 2004. "In April of 2004, three explosive laden boats targeted Iraqi's Khawr al-Amaya and Al-Basra Oil terminals, which together account for 80 percent of the nation's export capacity. The first vessel was intercepted by U.S. naval forces and targeted for inspection. The terrorists detonated their device, killing three American sailors. The other two vessels raced for their intended targets. Their explosives were detonated

by gunfire from US and Iraqi forces just shy of where they would have maximized the damage. The explosions damaged the pumping stations and cost the government about $28 million in lost revenues. If the attackers had made it just a few hundred yards more, Iraqi oil production would have been effectively shut down indefinitely."

20   *Each year, 310 million tons of grain:* Chris Talbott, "Low Water Levels Starting to Affect Mississippi River," Associated Press/New Orleans *Times-Picayune,* August 29, 2006.

20   *In 2005, more than eleven million containers:* Chris Koch, testimony before the Senate Committee on Commerce, Science, and Transportation, February 28, 2006, see http://www.worldshipping.org/testimony_senate _commerce_feb06.pdf.

20   *Once a week a ship:* Stephen Rosenberg, "Life Uneasy on 'the Line' with LNG," *The Boston Globe,* December 28, 2003.

20   *To get there, the vessel travels:* Richard A. Clarke, testimony before the Boston City Council, July 6, 2006; "City Officials Warned of LNG Terror Threat," *The Boston Globe,* July 6, 2006.

20   *The terminal has been on the receiving end:* "Suez Energy International, Distrigas Website," see http://www.distrigas.com.

20   *Through a direct pipe connection:* "Citizens Energy/Distrigas Heat Assistance Program Created to Help Natural Gas Customers in Need," press release, January 25, 2005, see http://www.cgi.tractebel.com./content /newsroom/pressreleases/detail.asp?id=41.

21   *The Port of Long Beach:* Port of Long Beach Annual Report 2005, Bulk Cargoes, p. 12, see http://www.polb.com/civica/filebank/blobdload .asp?BlobID=3012.

21   *Pier T accommodates:* The Port of Long Beach, BP Pipeline Pier-T, see http://www.polb.com/facilities/cargotenant/liquid_bulk/bp_piert.asp.

21   *First, building new refineries:* Jad Mouawad, "No New Refineries in 29 Years," *The New York Times,* May 9, 2006.

22   *They are three of the more than:* Boston-Logan International Airport, Monthly Airport Traffic Summary, March 2006, see http://www .massport.com/logan/about_stati.html.

22   *Three thousand miles away:* Los Angeles International Airport (LAX), Volume of Air Traffic, March 2006, see http://www.lawa.org/lax /volTraffic.cfm.

22   *Upon graduation:* Unemployment and underemployment among Europe's burgeoning Muslim youth population runs even higher in other EU countries. Radical Islam among Europe's Muslim youth is discussed extensively in Benjamin and Simon, *The Next Attack.* Figures on unemployment in the Netherlands are from: Islam in Europe, see http:// islamineurope.blogspot.com/2006/01/netherlands-40-unemployment -among.html.

23   *They immersed themselves in the writings:* In their first coauthored book, Daniel Benjamin and Steven Simon wrote an extensive account on the roots of terrorism in radical Islam. See *The Age of Sacred Terror* (New York: Random House, 2002).

24   *Now a businessman or tourist:* In the late eighties and early nineties, a series of treaties known as the Schengen Agreements went into effect, effectively eliminating all border checks between EU countries. For more information, see http://eulaw.edu.ru/english/papers/sch_agreem.htm.

24   *In 2004, the Spanish government:* Dominic Bailey, "EU Outposts Turn into Fortresses," BBC News, September 29, 2005.

25   *Pentagon experts are working:* Greg Grant, "Behind the Bomb Makers," *Aviation Week & Space Technology,* January 30, 2006. The Pentagon has created a Joint IED Detection Office to focus on this challenge, which

is the leading source of fatalities and serious injuries for U.S. servicemen in Iraq.

26 *If a small boat:* Howard, "Hazardous Seas."

26 *Osama bin Laden:* "Excerpts of Purported Statements by Bin Laden," *The Washington Post,* October 15, 2002. Bin Laden went on to state, "The fact that all this coincided with the one-year anniversary of the start of the Christian crusade is not a coincidence but a clear and strong message to all our enemies and friends alike that the Mujaheddin, thanks be to God, have not been weakened or exhausted and that God repaid those who sinned with their mischief."

27 *Liquefied natural gas:* Mike Hightower et al., "Guidance on Risk Analysis and Safety Implications of a Large Liquefied Natural Gas (LNG) Spill over Water," Sandia National Laboratory, December 2004, p. 28.

27 *After the briefing:* Ellen J. Silberman, "Menino Renews Call to Ban Tankers," *Boston Herald,* November 28, 2001.

27 *The agency then put into place:* Sean P. Murphy and Corey Dade, "Menino Urges More Study of LNG Risk; Industry Officials Say Shipments Safe," *The Boston Globe,* November 8, 2003.

28 *Menino accused federal and industry officials:* Ibid.

28 *A bit more research revealed:* Oregon Live maintains an online archive of news stories and information about the incident at http://www.oregonlive.com/special/newcarissa/.

29 *Too often, confusion over:* Author telephone interview with John Holmes, Captain, U.S. Coast Guard (retired), former captain of the Port of Los Angeles/Long Beach, October 12, 2006.

29 *In the five years since 9/11:* Through five rounds of port security grant programs since 2001, the Port of Los Angeles has been awarded

$26.2 million, out of total requests of $131.8 million. For fiscal year 2006, Congress appropriated $4.6 billion for the aviation security mission of the Transportation Security Administration (Public Law 109-90). "Acceptance of Assistance Award under Round Five Port Security Grant Program," Port of Los Angeles, November 21, 2005, see http://www.portoflosangeles.org/Board/Items/112105-item1.pdf.

29 *The one time when the reporter:* Alwyn Scott, "Piercing Port Security as Easy as Hitching a Ride," *The Seattle Times,* July 26, 2006.

30 *Admiral Thad Allen had publicly declared:* Corline Drees and Edgar Ang, "U.S. at Risk from Boats Packed with Explosives," Reuters, June 6, 2006.

30 *The United States has no national registry:* National Marine Manufacturers Association, "2005 Recreational Boating Figures," Industry statistics and research, see http://www.nmma.org/facts/boatingstats/2005/files/populationstats2.asp.

32 *However, most would likely be able:* Hightower et al., "Guidance on Risk Analysis," p. 51. The Sandia report maintains that the threshold for safe levels of thermal radiation for humans is five kilowatts per square meter. James Fay, a noted expert on LNG and an emeritus professor at MIT, maintains that this level of heat is like sticking your hand in a toaster oven when it is on. Five kilowatts per square meter is the thermal radiation level at which firefighters can begin to respond with protective clothing. Fay recommends a lower threshold of 1.6 kilowatts per square meter, which would significantly extend the hazard zones for LNG fires. This lower threshold would extend the radius of the danger zone beyond the distance cited in the Sandia report. See James A. Fay, "Public Safety Issues at the Proposed Pleasant Point LNG Terminal," August 5, 2004, p. 3.

37 *Outside of the Middle East:* Bali, October 12, 2002; Mumbai, India, July 11, 2006; Casablanca, Morocco, May 19, 2003; London, England, July 7, 2005.

3. INVITING DISASTER

38   *At that time, the prosperous citizens:* The story of John Damrell and the Great Boston Fire of 1872 is comprehensively depicted in a Docema documentary, *Damrell's Fire,* produced for national public television in 2006. See www.damrellsfire.com.

38   *The firefighters had to do:* A contemporary depiction of the horse epidemic can be found in *Frank Leslie's Illustrated Newspaper,* November 9, 1872, pp. 141–42, and November 16, 1872, p. 157.

39   *Only nine hours after:* Firemen and engines came from as far away as Biddeford, Maine; Portsmouth, New Hampshire; Newport, Rhode Island; and New Haven, Connecticut. One hand-engine from neighboring Wakefield, Massachusetts, was pulled twelve miles by hand because the fire company had no horse to pull it. Russell Conwell, *A Great Fire in Boston* (Boston: B. B. Russell, 1873), pp. 198–99.

40   *The ground shook for a little over a minute:* There is disagreement among scientists about the magnitude of the 1906 earthquake. One contemporary study holds it at magnitude 7.7, while another places it at 7.9. The traditional magnitude of 8.25 or 8.3 comes from Richter (1958). U.S. Geographical Survey, "Introduction: The Great 1906 San Francisco Earthquake," see http://quake.usgs.gov/info/1906/index.html.

40   *A Crack in the Edge of the World:* For a description of the human response to the earthquake, see Simon Winchester, *A Crack in the Edge of the World: America and the Great California Earthquake of 1906* (New York: HarperCollins, 2005), pp. 304–17.

41   *The largest hospital train:* Simon Winchester, "Before the Flood," *The New York Times,* September 8, 2005, A29.

41   *Congress made all this legal:* Winchester, *A Crack in the Edge of the World,* p. 310.

41   *In the end, San Francisco:* U.S. Geological Survey, "Casualties and Damage after the 1906 Earthquake," see http://quake.usgs.gov/info/1906/casualties.html.

41   *Yet it would take six days:* Christopher Cooper and Robert Block, *Disaster: Hurricane Katrina and the Failure of Homeland Security* (New York: Times Books, 2006), pp. 216–17.

41   *As the Pentagon dithered:* Douglas Brinkley, *The Great Deluge: Hurricane Katrina, New Orleans, and the Mississippi Gulf Coast* (New York: William Murrow, 2006), pp. 205–14, 261, 297–301, 372–81.

42   *By the early twentieth century:* Damrell founded and was elected first president of the National Association of Commissioners and Inspectors of Public Buildings (NACIPB). The National Model Building Code was established in 1905, shortly after his death that year. See http://www.damrellsfire.com/Damrell_timeline.html.

43   *Hardly any of the structures:* Winchester, *A Crack in the Edge of the World,* pp. 260–62.

45   *It was created as a result:* Norfolk (Virginia) Public Library, "A Page from the Past," see http://npl.lib.va.us/history/history65.html.

45   *At the very tip of the spit:* Harry Minium, "Norfolk Project Will Alter Landscape at Willoughby," *The Virginian-Pilot,* March 16, 2006, see http://home.hamptonroads.com/stories/story.cfm?story=101487&ran=819818&tref=po.Norfolk; Norfolk Public Library, "A Page from the Past."

45   *The years 1960 to 2000:* Eric S. Blake, Jerry D. Jarrell, and Edward N. Rappaport, "Number of Hurricanes by Category to Directly Strike the Mainland U.S. Each Decade," in *The Deadliest, Costliest, and Most Intense United States Tropical Cyclones from 1851 to 2005 (and Other Frequently Requested Hurricane Facts),* NOAA Technical Memorandum NWS TPC-4 (July 2006), table 6, see http://www.nhc.noaa.gov/Deadliest_Costliest.shtml.

45   *In theory, the NFIP was intended:* FloodSmart.gov, "About the NFIP," see
      http:www.floodsmart.gov/floodsmart/pages/aboutnfip.jsp.

45   *But in practice, the insurance often:* According to Robert P. Hartwig, chief
      economist of the nonprofit Insurance Information Institute, "There are
      hundreds of thousands of coastal structures today that would have
      never been built were it not for the implicit guarantees of a myriad
      of government-run insurance enterprises including the NFIP." See
      Hartwig, "The Future of the National Flood Insurance Program," writ-
      ten testimony before the U.S. Senate Committee on Banking, Housing
      and Urban Affairs, Washington, D.C., October 18, 2005, p. 4.

46   *Compounding the problem is the fact that:* Ibid. In 2005, plans were issued in
      thirty states. The NFIP issued approximately 6.6 million policies with a
      face value of $1.2 trillion.

46   *Hurricane Katrina would destroy:* Population growth figures were calcu-
      lated from U.S. Census data for Hancock, Harrison, Jackson, Pearl River,
      Stone, and George counties. See http://www.census.gov.

46   *Andrew made landfall:* Christopher W. Landsea et al., "A Reanalysis of
      Hurricane Andrew's Intensity," *American Meteorological Society,* 2004,
      pp. 1699–1712.

46   *The hurricane caused $26 billion:* The damage caused by 1992's Hurricane
      Andrew is estimated to be $37 billion (adjusted to 2005 dollars). Robert
      A. Murray, "Hurricane Katrina: Implications for the Construction Indus-
      try," McGraw-Hill Construction Special Report, September 20, 2005, see
      http://www.construction.com/AboutUs/20050909pr.asp.

46   *It was not until 2002:* Judy Stark, "New Building Code Brings Cost, Con-
      fusion," *St. Petersburg Times,* August 19, 2002, see http://www.sptimes
      .com/2002/webspecials02/andrew/day2/story1.shtml.

46   *Florida continues to be the fastest-growing:* Insurance Information Institute,

"Value of Insured Coastal Properties Vulnerable to Hurricanes by State," 2004, see http://www.iii.org/media/facts/statsbyissue/catastrophes/.

47   *A computer simulation of a hurricane:* Ken Kaye and Robin Benedick, "What if Hurricane Andrew Hit South Florida Today?" *South Florida Sun-Sentinel,* August 24, 2002, see http://sun-sentinel.com/news/weather /hurricane/sf-sandrew24aug24,0,1246678.story.

47   *The storm and the destruction of New Orleans:* The official reports include "A Failure of Initiative: The Final Report of the House Select Bipartisan Committee to Investigate the Preparation for and Response to Hurricane Katrina," February 15, 2006, and the White House, "The Federal Response to Hurricane Katrina," February 23, 2006. Brinkley, *The Great Deluge,* provides a comprehensive account of what happened at the local and state levels. Cooper and Block, *Disaster,* provides an outstanding analysis of the federal response.

47   *Through the combined forces:* Elizabeth Kolbert, "Watermark," *The New Yorker,* February 27, 2006.

47   *Now storm surges:* Mark Fischetti, "Drowning New Orleans," *Scientific American,* October 2001, see http://www.siam.com/article.cfm?articleID =00060286-CB58-1315-8B5883414B7F0000&sc=I100322.

47   *Many of the communities to the east:* As with so much of the damage associated with Hurricane Katrina, experts had been warning for years that the MRGO would be like a Trojan horse delivering floodwaters into the heart of the city and had urged officials to close the canal and restore the wetlands it impacted. Michael Grunwald, "Canal May Have Worsened City's Flooding," *The Washington Post,* September 14, 2005.

48   *New Orleans has been sinking:* University of New Orleans, "New Orleans . . . The New Atlantis?" *Science Daily,* January 21, 2000, see http:// www.sciencedaily.com/releases/2000/01/000121071306.htm.

48   *They were never built:* Fischetti, "Drowning New Orleans."

49   *With the arrival of the new millennium:* Sidney Blumenthal, "No One Can Say They Didn't See It Coming," Salon.com, August 31, 2005.

49   *Undeterred, the next year the White House:* Jim VandeHei and Peter Baker, "Critics Say Bush Undercut New Orleans Flood Control," *The Washington Post,* September 2, 2005, A16.

49   *Follow-up sessions were scheduled:* Cooper and Block, *Disaster,* p. 21. Cooper and Block cover the Hurricane Pam exercise extensively in chapter one of their book, "The Perfect Storm."

50   *There is no commitment by the federal government:* Congress has approved $122.5 billion for the Gulf region for rebuilding and restitution efforts. "The Tragedy of New Orleans," *The Wall Street Journal,* August 29, 2006, see http://www.opinionjournal.com/editorial/feature.html?id =110008860. Only $115 million has gone toward wetlands restoration. A coalition of environmental groups gave a D+ for wetlands restoration efforts in their report. Environmental Defense, Coalition to Restore Coastal Louisiana, National Wildlife Federation, Gulf Restoration Network, and Lake Pontchartrain Basin Foundation, "One Year After Katrina: Louisiana Still a Sitting Duck, a Report Card and Roadmap on Wetlands Restoration," August 28, 2006, see http://www.environmentaldefense.org /documents/5416_KatrinaReportCard.pdf. The groups say that $500 million to $1 billion per year is needed over the next decade to protect the coastal communities of New Orleans.

50   *At the local level:* Nicolai Ouroussoff, "In New Orleans, Each Resident Is Master of Plan to Rebuild," *The New York Times,* August 8, 2006.

50   *The FEMA guidelines:* The Advisory Base Flood Elevations (ABFE) for Orleans Parish, Louisiana, are available on the FEMA website. See http://www.fema.gov/pdf/hazard/flood/recoverydata/orleans_parish 04-12-06.pdf.

50   *According to Steven Bingler:* Ouroussoff, "In New Orleans."

50   *The "hundred-year storm":* Elizabeth Kolbert, *Field Notes from a Catastrophe* (New York: Bloomsbury Publishing, 2006), p. 123.

4. DANGER ON THE DELTA

53   *Al-Qaeda has even held:* I discuss the Ressam case in some detail in *America the Vulnerable: How Our Government Is Failing to Protect Us from Terrorism* (New York: HarperCollins, 2004), pp. 136–38.

53   *A geological analysis of sediments:* Jeffrey Mount and Robert Twiss, "Subsidence, Sea Level Rise, and Seismicity in the Sacramento–San Joaquin Delta," *San Francisco Estuary and Watershed Science,* March 2005, p. 3, see http://repositories.cdlib.org/cgi/viewcontent.cgi?article=1026&context=jmie/sfews.

53   *Within the Sacramento–San Joaquin River Delta:* Robert L. Reid, "Is California Next?" *Civil Engineering Magazine,* November 2005, p. 1, see http://www.pubs.asce.org/ceonline/ceonline05/1105feat.html.

54   *A 6.5-magnitude earthquake:* Department of Water Resources, "How a Delta Earthquake Could Devastate California's Economy," A Presentation before the Senate Subcommittee on Delta Resources, Senate Transportation and Housing Committee, Joint Committee on Emergency Services and Homeland Security, November 1, 2005, see http://www.publicaffairs.water.ca.gov/newsreleases/2005/11-01-05DeltaEarthquake.pdf.

54   *In the interim, 45 percent of:* Lester A. Snow, "Testimony to the Joint Hearing on Levees and Emergency Preparedness," November 1, 2005, see http://www.acwa.com/issues/levees_snow_testimony.asp.

55   *Three hundred thousand people:* "Levee Failure" video, California Department of Water Resources, March 8, 2006.

55   *Kenneth Kasprisin, the former deputy district engineer:* Author interview
     with Kenneth Kasprisin, former deputy district engineer, U.S. Army
     Corps of Engineers Sacramento District, September 26, 2006.

55   *Balanced against the need for supply:* For a thorough discussion of water in
     California, two books are particularly instructive: Marc Reisner lays the
     groundwork for understanding California's water system and its perpet-
     ual crisis in *Cadillac Desert: The American West and Its Disappearing Water*
     (New York: Penguin, 1993), and, for a more recent history, see David
     Carle, *An Introduction to Water in California* (Berkeley: University of Cali-
     fornia, 2004).

55   *The California Department of Water Resources:* Snow, "Testimony to the
     Joint Hearing."

56   *Not only are the levees under a growing strain:* Mount and Twiss, "Subsi-
     dence, Sea Level Rise, and Seismicity."

56   *In 2006, the Corps evaluated:* California Department of Water Resources,
     "State to Ensure that Levees Will Be Fixed," press release, July 27,
     2006, see http://www.publicaffairs.water.ca.gov/newsreleases/2006/07
     -27-06levees.cfm.

57   *In all, 120,000 people had to flee:* Department of Water Resources, "Re-
     sponding to California's Flood Crisis," A Flood Management White
     Paper Prepared by the Resource Agency, State of California, January
     2005, p. 7.

57   *Past levee failures have highlighted:* California Department of Water Re-
     sources County of Sacramento, "Multi-Hazard Mitigation Plan: 4.2 Vul-
     nerability Assessment," December 2004, p. 43.

58   *It took twenty-three days to repair:* Lester A. Snow, "Upper Jones Tract Levee
     Break," Department of Water Resources, see http://www.calwater.ca
     .gov/Levee_Break/Upper_Jones_Tract_Levee_Break.pdf.

58   *For one thing, the cost of repairs:* Department of Water Resources, "Responding to California's Flood Crisis," p. 5.

58   *Beginning in the 1970s:* California Proposition 13 was passed in 1978, amending the state constitution to place a cap on property taxes and putting in place high procedural hurdles for state lawmakers to raise them. The ensuing budget crisis is covered thoroughly in Peter Schrag's *California: America's High-Stakes Experiment* (Berkeley: University of California Press, 2006).

59   *Across the country, many Corps projects:* Nicole T. Carter et al., "Water Resources Development Act (WRDA): Corps of Engineers Authorization Issues," July 14, 2006. Current authorization legislation is being held up by Bush administration opposition to the estimated cost of carrying out the authorized projects. The Congressional Budget Office estimates "the cost to the federal government of S. 728 as passed by the committee at $4.1 billion from 2006 to 2010, and an additional $7.6 billion from 2011 to 2020. The agency estimated the cost of H.R. 2864 at $4.1 billion from 2006 to 2010 and an additional $5.9 billion from 2011 to 2020" (CRS: 4). The Bush administration is requesting changes to the authorization process that would make it a risk-based process and focus on priority projects.

59   *For the $90 million Congress:* Sacramento–San Joaquin Delta Report to Congress, Executive Summary, September 14, 2001, p. 1, see http://www.spk .usace.army.mil/organizations/cespk-pao/delta/report.html.

59   *Up until 1996, the Corps of Engineers:* Section 202 of the Flood Control Policy of the Water Resources Development Act of 1996 reads: "Subsections (a) and (b) of section 103 of the Water Resources Development Act of 1986 (33 U.S.C. 2213 (a) and (b)) are each amended by striking '25 percent' each place it appears and inserting '35 percent.'"

60   *More than 150,000 new people:* "Most of Nation's 10 Fastest-Growing

Counties in South," *U.S. Census Bureau News,* April 29, 2002. See also "Elk Grove, California, Named Fastest Growing City," *U.S. Census Bureau News,* June 21, 2006.

60   *Because California incorporated the levee:* Department of Water Resources, "Responding to California's Flood Crisis," p. 9.

60   *California had five severe storms:* Reid, "Is California Next?" pp. 39–46, 84–85.

61   *Also, there are fewer full-time professionals:* Ibid., p. 1.

61   *In January 2005, a report prepared for the state:* Department of Water Resources, "Responding to California's Flood Crisis," p. 11.

61   *On February 27, 2006, Governor Arnold Schwarzenegger:* The letter is available on the governor's website at http://gov.ca.gov/index.php?/press-release/267/.

61   *Governor Schwarzenegger signed:* "California Gov. Schwarzenegger Signs Legislation, Executive Order to Develop Strategic Vision for DeltaExecutive Order S-17-06 on September 28, 2006," see http://gov.ca.gov/index.php?/press-release/4150/.

62   *Drawing on research by Jeffrey Mount:* Snow, "Testimony to the Joint Hearing." A copy of the PowerPoint presentation of the scenario is available online at http://www.publicaffairs.water.ca.gov/newsreleases/2005/11-01-05DeltaEarthquake.pdf.

62   *There are less active faults:* California Department of Water Resources, "California Water Plan Update 2005 Volume 3—Regional Reports Public Review Draft," chapter 12, Sacramento–San Joaquin Region, see http://www.waterplan.water.ca.gov/docs/cwpu2005/Vol_3/12Delta/V3PRD12-Delta.pdf.

64–65   *Ten million Californians left:* Reid, "Is California Next?" p. 40.

65   *By way of comparison:* Snow, "Testimony to the Joint Hearing."

65   *The state has estimated:* Phil Angelides and Bill Edgar, "Governor's Slow
      Response Not Enough for Flood Control," *San Jose Mercury News*, March
      14, 2006.

66   *He argues that no amount of remediation:* Betina Boxall, "California's Lev-
      ees Are in Sorry Shape," *Los Angeles Times*, September 19, 2005.

67   *Kenneth Kasprisin, the former Army Corps deputy district engineer:* Author in-
      terview, September 26, 2006.

5. AILING FOUNDATIONS

69   *The final financial tally:* U.S. Canada Power System Outage Task Force,
      Final Report on the August 14, 2003 Blackout in the United States and Canada:
      Causes and Recommendations, April 2004. The Task Force investigated the
      causes of the 2003 blackout and recommended actions be taken to pre-
      vent future widespread outages. ICF Consulting, "The Economic Cost
      of the Blackout: An Issue Paper on the Northeastern Blackout, August
      14, 2003," see http://www.solarstorms.org/ICFBlackout2003.pdf.

69   *The power outage lasted several days:* Jake Wagman et al., "Measuring the
      Response; Assessing Officials," *St. Louis Post-Dispatch*, July 30, 2006, C1.

69   *An investigation into a four-day blackout:* Nicholas Kulish, "Things Fall
      Apart: Fixing America's Crumbling Infrastructure," *The New York Times*,
      August 23, 2006.

70   *Reportedly, none of the power lines:* "New York Blackout Spotlights Local
      System's Neglect," *The Wall Street Journal*, August 3, 2006.

70   *"We've got to keep our fingers crossed":* "Heat Pushes Power to Breaking
      Point," Reuters, July 25, 2006.

70   *Emergency rooms that stood by:* The Century Foundation, *The Forgotten
      Homeland*, A Century Foundation Task Force Report, June 2006, p. 43.

71   *Ninety-six people would perish:* William Grosshandler et al., *Report of the Technical Investigation of the Station Nightclub Fire* (NIST NCSTAR 2: Vol. 1), National Institute of Standards and Technology, U.S. Department of Commerce, June 2005. See http://fire.nist.gov/bfrlpubs/fire05/PDF /f05032.pdf.

71   *"Unfortunately, the deficiencies":* Rhode Island Office of Emergency Management, "Titan After-Action Report," see http://www.projo.com /extra/2003/stationfire/pdf/afteractionreport.pdf.

72   *At the time of the Station fire:* David J. Barillo et al., "Tracking the Daily Availability of Burn Beds for National Emergencies," *Journal of Burn Care and Rehabilitation* 26, no. 2, March/April 2005, p. 178.

72   *The nearest hospital to the nightclub:* Grosshandler et al., *Report.*

72   *Virtually every emergency medical helicopter:* G. Wayne Miller, "Most Severe Victims Treated at Mass General," *The Providence Journal,* February 22, 2003.

72   *was mobilized to transport victims:* Felice J. Freyer, "Treatment Costs for Fire Victims Straining System," *The Providence Journal,* May 26, 2003.

73   *This influx stressed the hospitals':* Stephen Smith, "After the Fire," *The Boston Globe,* August 12, 2003.

73   *The overall mortality rate:* Garrett, "The Next Pandemic?"

74   *the entire inventory:* Of the 970,000 staffed hospital beds and 100,000 ventilator beds, three quarters are already in use at any given time. Congressional Budget Office, "A Potential Influenza Pandemic: Possible Macroeconomic Effects and Policy Issues," July 17, 2006, p. 29.

75   *Hospitals in more than 40 percent:* Trust for America's Health, "Ready or Not? Protecting the Public's Health from Diseases, Disasters, and Bioterrorism," 2005, p. 3, see http://healthyamericans.org/reports/bioterror05.

75   *Public health employment:* Association of State and Territorial Health Officials (ASTHO), "State Public Health Employee Worker Shortage

Report: A Civil Service Recruitment and Retention Crisis," 2004, see http://www.astho.org/pubs/Workforce-Survey-Report-2.pdf.

75–76   *Thirty percent of all hospitals:* Thomas Inglesby, "All Hazards Medical Preparedness and Response," Senate Subcommittee on Bioterrorism and Public Health Preparedness Roundtable, April 5, 2006.

76   *In 2005, half of the nation's 4,000:* Frederick C. Blum, "Emergency Care Crisis: A Nation Unprepared for Public Health Disasters," testimony before the House Committee on Homeland Security, Subcommittee on Emergency Preparedness, Science, and Technology, July 26, 2006, see http://hsc.house.gov/files/TestimonyBlum.pdf; and American Hospital Association, "The State of America's Hospitals," Survey of Hospital Leaders, 2006, see http://ahapolicyforum.org /ahapolicyforum/resources/content/StateHospitalsChartPack2006 .PPT.

76   *Not surprisingly, 91 percent:* Committee on the Future of Emergency Care in the United States Health System, "Hospital-Based Emergency Care: At the Breaking Point," June 14, 2006. See http://www .nap.edu/execsumm_pdf/11621.pdf.

76   *In 2004, patients:* Benjamin Sun et al., "Effects of Hospital Closures and Hospital Characteristics on Emergency Department Diversion Los Angeles County, 1998 to 2004."

76   *Three quarters of hospitals:* Ibid.

76   *As of December 2005:* American Hospital Association, "The State of America's Hospitals."

76   *In New York City:* Anne Bove, testimony before the New York City Regional Advisory Committee of the Commission on Healthcare Facilities in the 21st Century, March 30, 2006.

77   *since 1980, the number of:* Kyusuk Chung and Ross Mullner, "Major Changes and Trends in Chicago Hospitals, 1980–2004," prepared for the

Conference on Chicago Research and Public Policy, May 2004, see http:
//www.about.chapinhall.org/uuc/presentations/MullnerChungPaper
.pdf.

77   *Forty-five percent of hospital:* Institute of Medicine of the National Academies, *Emergency Medical Services,* p. 3.

78   *In April 2005:* The U.S. Department of Homeland Security's Top Officials
Three Exercise (TOPOFF 3) is a congressionally mandated exercise designed to strengthen the nation's capacity to prevent, prepare for, respond to, and recover from large-scale terrorist attacks involving
weapons of mass destruction. Department of Homeland Security, "Top
Officials Three Exercise (TOPOFF 3)," April 4–8, 2005, see http://www
.dhs.gov/xprepresp/training/editorial_0588.shtm.

80   *Second, the private sector:* Author interview with Laurie Garrett, senior fellow for global health, Council on Foreign Relations, September 29, 2006.

80   *A week after the exercise:* New Jersey Business Force, "TOPOFF 3 Private
Sector Roundtable After Action Report," July 27, 2005.

82   *But the overall grade:* Trust for America's Health, "Ready or Not?"

83   *Even power surges:* Siobhan Gorman, "NSA Risking Electrical Overload,"
Baltimore *Sun,* August 6, 2006.

83   *The official name of our highway network:* U.S. Department of Transportation, "The Dwight D. Eisenhower National System of Interstate and Defense Highways," Route Log and Finder List, November 2002, see
http://www.fhwa.dot.gov/reports/routefinder/.

84   *The estimated cost:* Kulish, "Things Fall Apart."

84   *A single barge:* Norb Whitlock, "Inland Waterway Users Board 19th Annual
Report," March 2005, presented to the Transportation Research Board
Marine Board Spring Meeting, April 13, 2005, Memphis, Tennessee, see
http://gulliver.trb.org/conferences/MB/Spring05/Whitlock.pdf.

84   *Altogether, this towing arrangement:* Brian Hayes, *Infrastructure: A Field Guide to the Industrial Landscape* (New York: W. W. Norton, 2005), p. 472.

84   *The U.S. Army Corps of Engineers:* American Society of Civil Engineers, "Report Card."

85   *As a result, the total time:* Whitlock, "Inland Waterway Users."

85   *Every year that there is a delay:* Ibid.

85   *Based on the current budget trajectory:* American Society of Civil Engineers, "Report Card."

85   *The Corps engineers determined:* U.S. Army Corps of Engineers, "Meeting on the McAlpine Lock Closure," August 2005; U.S. Army Corps of Engineers, "Shipper and Carrier Response, Results of Surveys," May 27, 2004, Louisville, Kentucky, IWR Report 05-NETS-R-08, September 2005.

86   *By one estimate:* Chuck Parrish, "Navigation Mission Is Old and Continuing," *Engineer Update,* February 2001, see http://www.hq.usace.army .mil/cepa/pubs/feb01/story7.htm.

86   *One of the most important commodities:* U.S. Army Corps of Engineers–Huntington District, McAlpine Locks and Dam, "McAlpine Locks—2004 Commodity Distribution," see http://outreach.lrh.usace.army.mil /Locks/McAlpine/Default.htm.

86   *A single large power plant:* Hayes, *Infrastructure,* p. 186.

87   *"We have not yet had":* Katherine McIntire Peters, "Army Corps Closes Ohio River for Critical Lock Repairs," August 6, 2004, see http://www .govexec.com/dailyfed/0804/080604kp1.htm.

89   *Last, the society:* Jared Diamond, *Collapse: How Societies Choose to Fail or Succeed* (New York: Penguin, 2005), p. 421.

90   *In addition to the meteoric cost overruns:* Glen Johnson, "Governor Seeks to Take Control of Big Dig Inspections," *The Boston Globe,* July 13, 2006.

90   *Culminating with the collapse:* Jay Lindsay, "Big Dig Collapse Prompts Re-
     newed Scrutiny," *The Boston Globe,* July 11, 2006.

90   *Tired of its frequent blackouts:* Morgan Stanley, "India and China: New
     Tigers of Asia, Part II," June 2006, p. 84.

90   *According to the investment firm Morgan Stanley:* Ibid., p. 40.

91   *I cleared immigration and customs:* The Airport Express provides a swift
     link between Hong Kong International Airport and the heart of Hong
     Kong. It is one of the few dedicated airport railways in the world, cover-
     ing the twenty-two miles between the airport at Chek Lap Kok and
     central Hong Kong in about twenty-four minutes. MTR Corporation,
     "Airport Express Service: Information," see http://www.mtr.com
     .hk/eng/train/ae_intro.htm.

91   *Our freight rail systems:* American Society of Civil Engineers, "Report
     Card."

6. THE BEST DEFENSE IS A GOOD DEFENSE

93   *"The real danger lies":* This view is also shared by terrorism expert Brian
     Jenkins: "The greater danger is the reaction the attacks may provoke.
     Terror, not terrorists, is the principal threat." Brian Michael Jenkins, *Un-
     conquerable Nation: Knowing Our Enemy, Strengthening Ourselves* (Santa
     Monica: RAND, 2006), p. 16.

94   *Any serious effort to protect:* Lee Hamilton, "Remarks on Homeland
     Security and Public/Private Cooperation," Brookings Institution
     Seminar, September 5, 2003, see http://www.wilsoncenter.org/docs
     /staff/Hamilton_pubpriv.doc.

94   *As has been well documented:* 9/11 Commission Report.

95   *Further, this recruitment is not limited:* The White House, "National Strat-
     egy for Combating Terrorism," September 2006, see http://www
     .whitehouse.gov/nsc/nsct/2006/nsct2006.pdf.

95   *The foreign participants who joined:* "Who Is Osama bin Laden?" BBC News, September 18, 2001, see http://news.bbc.co.uk/2/hi/south_asia /155236.stm.

95   *Between January 2004:* Tom Doggett, "U.S. Says Attacks Cost Iraq $16 Billion in Oil Exports," Reuters, September 28, 2006, see http://www .alertnet.org/thenews/newsdesk/N28375111.htm. To view a comprehensive list of all attacks against Iraqi pipelines, oil installations, and oil personnel, see Institute for the Analysis of Global Security, "Iraq Pipeline Watch," October 2, 2006, http://www.iags.org/iraqpipelinewatch.htm.

95   *Successful attacks on the electrical grid:* Carlye Murphy and Bassam Sebti, "Power Grid in Iraq Far from Fixed," *The Washington Post,* May 1, 2005.

95   *The terrorist skills acquired:* Gabriel Weimann, "www.terror.net: How Modern Terrorism Uses the Internet," United States Institute of Peace Special Report 116, March 2004, see http://www.usip.org/pubs /specialreports/sr116.pdf.

96   *American taxpayers contributed:* Amy Belasco, "The Cost of Iraq, Afghanistan, and Other Global War on Terror Operations Since 9/11," Order Code RL33110, June 16, 2006, Congressional Research Service, see http://www.fas.org/sgp/crs/natsec/RL33110.pdf.

96   *"Meaning that every dollar":* "Full Text of Osama bin Laden's Remarks," Aljazeera, November 1, 2004, see http://english.aljazeera.net/NR /exeres/79C6AF22-98FB-4A1C-B21F-2BC36E87F61F.htm.

98   *What those priorities should be:* Department of Homeland Security, "National Infrastructure Protection Plan," June 2006, see http://www .dhs.gov/xlibrary/assets/NIPP_Plan.pdf.

100   *After September 11, 2001:* Stephen Kurkjian, Kevin Cullen, and Thomas Farragher, "Despite Millions Spent, Boston is Vulnerable," *The Boston Globe,* September 10, 2006, A1.

101 *In 1990, a year after:* U.S. Congress, *Oil Pollution Act of 1990*, see http://www.access.gpo.gov/uscode/title33/chapter40_.html.

103 *In 2006, there were 30,000 members:* "U.S. Coast Guard Auxiliary," see http://nws.cgaux.org/visitors/ps_visitor/index.html.

103 *There are an estimated eighteen million:* National Marine Manufacturers Association, "Industry Statistics and Research, Recreational Boating Figures," 2005, see http://www.nmma.org/facts/boatingstats/2005 /files/populationstats2.asp.

104 *But the service is responsible:* "U.S. Coast Guard Website, FactFile," see http://www.uscg.mil/hq/g-cp/comrel/factfile/index.htm.

106 *Police departments are finding:* At of the end of fiscal year 2004, COPS funded more than 118,768 community policing officers and deputies. Department of Justice, "Office of Community Oriented Policing Services," see http://www.cops.usdoj.gov/.

107 *At the same time, the number:* Terry Frieden, "Violent Crime Takes First Big Jump since '91," CNN Law Center, June 12, 2006, see http://www .cnn.com/2006/LAW/06/12/crime.rate/index.html.

107 *The federal government:* A Century Foundation Task Force, co-chaired by Richard A. Clarke and Rand Beers, of which the author was a member, proposes that "Congress should establish a COPS II first preventers program to hire and train local law enforcement to do counterterrorism and gather intelligence." See Richard A. Clarke, Rand Beers, et al., "The Forgotten Homeland," Century Foundation Task Force Report, July 2006, p. 248.

107 *The bombs were actually constructed:* Kiran Randhawa, "Revealed: The Bath Where the 7/7 Bombs Were Made," *Evening Standard* (London), June 15, 2006, see http://www.findarticles.com/p/articles/mi_qn4153 /is_20060615/ai_n16496752/print.

7. GETTING IT RIGHT

110   *By one estimate, in 2006:* Brian M. Riedl and Alison Acosta Fraser, "The Senate's Deadly Sins: Larding Up Emergency Appropriations," Heritage Foundation, April 17, 2006.

111   *Taking a page from the Department:* U.S. Congress, *Defense Base Closure and Realignment Act of 1990* (as Amended through FY05 Authorization Act), Pub.L. 100-526; and Trade Act of 2002, Pub.L. 107-210. In addition to the BRAC process, another example of this thumbs-up-or-down approach is the fast-track negotiating authority provided to recent presidents to support negotiating international trade agreements.

112   *The national academies draw on experts:* "The National Academy of Sciences was born in the travail of the Civil War. The Act of Incorporation, signed by President Lincoln on March 3, 1863, established service to the nation as its dominant purpose. . . . Over the years, the National Academy of Sciences has broadened its services to the government. In 1916 the Academy established the National Research Council at the request of President Wilson to recruit specialists from the larger scientific and technological communities to participate in that work. . . . Under the authority of its charter, the National Academy of Sciences established the National Academy of Engineering in 1964 and the Institute of Medicine in 1970. Much like the National Academy of Sciences, each of these organizations consists of members elected by peers in recognition of distinguished achievement in their respective fields. The National Academy of Sciences includes about 1,800 members, the National Academy of Engineering about 1,900, and the Institute of Medicine about 1,200. All three organizations also elect foreign associates." See http://www .nationalacademies.org/about/history.html.

112   *The National Academy:* "The National Academy of Public Administration is an independent, non-partisan organization chartered by Congress to assist federal, state, and local governments in improving their effective-

ness, efficiency, and accountability. For more than 35 years, the Academy has met the challenge of cultivating excellence in the management and administration of government agencies." See http://www.napawash.org/about_academy/index.html.

113 *In addition to the extensive survey:* "The American Society of Civil Engineers (ASCE) supports sustained efforts to improve professional and related practices in planning, design, construction, operation and maintenance that will mitigate the effects of natural and man-made hazards. ASCE is committed to participating in national and international activities that encourage mitigation of the effects of hazards and provide improved warning of impending hazards. ASCE will collaborate and cooperate with government and private agency initiatives and activities for hazard mitigation, preparedness and disaster recovery." American Society of Civil Engineers, "Mitigating the Impacts of Natural and Man-Made Disasters," ASCE Policy Statement 389, see http://www.asce.org/pressroom/news/policy.cfm.

113 *The Institute of Medicine:* The nonprofit Association of State and Territorial Health Officials (ASTHO) is comprised of senior state health officials from the entire United States and is concerned with issues affecting public health agencies, such as patient access to care, disease prevention, environmental health, and public health preparedness. Based in Washington, D.C., the ASTHO helps to formulate and influence public health policy and forward quality state-based public health practices. See http://www.astho.org.

113 *This information would then be presented:* "The Federal Reserve System uses advisory and working committees in carrying out its varied responsibilities. Three of these committees advise the Federal Reserve Board directly: the Consumer Advisory Council, the Federal Advisory Council, and the Thrift Institutions Advisory Council. The first two were established by law, and the third was created by the Federal Reserve Board.

Each Federal Reserve Bank also uses advisory committees. These committees advise the Bank on matters of importance in the Bank's District, such as agriculture and small business." See http://www.federalreserve.gov/general.htm.

115 *The American Society of Civil Engineers:* This figure is extrapolated from the $1.6-trillion-over-five-years figure included in the ASCE report. The $1.6 trillion includes funding for schools, which fall out of the traditional definition of infrastructure. Though the problems with public funding of education continue, more than just crumbling buildings are responsible. American Society of Civil Engineers, "Report Card."

115 *Another $12 billion is needed:* The Public Health Foundation, a nonprofit organization that provides research, training, and technical assistance on public health issues, estimates that an infusion of $10 billion is necessary to bring our public health systems up to where they meet minimum requirements. However, other organizations believe the number could be much higher. Public Health Foundation, "A Strong Public Health Infrastructure Can Help Save Lives," see http://phf.org/infrastructure/resources/PHFactSheet.pdf.

115 *Recognizing that they have only a limited capacity:* Kate Milani, "PE Interest Grows in Public Infrastructure Projects," *LBO Wire,* September 6, 2006.

115 *Macquarie is extending its investments:* Andrew Bary, "Toll Road Sales," *Barrons* online, May 8, 2006.

116 *The first might be the roughly:* Between 2001 and 2011, the estate tax is projected to yield $409 billion. Jane G. Gravelle, "Economic Issues Surrounding the Estate and Gift Tax: A Brief Summary," Congressional Research Service (CRS) RS20609, Report for Congress, January 23, 2006, see http://www.nationalaglawcenter.org/assets/crs/RS20609.pdf.

116 *However, the estate tax is set:* Ibid., p. 2. "The Economic Growth and Tax Relief Reconciliation Act of 2001 (EGTRRA) repeals the estate tax in

2010. . . . However, the estate tax provision in the EGTRRA automatically sunsets December 31, 2010. Thus the estate and gift tax will be reinstated as it existed before EGTRRA."

117 *This would generate approximately:* Figures are calculated based on data from David Cay Johnston, "Big Gain for Rich Seen in Tax Cuts for Investments," *The New York Times,* April 5, 2006; Aviva Aron-Dine and Joel Friedman, "The Skewed Benefits of the Tax Cuts, 2007–2016: If the Tax Cuts Are Extended, Millionaires Will Receive More than $600 Billion over the Next Decade," Center on Budget and Policy Priorities, March 15, 2006, see http://www.cbpp.org/2-23-06tax.htm.

117 *This recommendation has been proposed:* N. Gregory Mankiw, "Raise the Gas Tax," *The Wall Street Journal,* October 20, 2006, A12.

117 *The AASHTO recommends that an additional:* American Society of Civil Engineers, "Report Card."

118 *To put my proposal into a global perspective:* In 2005, China's total capital spending on electricity, railways, roads, airports, seaports, and telecoms was $201 billion (9.0 percent of GDP). Morgan Stanley, "New Tigers of Asia, Part II," June 2006, p. 40.

119 *Indeed, it required the prodding:* "The Goldwater-Nichols Department of Defense Reorganization Act of 1986, sponsored by Senator Barry Goldwater and Representative Bill Nichols, caused a major defense reorganization, the most significant since the National Security Act of 1947. Operational authority was centralized through the Chairman of the Joint Chiefs as opposed to the service chiefs. The chairman was designated as the principal military advisor to the president, National Security Council and secretary of defense. The act established the position of vice-chairman and streamlined the operational chain of command from the president to the secretary of defense to the unified commanders." See http://www.ndu.edu/library/goldnich/goldnich.html.

120   *For instance, FEMA's Region IV:* Federal Emergency Management Agency, "Region IV," Department of Homeland Security, see http://www .fema.gov/about/regions/regioniv/index.shtm.

120   *"You need to make sure":* Cooper and Block, *Disaster,* p. 56.

121   *"It's not your fault":* Ibid., pp. 279–80.

121   *What follows is a description:* See the U.S. Coast Guard Aviation Association's website: http://uscgaviationhistory.aoptero.org/images/ Hurricane_Katrina_Cos_message.pdf.

129   *Coast Guard officers have the power:* The Reconstruction-era Posse Comitatus Act of 1878 prohibits federal troops from acting in a domestic law enforcement capacity unless specifically authorized by Congress. The Coast Guard has a number of statutory authorities that assign it a domestic law enforcement role. They include 14 USC 2, stating that law enforcement is the primary duty of the Coast Guard; 14 USC 89, giving the Coast Guard general boarding, search, and arrest authority; 14 USC 141, specifying Coast Guard cooperation with federal/state agencies; and 14 USC 143/19 USC 1401(i), stating that certain Coast Guard personnel also may be deemed "Officers of the Customs."

8. TAPPING THE PRIVATE SECTOR

132   *Singapore now tops the list:* Port of Singapore, "Total Container Throughput," see http://www.mpa.gov.sg/infocentre/pdfs/container-throughput .pdf; Port of Los Angeles, "Frequently Asked Questions," Port of Los Angeles Annual Container Volume, see http://www.portoflosangeles .org/about_faq.htm#5.

132   *Gathered at the venue were:* For a list of the top shipping companies see World Shipping Council, "Linear Shipping: Facts and Figures," Annual TEU figures for May 1, 2003–April 30, 2004, p. 3, see http://www .worldshipping.org/liner_shipping-facts&figures.pdf.

137 *Government agencies collect:* For an in-depth discussion of information sharing with the private sector, see Daniel B. Prieto, "Information Sharing with the Private Sector: History, Challenges, Innovation, and Prospects," in Philip Auerswald, Lewis M. Branscomb, Todd M. La Porte, and Erwann Michel-Kerjan, eds., *Seeds of Disaster, Roots of Response: How Private Action Can Reduce Public Vulnerability* (Cambridge, England: Cambridge University Press, 2006), pp. 404–28.

139 *The strategy declares that:* Office of Homeland Security, the White House, *National Strategy for Homeland Security,* July 16, 2002, see http://www.whitehouse.gov/homeland/book/nat_strat_hls.pdf. The strategy assigns most of the responsibility for funding the protection of potential targets within U.S. borders to the private sector. It lays out "the broad principles that should guide the allocation of funding for homeland security [and] help determine who should bear the financial burdens" and states that "the government should only address those activities that the market does not adequately provide—for example, national defense or border security. . . . For other aspects of homeland security, sufficient incentives exist in the private market to supply protection. In these cases we should rely on the private sector."

139 *Of the 11 million cargo containers:* World Shipping Council, "Linear Shipping," p. 3.

139 *And as the Dubai Ports World controversy:* Calculated from data provided by the U.S. Department of Transportation Maritime Administration, Foreign and Domestic Container Terminal Operation in the U.S., March 2, 2006.

143 *The city of Los Angeles:* Author interview with Maurice Suh, deputy mayor of public safety, city of Los Angeles, on July 20, 2006.

143 *Under the Civil Reserve Air Fleet program:* White House, "Executive Order 11090 Assigning Emergency Preparedness Functions to the Civil Aero-

nautics Board," 1963, see http://www.lib.umich.edu/govdocs/jfkeo
/eo/11090.htm.

145 *This evidence, in the form:* Flynn, *America the Vulnerable,* pp. 152–54.

147 *The consensus among corporate:* For examples of recommendations that
have been made since 9/11 to improve information sharing with the private sector, see Harold C. Ralyea and Jeffrey W. Seifert, "Information
Sharing for Homeland Security: A Brief Overview," RL32597, Congressional Research Service, updated September 30, 2004, pp. 22–25,
http://www.fas.org/sgp/crs/RL32597.pdf; U.S. General Accounting
Office, "Critical Infrastructure Protection: Establishing Effective Information Sharing with Infrastructure Sectors, Testimony," GAO-04-699T,
April 21, 2004, see http://www.gao.gov/new.items/d04699t.pdf; U.S.
General Accounting Office, "Critical Infrastructure Protection: Improving Information Sharing with Infrastructure Sectors, Report to Congressional Requesters," GAO-04-780, July 2004, see http://www.gao.gov
/new.items/d04780.pdf; ISAC Council, "A Functional Model for Critical
Infrastructure Information Sharing and Analysis: Maturing and Expanding Efforts," White Paper, January 31, 2004, see http://www.isaccouncil
.org/pub/Information_Sharing_and_Analysis_013104.pdf; and ISAC
Council, "Government–Private Sector Relations," White Paper, January 31, 2004, see http://www.isaccouncil.org/pub/Government_Private
_Sector_Relations_013104.pdf.

147 *An exception to this rule:* NYPD Shield is an umbrella program for a series
of Police Department initiatives that pertain to private sector security
and counterterrorism. "NYPD Shield," see http://www.nypd2.org
/nyclink/nypd/html/ctb/index.html.

148 *In this way, everyone receives:* "Regional Alliances for Infrastructure and
Network Security," see http://www.oregonrains.org/.

148 *Inspired by the painful example:* Author interview with Michael Laden,
president of Trade Innovations Inc., September 20, 2005.

149 *For example, the nonprofit:* "Business Force Regions," see http://www
.bensbusinessforce.org/NBFregions.htm.

150 *At a speed of 10 mph:* The technology demonstrated that it was possible to
collect a gamma ray image and the radiographic information of containers moving at speeds of 10 mph; however, there is still room for improvement in increasing the sensor capabilities. Yet the biggest challenge lies
not with the technology, which is evolving quickly, but with adapting inspection protocols to capitalize on the tremendous amount of new data
that is being generated.

150 *Six months later, President Bush signed:* "President Bush Signs SAFE Port
Act," October 13, 2006, see http://www.whitehouse.gov/news/releases
/2006/10/20061013-2.html; and U.S. Congress, Security and Accountability for Every Port Act of 2006, see http://frwebgate.access.gpo.gov/cgi
-bin/getdoc.cgi?dbname=109_cong_bills&docid=f:h4954enr.txt.pdf.

9. PREPARING FOR THE WORST

153 *More than 40,000 Americans:* There was a total of 42,443 deaths from automobile accidents in the United States in 2001. Centers for Disease Control, "Deaths from Automobile Accidents Injury," 2001 (most current
data), see http://www.wrongdiagnosis.com/a/automobile_accidents
_injury/deaths.htm.

154 *Unfortunately, nearly half of those surveyed:* The study was conducted by
the Advertising Council on behalf of the Department of Homeland Security's Ready Campaign. "Homeland Security and Coalition of More
than 1,150 Launch National Preparedness Month 2006," August 31,
2006, see http://www.ready.gov/america/npm/083106_release.htm.

154 *In an August 2006* Time *poll:* Mark Schulman, "Katrina One Year Later:
Still Not Prepared," SRBI Public Affairs, August 11, 2006, see http://www
.srbi.com/time_poll_arc30.html.

154 *But 91 percent of Americans live:* Amanda Ripley, "Time Poll."

156 *They use catastrophe modeling:* Patricia Grossi and Howard Kunreuther, "New Catastrophe Models for Hard Times," *Contingencies,* March/April 2006.

156 *Economists calculate that every dollar:* "Interview with Sir David King, Chief Scientific Adviser to HM Government of the United Kingdom," see http://www.wmo.ch/web/Press/SirDave.pdf.

156 *For the average citizen:* Federation of American Scientists, "Analysis of Ready.gov: Disabled and Special Needs," see http://www.fas.org /reallyready/analysis.html#disabled and http://www.wmo.ch/web /Press/SirDave.pdf.

160 *Project Impact provided small:* Shane Harris, "What FEMA May Have Gotten Right?" *National Journal,* September 17, 2005.

161 *What began as a pilot in seven cities:* "Congresswoman Capps Introduces Legislation to Help Local Communities Prevent and Prepare for Natural Disasters," States News Service, September 15, 2005.

161 *However, when the Bush administration:* Harris, "What FEMA May Have Gotten Right?"

161 *However, according to the congressional testimony:* Pamela Pogue, "Emergency Preparedness and Response System as Related to the Stafford Act," testimony before the Senate Environment and Public Works Committee, July 27, 2006.

161 *at the same time lost one:* Tamara S. Little, "Emergency Preparedness and Response System as Related to the Stafford Act," testimony before the Senate Environment and Public Works Committee, July 27, 2006.

161 *Senator Murray issued a press release:* "Senator Murray, Democratic Leaders Call for Renewed Emphasis on Emergency Preparedness," *US Fed News,* September 12, 2005.

161 *"We've strengthened infrastructure":* Greg Nichols, "City of Seattle, Emergency Management," see http://www.seattle.gov/emergency/.

161 *Part of Seattle's effort includes:* "City of Seattle Emergency Preparedness," see http://www.seattle.gov/economicdevelopment/biz_district_guide/biz_dist_pages/emergency_prep.htm.

162 *Moreover, Seattle's DRB:* "Business Emergency Network," see http://www.seattle.gov/projectimpact/pdfs/what-is-ben.pdf.

162 *One of the main reasons why:* Armond Mascelli, "Emergency Preparedness and Response System as Related to the Stafford Act," testimony before the Senate Environment and Public Works Committee, July 27, 2006.

162 *Launched as a national initiative in 2002:* "Citizen Corps," see http://www.citizencorps.gov/.

163 *The medical reserve corps:* "Medical Reserve Corps," see http://www.medicalreservecorps.gov/HomePage.

10. A RESILIENT SOCIETY

169 *While only the smallest percentage:* Terrorism expert Brian Jenkins points out that the average American has about 1 chance in 9,000 of dying in an automobile accident in a given year and about 1 chance in 18,000 of being murdered. During the past five years, the average American had a 1 in 500,000 chance of being killed in a terrorist attack. Jenkins, *Unconquerable Nation,* p. 154.

170 *Poor road conditions cost:* Poor road conditions cost U.S. motorists $54 billion a year in repairs and operating costs, or $275 per motorist. Americans spend 3.5 *billion* hours a year stuck in traffic, at a cost of $63.2 billion a year to the economy. Total spending of $59.4 billion annually is well below the $94 billion needed annually to improve transportation infrastructure conditions nationally. Long-term federal transportation programs remain unauthorized since expiring on September 30, 2003, and

the nation continues to shortchange funding for needed transportation improvements. American Society of Civil Engineers, "Report Card."

171 *America's gross domestic product:* The GDP of the U.S. was $12,455.8 billion in 2005. U.S. Department of Commerce, "National Income Product Accounts Table, Gross Domestic Product in Billions of Dollars," Bureau of Economic Analysis, see http://www.bea.gov/bea/dn/nipaweb/TableView.asp#Mid.

175 *But even in the face of such compelling:* Amanda Ripley, "Floods, Tornadoes, Hurricanes, Wildfires, Earthquakes: Why We Don't Prepare," *Time,* August 28, 2006, p. 54, see http://www.time.com/time/magazine/article/0,9171,1229102,00.html.

176 *If avian flu became highly contagious:* The World Bank, "Speak Out: Interview with Milan Brahmbhatt on Avian Flu," see http://discuss.worldbank.org/content/interview/detail/2739/.

178 *Early in the 1990s, the economist:* Robert Heilbroner, *21st Century Capitalism* (New York: W. W. Norton, 1993), p. 104.

INDEX

ABOUT THE AUTHOR

STEPHEN FLYNN is among the world's most widely cited experts on homeland security and trade and transportation security issues. He has been a senior fellow with the National Security Studies Program at the Council on Foreign Relations since 1999. The author of the critically acclaimed national bestseller *America the Vulnerable*, Dr. Flynn lives in Connecticut with his wife and daughter.

ABOUT THE TYPE

This book was set in Monotype Dante, a typeface designed by Giovanni Mardersteig (1892–1977). Conceived as a private type for the Officina Bodoni in Verona, Italy, Dante was originally cut only for hand composition by Charles Malin, the famous Parisian punch cutter, between 1946 and 1952. Its first use was in an edition of Boccaccio's *Trattatello in laude di Dante* that appeared in 1954. The Monotype Corporation's version of Dante followed in 1957. Though modeled on the Aldine type used for Pietro Cardinal Bembo's treatise *De Aetna* in 1495, Dante is a thoroughly modern interpretation of that venerable face.